Josef Schwelifs
,1977

Grasshoppers & Elephants

The Viet Cong account of the last 55 days of the war

BY WILFRED BURCHETT

Pacific Treasure Island   1941
Bombs over Burma   1944
Wingate Adventure   1944
Democracy with a Tommy-Gun   1946
Cold War in Germany   1950
Peoples Democracies   1951
The Changing Tide [play]   1951
China's Feet Unbound   1952
This Monstrous War   1953
Koje Unscreened [with Alan Winnington]   1953
Plain Perfidy [with Alan Winnington]   1954
North of the 17th Parallel   1955
Mekong Upstream   1959
Come East Young Man   1962
The Furtive War: The United States in Viet Nam and Laos   1963
My Visit to the Liberated Zones of South Viet Nam   1964
Viet Nam: Inside Story of the Guerilla War   1965
Viet Nam North   1966
Viet Nam Will Win   1968
Again Korea   1968
Passport   1969
The Second Indochina War   1970
My War with the CIA [with Prince Norodom Sihanouk]   1973
Portugal After the Captains' Coup   1975
China: The Quality of Life [with Rewi Alley]   1976
Grasshoppers and Elephants   1977

Grasshoppers & Elephants

Why Viet Nam Fell

by Wilfred Burchett

Urizen Books   New York

© Wilfred Burchett 1977

First published by
Urizen Books
66 West Broadway
New York, New York 10007

Printed in U.S.A.

Library of Congress Cataloging in Publication Data

Burchett, Wilfred G   1911-
    Grasshoppers and Elephants.

      1. Vietnamese Conflict, 1961-1975.
2. Guerrilla warfare.   I. Title.
DS557.7.B87   959.704'3   76-30911
ISBN 0-916354-65-2
ISBN 0-916354-66-0 pbk.

Contents

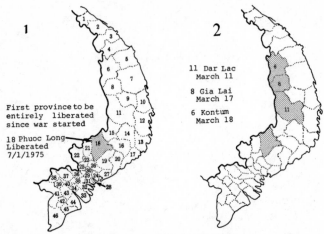

1

First province to be
entirely liberated
since war started

18 Phuoc Long
Liberated
7/1/1975

2

11 Dar Lac
March 11

8 Gia Lai
March 17

6 Kontum
March 18

KEY TO THE PROVINCE NAMES
(Liberated provinces shown in gray)

1	Quang Tri	24	Gia Dinh
2	Thua Thien	25	Hau Nghia
3	Quang Nam	26	Bien Hoa
4	Quang Tin	27	Phuoc Le
5	Quang Ngai	28	Rung Sat
6	Kontum	29	Long An
7	Binh Dinh	30	Saigon
8	Gia Lai	31	Go Kong
9	Phu Bon	32	Kien Hoa
10	Phu Yen	33	Vinh Binh
11	Dar Lac	34	Vinh Long
12	Khan Hoa	35	Dinh Tuong
13	Ninh Thuan	36	Kien Tuong
14	Tuyen Duc	37	Kien Phong
15	Quang Duc	38	Chau Doc
16	Lam Dong	39	An Giang
17	Binh Thuan	40	Sa Dec
18	Phuoc Long	41	Kien Giang
19	Long Khanh	42	Chuong Thien
20	Binh Tuy	43	Phong Dinh
21	Binh Long	44	Ba Xuyen
22	Tay Ninh	45	Bac Lieu
23	Binh Duong	46	An Xuyen

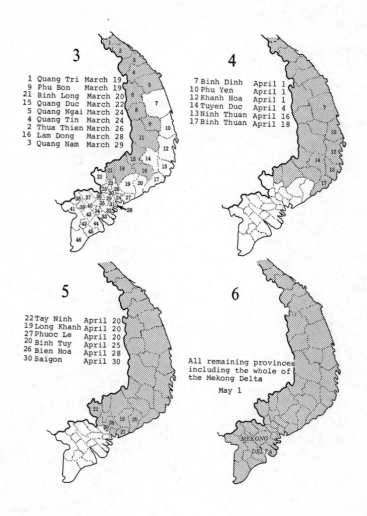

3

1	Quang Tri	March 19
9	Phu Bon	March 19
21	Binh Long	March 20
15	Quang Duc	March 22
5	Quang Ngai	March 24
4	Quang Tin	March 24
2	Thua Thien	March 26
16	Lam Dong	March 28
3	Quang Nam	March 29

4

7	Binh Dinh	April 1
10	Phu Yen	April 1
12	Khanh Hoa	April 1
14	Tuyen Duc	April 4
13	Ninh Thuan	April 16
17	Binh Thuan	April 18

5

22	Tay Ninh	April 20
19	Long Khanh	April 20
27	Phuoc Le	April 20
20	Binh Tuy	April 25
26	Bien Hoa	April 28
30	Saigon	April 30

6

All remaining provinces
including the whole of
the Mekong Delta

May 1

MEKONG
DELTA

Grasshoppers & Elephants

The Viet Cong account of the last 55 days of the war

Chronology

20 JANUARY 1961

John F. Kennedy takes office as President of the U.S.A.

16 DECEMBER

Two American helicopter companies with 36 Shawnee helicopters, 7 T.28 combat aircraft and 370 officers and men arrive in Saigon.

Throughout 1961, 41 U.S. military missions visit South Vietnam.

8 FEBRUARY 1962

The United States sets up MACV (Military Assistance Command Vietnam) in Saigon, under General Paul D. Harkins, to direct military operations.

By the end of 1962, there are 11,000 U.S. military personnel in South Vietnam; U.S. planes and helicopters carry out 50,000 sorties.

22 AUGUST 1963

Henry Cabot Lodge replaces Frederick D. Nolting as U.S. ambassador to Saigon.

1 NOVEMBER

President Ngo Dinh Diem of South Vietnam and his brother Ngo Dinh Nhu are assassinated in Saigon with the complicity of the CIA.

22 NOVEMBER

President Kennedy assassinated; replaced as president of the U.S.A. by Lyndon B. Johnson.

During 1963, over 40 U.S. military missions visit South Vietnam and some 37,000 military operations are carried out by South Vietnamese and American troops.

25 APRIL 1964

General William C. Westmoreland replaces General Harkins as U.S. Commander-in-chief in South Vietnam.

23 JUNE

General Maxwell D. Taylor, till then Chairman of the U.S. Joint Chiefs of Staff, is named ambassador to Saigon to replace Cabot Lodge.

5 AUGUST

American planes and naval vessels bombard coastal regions of North Vietnam on the pretext that North Vietnamese patrol boats had attacked the U.S. destroyers, *Maddox* and *Joy* in the Gulf of Tonkin.

7 AUGUST

President Johnson pushes through the famous "blank check", Gulf of Tonkin resolution by 414-0 in the House of Representatives and 88-2 (Senators Wayne Morse and Ernest Gruening opposing) in the Senate.

8 JANUARY 1965

2,000 South Korean troops arrive in South Vietnam.

7 FEBRUARY

U.S. planes start the systematic bombing of North Vietnam under the pretext of a reprisal for an NLF commando raid against the U.S. Holloway air base at Pleiku in the Central Highlands area of South Vietnam.

7 MARCH

4,000 U.S. Marines belonging to two battalions of the 1st Marine Division disembark at Danang, thus starting the commitment of U.S. combat troops.

2 AUGUST

6,000 U.S. Marines supported by 60 tanks and 100 aircraft start a major operation, just south of Danang, the first combat action by American military units.

By the end of 1965, there are 185,000 U.S. combat troops in South Vietnam; 250,000 tons of bombs are dropped on North Vietnam.

14 APRIL 1966

Defense Secretary Robert S. McNamara announces that 638,000 tons of bombs will be dropped on Vietnam during 1966, that is, 91 percent of the total dropped on Korea during 37 months of war there.

12 JUNE

4,000 Australian troops arrive in South Vietnam.

12 JULY

The U.S. Senate accords 17.4 billion dollars for the Vietnam War.

11 SEPTEMBER

2,000 Philippine troops arrive in South Vietnam.

17 NOVEMBER

President Johnson announces that from that date the U.S. expeditionary corps will take over military operations while South Vietnamese troops will be used for "pacification" work.

By the end of 1966, there are 390,000 U.S. troops in South Vietnam. 637,000 tons of bombs had been dropped, compared to 656,000 tons dropped in the Pacific area during World War II. 500,000 tons of shells had been fired, exceeding the total fired by the U.S. army during World War II. From 1961–1966, the U.S. had spent over 40 billion dollars on the war in Vietnam. Over one million acres of forest and orchards in South Vietnam were laid waste by chemical products during 1966.

3 JANUARY 1967

The government of Thailand announces the dispatch of 1,000 Thai troops to South Vietnam.

28 JANUARY

Nguyen Duy Trinh, foreign minister of the DRV (Democratic Republic of Vietnam) announces that talks with the United States to end hostilities in Vietnam could start on condition that the bombing of North Vietnam halt.

26 MAY

The *New York Times* reported that there were 453,000 U.S. troops in South Vietnam and that as of 20 May 1967, 10,253 had been killed and 61,452 wounded, making it for the first two years of direct engagement the fifth costliest war in American history.

3 AUGUST

President Johnson announces that a further 45,000 troops would be sent to South Vietnam

29 DECEMBER

Nguyen Duy Trinh repeats his offer of talks on condition that the U.S. halt the bombing and "other acts of war" against the DRV.

31 JANUARY 1968

The "Tết" offensive, launched on the Vietnamese Lunar New Year's Day, in which some 140 cities and towns and most U.S. and South Vietnamese bases are attacked simultaneously.

22 MARCH

General Creighton W. Abrams replaces Westmoreland.

31 March

President Johnson announces a limited bombing halt in the attacks against North Vietnam, his readiness for negotiations and that he will not be a candidate for the November 1968 presidential elections.

13 May

Talks start in Paris between a U.S. delegation headed by Governor William Averell Harriman and Cyrus R. Vance and a North Vietnamese delegation headed by Minister Xuan Thuy and Ambassador Ha Van Lau on ending the bombing of North Vietnam as a precondition to full-scale peace talks to end the war.

31 October

President Johnson announces that full agreement has been reached and that four-party talks to end the war will start on 6 November 1968.

5 November

U.S. presidential elections in which Richard M. Nixon beat Hubert H. Humphrey by 335,000 votes.

2 December

President-elect Nixon appoints Dr. Henry A. Kissinger, professor of Government at Harvard University, his Adviser on National Security.

5 January 1969

President-elect Nixon announces that Henry Cabot Lodge will replace Harriman as head of the U.S. negotiating team for the Paris talks.

20 January

Nixon takes over as President of the United States.

25 January

Four-party negotiations start in Paris with the addition of delegations from the National Liberation Front and the Saigon régime. The time between 6 November 1968, when they should have started, and 25 January 1969 was deliberately wasted because the Saigon authorities had been "advised" not to start negotiations until Nixon was in charge at the White House and Cabot Lodge in charge in Paris.

10 June

Formation of the Provisional Revolutionary Government of South Vietnam, from elements of the National Liberation Front and the Alliance of National, Democratic and Peace Forces—formed shortly after the Tết offensive by intellectuals from Saigon, Hue and other urban centers.

3 September

President Ho Chi Minh dies in Hanoi at the age of 79 and is succeeded by the 81 year-old Vice-President Ton Duc Thang.

3 NOVEMBER

In a nationwide broadcast, President Nixon reveals that when he became President, there were 540,000 Americans in Vietnam and 31,000 Americans had been killed. By 15 December 1969, U.S. troops will be reduced by 60,000. The forces of the Saigon regime will be expanded proportionately under the "Vietnamization" of the war.

18 MARCH 1970

Prince Norodom Sihanouk, the neutralist Head of State of Cambodia, is overthrown by pro-U.S. rightwingers headed by former Defense Chief General Lon Nol.

1 MAY

Tank and air-supported U.S. troops invade Cambodia, two days after a strong force of Saigon troops carried out a spearhead operation. At least 50,000 U.S.-Saigon troops are involved.

8 FEBRUARY 1971

U.S.-Saigon troops lauch a major operation into South Laos in a proclaimed attempt to "cut the Ho Chi Minh trail". The operation is the greatest military disaster of the war from the U.S.-Saigon viewpoint.

3 OCTOBER

Presidential "elections" in South Vietnam in which the reigning dictator, Nguyen Van Thieu, is the only candidate, one rival, vice-president Nguyen Cao Ky having been ruled ineligible as a candidate, and the other, Duong Van "Big" Minh having withdrawn because of impossible conditions for campaigning.

By the end of 1971, 45,629 American servicemen have been killed; another 1,491 are listed as "missing" since the start of U.S. involvement. The U.S.-Saigon Command reveal that aircraft losses for 1971 alone are 8,051.

25 JANUARY 1972

President Nixon reveals that between 30 May and 13 September 1971, there were five secret meetings between Le Duc Tho, the senior adviser to the DRV delegation to the Paris talks and Henry Kissinger. A sixth meeting for November 20 is cancelled by the United States on 24 hours' notice.

21–28 FEBRUARY

President Nixon visits People's Republic of China.

23 MARCH

Indefinite suspension of the Paris talks by the United States.

30 MARCH

The North Vietnamese and NLF forces launch the biggest offensive of the war until that time, overrunning all South Vietnamese positions immediately south of the demilitarized zone along the 17th parallel, seizing important positions in the Central Highlands and along the frontiers with Laos and Cambodia.

3 APRIL

The United States resumes large-scale bombing over the whole of North Vietnam for the first time since November 1968.

16 APRIL

B-52 bombers are used for the first time against Haiphong. Hanoi is also heavily bombed.

26 APRIL

President Nixon announces three decisions. (1) American troop withdrawals will continue. (2) Ambassador William Porter who had succeeded Ambassador David K.E. Bruce who had replaced Henry Cabot Lodge as head of the U.S. delegation, will return to the negotiating table on 27 April. (3) The bombings of North Vietnam will continue "until the North Vietnamese stop their offensive in South Vietnam..."

27 APRIL

Four-party talks resume in Paris.

2 MAY

Secret meeting between Kissinger and Le Duc Tho.

4 MAY

Talks again indefinitely suspended at U.S. initiative.

8 MAY

President Nixon announces that all North Vietnamese ports are to be mined and bombings stopped up until American prisoners are released and an "internationally supervised cease fire" in effect throughout Indochina.

9 MAY

U.S. mining operations against Haiphong and six other North Vietnamese ports are carried out by naval aircraft.

22–30 MAY

President Nixon visits the Soviet Union.

13 JULY

Four-party talks resume in Paris.

19 JULY & 1 & 14 AUGUST

Secret talks between Kissinger, Le Duc Tho and Xuan Thuy in Paris.

17–18 AUGUST

Kissinger has discussions with President Nguyen Van Thieu in Saigon.

11–14 SEPTEMBER

Kissinger visits Moscow.

14–15 SEPTEMBER

Kissinger visits London.

8–17 OCTOBER

Secret talks in Paris by Dr. Kissinger, Major-General Alexander Haig, his deputy at the National Security Council, Le Duc Tho and Xuan Thuy.

26 OCTOBER

The Government of the DRV releases the text of a Draft Agreement to end the war to be signed in Paris on 30 October. The texts of an exchange of telegrams between President Nixon and Prime Minister Pham Van Dong, in which Nixon proposes and Pham Van Dong accepts, a postponement of the signing by 24 hours. At a Washington press conference, Kissinger confirms the accuracy of the text but claims that 31 October was not a firm date for signing the Agreement.

2 NOVEMBER

Statement by President Nixon that: "We are going to sign the agreement when the agreement is right, not one day before..."

7 NOVEMBER

Presidential elections in which Nixon heavily defeats his Democratic Party rival, George S. McGovern.

20 NOVEMBER

Start of a new series of meetings between Le Duc Tho and Kissinger, fourteen in all, ending on 13 December.

13 DECEMBER

Kissinger returns to Washington.

14 DECEMBER

Le Duc Tho returns to Hanoi.

16 DECEMBER

Kissinger tells Washington press conference that Paris talks have broken down because of North Vietnam's "obstructive tactics". Xuan Thuy tells Paris press conference that the DRV is ready to sign the Agreement as drafted: "the sooner the better".

18 DECEMBER

Premier Pham Van Dong receives ultimatum from Nixon that either the DRV accept changes in the Agreement as proposed by Kissinger or Hanoi will be bombed. Within minutes, the first waves of B-52's start bombing Hanoi. The bombings last until December 30, by which time

40,000 tons of bombs had been dropped on Hanoi and 15,000 tons on Haiphong.

8 JANUARY 1973

Kissinger and Le Duc Tho start final series of talks on drafting Agreement.

27 JANUARY

Paris Agreement on Ending the War and Restoring Peace in Vietnam signed in Paris by DRV Foreign Minister Nguyen Duy Trinh, U.S. Secretary of State William Rogers, PRG Foreign Minister Madame Nguyen Thi Binh and Foreign Minister Tran Van Lam of the Republic of Vietnam.

10 FEBRUARY

Henry Kissinger arrives in Hanoi for a four-day visit. Agreement was reached to set up a Joint Economic Commission to handle U.S. reparation payments, as provided for in the Paris Agreement, and to be "charged with the task of developing economic relations between the two countries".

12 FEBRUARY

The first batch of U.S. pilot POW's leave Hanoi's Gia Lam airport for the U.S.A.

26 FEBRUARY

An International Conference to ratify the Peace Agreement opens in Paris attended by the U.S. Secretary of State and the foreign ministers of the USSR, China, the United Kingdom, France, the Democratic Republic of Vietnam, the Provisional Revolutionary Government, the Republic of Vietnam (Saigon), and of the four governments that are to constitute the International Commission of Control and Supervision (ICCS), Canada, Hungary, Poland and Indonesia.

1 MARCH

In the presence of UN Secretary-General Dr. Kurt Waldheim, the foreign ministers sign a 9-point Declaration supporting the Peace Agreement and demanding its strict application.

15 MARCH

Talks start in Paris between economic delegations of the U.S.A. and DRV on the detailed implementation of the pledge given by President Nixon to premier Pham Van Dong that the United States would furnish 3.25 billion dollars of economic aid to the DRV as a contribution towards "healing the wounds of war". Heading the U.S. team is Maurice Williams, deputy director of the Agency for International Development. The DRV Finance Minister, Dang Viet Chau, headed the DRV delegation.

19 MARCH

Talks started in LaCelle–St. Cloud (Paris) between the PRG and the

Saigon government for the implementation of the political clauses of the Paris Agreement. Heading the PRG delegation is Nguyen Van Hieu, Minister of State, while the Saigon delegation is headed by Deputy-Premier, Nguyen Luu Vien.

29 MARCH

President Nixon announces that all remaining U.S. servicement have been withdrawn from South Vietnam. In fact, about 100,000 still remain in the general area, 30,000 serving 50 warships of the 7th Fleet; 48,000 in Thailand and 20,000 on Guam, flying and servicing about 800 aircraft.

30 MARCH

The DRV accuses the U.S.A. of leaving 10,000 U.S. servicemen behind disguised as civilian "advisers". A few hours later, the State Department says there are "only" 8,500, including 5,000 Defense Department personnel on contract to the Saigon Government for "maintenance, logistics, communications, and similar operations" for the Saigon armed forces, more than 1,000 employees of the Agency for International Development (a CIA front organization) and some 50 military attachés.

(Throughout March–April 1973, there is continual fighting and refusal by the Saigon Government either to delimit the areas controlled by one side or the other, or to agree to setting up the Council for National Reconciliation and Concord, both of which are key provisions of the Paris Agreement).

16 APRIL

The DRV government sends a Note to all parties to the Paris Agreement charging that the Saigon Government with the backing of the U.S.A. has launched tens of thousands of operations into PRG-controlled areas, that the U.S.A. has not dismantled their military bases but handed them over, together with the equipment of the U.S. troops withdrawn, to the Saigon forces and many other charges of U.S.–Saigon violation of the Paris Agreement.

17 MAY

A new round of talks starts in Paris between Dr. Kissinger and Le Duc Tho, aimed at insuring respect for the Paris Agreement.

13 JUNE

A new Agreement is signed, in effect endorsing the previous one, by Kissinger and Le Duc Tho and also by representatives from the PRG and Saigon regime.

5–9 SEPTEMBER

Summit Meeting in Algiers of Non-Aligned States at which the PRG is accepted as a full member despite energetic protests from the Saigon regime.

11 OCTOBER

PRG issues an "Order of the Day" that in future its armed forces are to resist "landgrabbing" operations by the Saigon forces and "punish" the bases from which such attacks are launched.

4 NOVEMBER

PRG forces attack and capture two of three important bases near the Cambodian border, Bu Prang and Bu Bong, which had been seized by Saigon troops after the ceasefire agreement.

5 NOVEMBER

The Saigon Air Force bombs Loc Ninh, the unofficial "capital" of PRG-held territory.

6 NOVEMBER

PRG forces launch a rocket attack on the big Bien Hoa air base destroying a number of jet fighter-bombers.

7 NOVEMBER

PRG forces capture the third Saigon-seized base of Dak Sone.

23 NOVEMBER

Wave after wave of bombers is launched against a PRG base area, 60 miles north of Saigon in Tay Ninh province.

3 DECEMBER

PRG commandos attack the huge Nha Be oil storage depot in the Saigon outskirts, destroying 18 million gallons of gasoline.

20 DECEMBER

Five-hour meeting between Kissinger and Le Duc Tho in Paris, described by North Vietnamese later as an "empty exercise in demagogy" by Kissinger who initiated the meeting.

29 DECEMBER

In an "end of the year" speech, President Nguyen Van Thieu announced that there would be no general elections—as stipulated in the Paris Agreement—nor any negotiated political settlement at the Paris talks.

4 JANUARY 1974

In a "New Year's" speech, President Thieu orders his armed forces into intensified offensive operations against PRG forces throughout the country. They are above all to strike deep into PRG base areas and wipe them out.

16–18 MARCH

Big battle 10 miles northeast of Kontum when about 3,000 Saigon troops attacked and penetrated a PRG base area, being driven back with very heavy losses.

11 APRIL

Subpoena is served on President Nixon, ordering him to surrender the tape-recordings of 42 presidential conversations related to the Watergate scandal.

16 APRIL

The Saigon government unilaterally and indefinitely suspends the Paris talks.

17 MAY

Start of a three-month battle in the Ben Cat area about 30 miles north of Saigon, initiated when PRG forces took three Saigon military outposts. In the battle that follows, troops of Saigon's 18th division succeed in re-taking one but after at least 2,000 casualties in vainly trying to retake the other two, the 18th division is forced to withdraw from the area.

23 JUNE

The PRG withdraws from the two-party Joint Military Commission and the four-party Joint Military Team, part of the machinery to supervise the Paris Agreement. The ICCS which could carry out its work only at the request of these bodies ceases to function.

JULY–AUGUST

The United States Congress reduces President Nixon's request for 1.4 billion dollars for the 1974–75 financial year (starting 30 June 1974) to 770 million dollars with the stated hope that the cut will force President Thieu to negotiate a military solution. A move by Senator Proxmire to have it further reduced to 550 million dollars is defeated in the Senate 47–44.

5 AUGUST

President Nixon admits that he withheld information on the Watergate Affair.

8 AUGUST

President Nixon announces intention to resign.

9 AUGUST

Vice-President Gerald Ford is sworn in as President of the United States.

14 DECEMBER

PRG forces launch an offensive in the province of Phuoc Long and within twelve days takes over the whole province except its capital, Phuoc Binh, 75 miles north of Saigon.

7 JANUARY 1975

Phuoc Binh is captured and for the first time since the war started, the PRG-NFL forces control an entire province.

PRG forces storm the strategic 3,000 foot Ba Den (Black Virgin) mountain, seven miles northeast of Tay Ninh, provincial capital of the province with the same name.

7 MARCH

The Vietnam's People's Army (VPA), into which the PRG forces had been integrated by this time, captures two strategic district towns, Thuan Man and Duc Lap, in Pleiku and Ban Me Thuot provinces respectively, thus initiating the 55 days and nights of battle which ends with the collapse of the Saigon regime.

10 APRIL

President Ford asks for an additional 977 million dollars, 722 million of it for direct military aid for South Vietnam. Further military aid, however, is refused by Congress.

21 APRIL

President Thieu resigns, bitterly attacking the United States for violating a secret pledge by former President Nixon to "react violently and immediately" in the event of a North Vietnamese offensive. Thieu is replaced as President by Vice-President Tran Van Huong.

26 APRIL

Start of the battle for Saigon.
Nguyen Van Thieu flies off to Taiwan.

28 APRIL

Le Duc Tho and Pham Hung, veteran members of the Political Bureau of the Lao Dong (now Communist) Party arrive at the forward headquarters of General Van Tien Dung, who personally directed the whole campaign, to help with the final stages of the battle.

General Duong Van "Big" Minh becomes president, Tran Van Huong having resigned the previous day.

30 APRIL

Saigon is taken by assault. The following day, the VPA is in control of the Mekong Delta and thus of the whole of the country's 44 provinces.

11 AUGUST

The DRV and the South Vietnam applications to join the UN are approved 13 to 1 (the United States) with Costa Rica abstaining. The U.S.A. applies the veto.

30 SEPTEMBER

The applications are renewed with a 14 to 1 (U.S.A.) vote in favor. The U.S.A. applied the veto.

25 APRIL 1976

Nationwide elections are held to elect a National Assembly of 249 deputies from the North and 243 from the South.

24 JUNE

First session of the all-Vietnam National Assembly.

2 JULY

The reunification of the country is formally declared under the name: The Socialist Republic of Vietnam, its capital Hanoi. Pham Van Dong is elected prime minister. Saigon is renamed Ho Chi Minh City.

14–20 DECEMBER

The Fourth Congress of the newly named Vietnam Communist Party is held in Hanoi with 1,038 elected delegates taking part. The Congress charted the course of building up a modern, advanced socialist state over the next 20 years. This is to be carried out "under a regime of collective rule by the toiling people", and will be based essentially on three simultaneous revolutions: in relations of production, in ideology and culture, and in science and technology, with the greatest stress on the last. Within the next twenty years Vietnam will have to move from present small-scale production to large-scale socialist production in agriculture and industry, although traditional handicrafts will have their place. The tasks are to be accomplished by a series of five-year plans, the first one of which began immediately after the end of the war.

Introduction

"Because of the imbalance of forces, some people at one point compared our resistance to a fight of 'grasshoppers against elephants.' To a certain extent, for those who saw only the material side and transitory aspect of things, the situation really seemed like that. Against enemy planes and artillery we had only bamboo spears. But our party is Marxist-Leninist. We look not only at the present, but also the future; we place our trust in the strength and morale of the masses and people. Thus we resolutely reply to the waverers and pessimists:

" 'Today, yes, it's the grasshoppers that dare stand up to the elephants.
" 'Tomorrow, it's the elephant that leaves its skin behind.'

"Reality has shown that the colonialist 'elephant' is starting to run short of breath, while our army has grown up into a majestic tiger."

Thus, Ho Chi Minh, founder and incomparable leader of the Vietnamese national independence struggle for half a century, described the situation in February 1951[1], at the mid-way

---

1. From the political report to the 2nd National Congress of the Lao Dong (Workers) party, February 1951. Ho Chi Minh, *Oeuvres Choisis* Hanoi: Foreign Languages Publishing House, 1962, vol. 2, p. 219.

point in the fierce, unequal struggle against French colonialism in the first resistance war.

It was this unswerving faith in the people and the decisive role of people's participation at every stage and phase of 30 years of armed struggle that is the distinguishing trait of the Vietnamese revolution. It was not by chance that the final, tempestuous storming of their adversary's bastions of power was officially designated: "General Offensive and People's Uprisings." For that is what it was. Perhaps because of the breathless speed with which everything happened, with an average of three provincial capitals falling every two days for 55 days on end, and because of the sheer technical brilliance of the military part of the operations, the people's uprisings aspect was overlooked. Certainly it was not something which would be admitted by the briefings officers at the U.S. Embassy or Saigon Command headquarters. It would have ruined the simplistic official version that all that was happening was a "North Vietnamese" invasion. Agence France Presse (AFP) correspondent, Paul Léandri, was brutally murdered by the Saigon police, in the first days of the offensive for reporting facts which refuted that official version! People's participation even in the liberation of Saigon could not be felt by those who remained in their hotels or conceived "people's uprisings" exclusively in terms of masses raging down the streets with axes and meat choppers to storm a Saigon equivalent of the Bastille!

In the book that follows, I have tried to place in perspective the role of the people, not only in that historic offensive which resulted in the final and total victory of the forces of national liberation, but throughout the decades of struggle and sacrifice which led up to that final offensive and made victory certain. It is the product of numerous firsthand observations of that struggle, starting with my first visit to the Liberated Zones of the North, at the start of the battle of Dien Bien Phu in the spring of 1954 and ending with two months in the Liberated South in the summer of 1975, with many visits to the North and the Liberated Zones of the South, in between.

Another aspect dealt with in the following chapters is the total defeat—by superior intelligence and morale—of the United States in every field: military, political, diplomatic and psychological. Parallel to this were the repeated blunders of American leadership in rejecting at every phase, solutions which were the most advantageous from their own viewpoint, in favor of an illusory military victory. From Presidents Eisenhower to Ford, with Presidents Kennedy, Johnson and Nixon in between, each believed in turn that he could do better than the president he succeeded and bring the Vietnamese to their knees. They were encouraged to believe so by the chiefs of the country's military and intelligence services.

Although this book deals almost exclusively with the struggle of the Vietnamese people, Cambodian and Laotian "grasshoppers" also dared to stand up to the American "elephant" and were transformed into "majestic tigers" in the course of the struggle while the "elephant" blundered into the inextricable quagmire of defeat. The saga of the struggles of the Cambodian and Laotian peoples will be dealt with in a subsequent work.

Wilfred Burchett
Paris,
April 30, 1976

Part I

The People's Uprising

Chapter 1.

Reaping the Whirlwind

During a two-months visit to liberated South Vietnam from mid-July to mid-September, 1975, I had innumerable discussions with soldiers from generals on down, as well as with members of local people's forces and organizations to piece together what really happened and how. Not just the strictly military operational side, but the interrelation between military force and people's participation in what was the fullest expression of People's War. It would take far more than two months' research to put together the whole story. Some key elements of the mosaic however, can give an idea of the pattern and color of the whole. From this point on the revolutionary forces will generally be referred to as the VPA (Vietnam People's Army), the NLF and North Vietnamese forces, while retaining their separate unit identity, having been fused into one single military machine operating under a single unified command of the Vietnam People's Army—as they had done up till the time of the historic battle of Dien Bien Phu. There was no longer a 17th parallel cutting through the VPA, nor was there one cutting through the Vietnamese Lao Dong (Workers') party. By the time the decisive general offensive was launched, the People's Revolutionary party in the South was operating under its real colors as the southern branch of the Lao Dong Party which it had always been.

On March 7, 1975, the VPA captured the two Saigon-controlled district centers of Thuan Man, 60 miles south of Pleiku in the Central Highlands and dominating a junction of Highways 14 and 7 (the latter linking Pleiku with Tuy Hoa on the coast) and Duc Lap, about 30 miles south of Ban Me Thuot on Highway 14. (Ban Me Thuot, Pleiku and Kontum are the three main cities of the strategic Central Highlands. Situated on an almost straight north-south line, they are linked by Highway 14. Ban Me Thuot is the southernmost, with Pleiku some 90 miles to the north, and Kontum 25 miles north of Pleiku). A couple of days previously, a feint attack had been launched towards Pleiku from the west. Such were the opening shots in a campaign of 55 days and nights that shook the world, shattering U.S. dreams of tele-guided domination of South Vietnam. It was an odd coincidence, but 21 years earlier, Vo Nguyen Giap, who certainly master-minded this operation, directed another battle of 55 days and nights which shook the world and shattered French dreams of hanging on to its Indochina colonies. Dien Bien Phu was an historic victory in its day because the elimination of some 16,000 élite French troops there was sufficient to bring France to the conference table and resulted in the subsequent signing of the 1954 Geneva Agreement. This time Giap was taking on some 1,100,000 troops, superbly equipped with the most of the best that the U.S. could provide, on a battlefield which ranged over the whole of South Vietnam.

"On the eve of the general offensive and people's uprisings" continued the Giap-Dung analysis, "the enemy still possessed very powerful military forces on all battle-fronts of the South. He still had very modern arms at his disposal, including relatively strong air and naval forces . . . His armed forces were disposed according to the exigencies of what is known as positional warfare, aimed at defending 'the maximum of territorial security,' linked with an integrated system of military control through some 8,000 posts of all sorts, even down to village and hamlet level. Great efforts had been made to multiply their regional forces in order to be able to mobilize the entirety of their regular troops to cope with our offensives and also to launch large-scale operations into the liberated zones . . ."

Thieu and his U.S. advisers misread what was going on, as Giap had guessed they would, and weakened the Ban Me Thuot garrison by rushing a regiment of the 23rd division—ear-marked for the city defense—towards Pleiku, and a regiment of the 23rd division together with a Ranger's regiment from the Coastal Plains to try to recapture Thuan Man and remove the threats to Highway 14 and 7. On March 8, the VPA with local guerillas struck at Ban Me Thuot, capturing that very heavily defended base-city on March 10. It was the most important base in the Central Highlands, the Americans at one time planning to transfer all headquarters installations there in case Saigon was endangered. Prime Minister Huynh Tan Phat stated that the case of Ban Me Thuot represented the second of the "seven fatal errors."*

The enemy was taken entirely by surprise when we attacked Ban Me Thuot. Thieu did not realize we could go over to the offensive so early and his forces were not ready. Their morale had been lowered by our counter-offensives from the end of 1973 onwards. They had nothing like their previous air and artillery support, and their own stocks of munitions were somewhat diminished.[2] They couldn't throw it away as they used to. And they could not react as promptly as before. These were also factors in influencing our decision to advance the date of the general offensive. Ban Me Thuot was defended by two divisions. The 23rd Infantry division was weakened because Thieu and his US advisers were fooled by our feint attack and thought either Pleiku or Kontum was our real target. We knew that if we captured the more heavily-defended Ban Me Thuot, at the same time cutting the enemy's line of retreat, this would lead to a further big deterioration of enemy morale and this could be decisive.

The third error was that after Thieu lost Ban Me Thuot, he lost his head and ordered his forces to withdraw to the Coastal Plains. But we had already cut the roads to prevent this. Thieu's strategy was to consolidate at all costs in the Coastal Plains, which meant abandoning Pleiku and Kontum and virtually the whole of the Central Highlands where the local people were rising up and taking things into their own hands. Thieu and his Americans could not foresee that each retreat or withdrawal, or whatever they want-

---

*The first and most significant of these is discussed in Chapter Thirteen.

2. It was estimated by American experts at that time that the Saigon forces normally expended 18 times as many artillery shells as the VPA, except in the Central Highlands, where the ratio was estimated at twenty-three to one.

ed to call it, further demoralised their troops. It appears that their computers have no equations for morale factors. In any case, we had no intention of allowing the enemy to consolidate in the Coastal Plains.

A measure of the panic which seized Saigon when the fall of Ban Me Thuot was announced was the brutal murder of Agence France Presse correspondent Paul Léandri on March 14, for having reported on the role of local Montagnard tribespeople in liberating the city. Called in to Saigon police headquarters to explain why he had sent the story, Léandri apparently reacted like any other journalist should and defended his sources and professional rights. As he left the building to get into his car, he was shot dead by a police guard. Four days later, a Catholic priest, Father Tran Tuu Thanh[3] held a press conference in Saigon and confirmed that the first troops to enter Ban Me Thuot were some thousand FULRO[4] Montagnards, supported by local residents. Tank-supported VPA troops entered the city after it had already been liberated largely by the local population. Father Thanh explained that the main reason for the speedy fall of the city was Saigon's repressive policy towards the Montagnard tribespeople.

Before the battle for Ban Me Thuot was over, some VPA units dashed off to block reinforcements reaching Pleiku or Kontum, or forces from either of the three cities withdrawing to the coastal Plains. By the time Thieu started withdrawing his forces from Kontum and Pleiku, local people's organizations had seized strategic passes and blown up bridges on the only roads along which Thieu's entirely motorized troops could pass. The Paris daily, *Le Monde* was later to comment (April 2) that "the local population played a decisive role in expelling the gov-

---

3. Father Tran Tuu Thanh headed the "Peoples Anti-Corruption Movement" in Saigon which became very active after the signing of the Paris Agreement.

4. FULRO (United Front for the Struggle of the Oppressed Races) was originally sponsored by French, based in Cambodia, mainly those with interests in rubber plantations in Cambodia and the other side of the frontier in South Vietnam. They hoped to use it to win back some French influence in the Central Highlands, home of the Montagnards. Later it was taken over by the CIA, but betrayed, due to pressures from the Saigon régime. Decimated in a series of uprisings in 1965, FULRO later rallied to the NLF mainly because of the latter's policy of an autonomous state for the tribespeople after Liberation. Several outstanding Montagnard leaders are members of the NLF's Central Committee.

ernment troops from the Central Highlands," the sort of comment for which Paul Léandri had been shot.

The regiment from the 23rd division that had been despatched to Pleiku turned back towards Ban Me Thuot, when its commander realized the main thrust was there. It found the road cut and was quickly encircled and wiped out. The remnants of the other two regiments tried to withdraw along Highway 21, linking Ban Me Thuot with the Coastal plains just north of Nha Trang, but were cut to pieces. Four battalions of Montagnard troops integrated in these regiments mutinied and joined in the attack against the fleeing survivors of the Ban Me Thuot garrison. The account of Generals Vo Nguyen Giap and Van Tien Dung continues:

> Confronted with our strong attacks the enemy's strategic retreat from the Central Highlands developed into a panic-stricken rout rarely known in military history. After the Ban Me Thuot victory we noted that, faced with decisive defeat, the enemy's morale had again fallen considerably and this was a favorable occasion to press on with our general offensive and pull off a great victory.
>
> From March 13, we were involved in blocking the enemy retreat from the Central Highlands. On March 16, when the enemy started to withdraw from Pleiku and Kontum via Highway 7 (linking Pleiku with Tuy Hoa on the coastal plains, W. B.), we mobilized our tank forces to seize positions along Highways 14 and 7, to block the enemy in time, at points east and west of the Cheo-Reo pass. A unit of regional forces from Phuc Yen province had cut the Son Hoa bridge, completely blocking the enemy's escape route. Thus the fate of the retreating enemy forces from the Central Highlands was sealed.
>
> Between March 18 and 20, we encircled, split up and attacked the retreating enemy forces, at the same time liberating Cheo-Reo (the capital of Phu Bon province and squarely astride Highway 7, W. B.). Following that, we quickly destroyed the remaining enemy forces withdrawing towards Cung Son district, (which flanked Highway 7 as it came down to the sea at Tuy Hoa, capital of Phu Yen province, W. B.). By March 24, the enemy forces withdrawing from Kontum, including 6 regiments of Rangers and 3 armoured regiments, together with some other miscellaneous units, were completely destroyed.

The battles for the Central Highlands represented a great

victory. The whole zone had been liberated and more than 112,000 puppet troops eliminated. Over 600,000 local inhabitants regained the right to be masters in their villages. We had seized all enemy arms and munitions. After this victory we were in a position to directly threaten the enemy's defense lines in the coastal areas. The whole enemy tactical defense system for the battlefronts in South Vietnam were in danger of being sliced in two . . .

The rapidity of action which constantly took the Saigon troops by surprise was made possible by the support role of the local population. They took care of the wounded, buried the dead, handled mopping-up operations, occupied all enemy installations, securing the surrender of local defense units, installing organs of revolutionary power while battles were still in progress. The VPA had élite commando units whose speciality it was to suddenly appear behind the lines in Saigon army uniforms; blowing up bridges to prevent an enemy retreat or securing them for the advance of their own forces, relying on local people to guide them to their targets. The high degree of people's participation enabled the regular forces to concentrate on the main job of dealing with the enemy forces with great dash and speed.

Even following the course of the advance from afar it was clear that there was great flexibility in the command of the VPA and, in a later discussion with the participants, an impressive factor was the amount of latitude in the hands of local commanders so they could immediately exploit enemy mistakes or weaknesses. And if the enemy did not make mistakes on his own initiative, he was lured into doing so by feint attacks and a hundred other ruses to keep him looking the "other way" while decisive positions were taken. The Saigon forces, despite their U.S. advisers, were constantly outmanouevred and induced into making disastrous and irreversible errors.

The example of persuading Thieu that Pleiku was the main target and then making a surprise attack against Ban Me Thuot was a case in point. More important was that Thieu's overall strategy was based on an attack from the North, against the 1st Military Region which adjoins the 17th parallel and includes Quang Tri, Hue and Danang. But the northern sector was bypassed and what Thieu received was a terrible punch in the belly which so doubled him up that he never did recover. While the final battles in the Central Highlands were still raging, VPA units swung North and cut the main north-south Highway 1 between Danang and Hue.

In the meantime pressure was being exerted against the Saigon sector from the South, in the Mekong Delta where there were stepped-up attacks against Highway 4—the "Foodline" along which passed the capital's daily food supplies—and from the North, where the district center Tri Tam, in Tay Ninh province, had been taken on March 11. All roads linking Saigon with Tay Ninh being cut on the 17th. By this time Thieu's conduct of military affairs was being more and more criticized, especially by some high-ranking officers. Fearing a coup coinciding with increasing military pressure against the capital. Thieu panicked again and withdrew the 1st Airborne division, considered one of the best, from Quang Tri to help defend Saigon, considerably weakening the northern sector. Meanwhile propaganda groups, mainly girls and old women, were working hard on the garrisons in the North, urging them to desert and return to their villages.

On March 19, before the road-cutting operations in the Hue-Danang sector had been effected, it was decided to open up a major attack against the whole northern area. The decision was taken on the basis of the declining state of enemy morale, Quang Tri having fallen that day without a fight. In response to effective work by the propaganda groups, mobile units supposed to be holding a defense line along the My Chanh river to the north of Hue simply abandoned their defenses and made off for their homes in now liberated Quang Tri! By March 22, Hue having been completely encircled, an assault was simultaneously launched from all sides. There was little resistance, a large part of Thieu's troops being evacuated by landing craft to Danang. Hue was completely liberated on the afternoon of the 26th. Two more provincial capitals, Quang Ngai, of the old revolutionary province of that name, birthplace of premier Pham Van Dong, and Tam Ky, capital of Quang Tin province, had been taken over by people's organizations on the 24th, the garrisons fleeing in disorder at the sudden appearance of NLF flags over all public buildings and leaflets showering down urging them to surrender "or else. . . ."

Western press reports often referred to the abandonment of a district center or provincial capital "without a fight," with garrisons inexplicably fleeing when there were no VPA troops even within artillery range. Trying to follow what was happening through official briefings in Saigon, with the location of units pin-pointed on military maps, it must have looked that way. But in fact the precipitate flight or surrender of garrisons was due to the people's uprisings element in what was officially and properly designated the "General Offensive and People's Uprisings." This aspect was almost entirely overlooked—or simply denied—in the western press, but not by Vo Nguyen Giap who, great classical strategist that he is, is also an ardent advocate and initiator of people's war.*

A few hours after the fall of Hue, Thieu broadcast that familiar formula for armies in retreat—a new "shortened defense line" was being established at Danang which would be "defended to the last." The account by Generals Vo Nguyen Giap and Van Tien Dung describe what really happened:

> The victories at Quang Ngai and Tam Ky had pushed the big military base complex at Danang into complete isolation. After having lost Hue, Thieu declared that he was determined to defend Danang cost what it may. The base complex was defended by the 1st Infantry division, remnants of the 2nd Infantry division, a Marine brigade, several Ranger battalions and artillery, tank and armoured car regiments. Over 100,000 troops altogether, plus one Air Force division based on the airport, as well as a number of warships anchored in the harbor and cruising offshore.

> Thieu and his U.S. advisers considered we would need at least one month's preparations to mount an attack on Danang. In fact, by mid-March our people and armed forces were well advanced with their plans to attack the huge base complex . . .

> On the morning of the 28th, the commanders of the puppets' 1st Army Corps (the total of main-force units in each of the four military regions constituted an Army Corps, W.B.) were still meeting to discuss their defense plans for Danang. We had come to the conclusion that the enemy had only two alternatives: to withdraw rapidly or to fight a delaying action and withdraw according to a pre-arranged plan. We prepared our attack as if they had chosen the first alternative, but also prepared to wipe them out in case they chose to fight a defensive, delaying action.

> Our people and armed forces were operating under the slogan: "Strike at the right moment, quickly, audaciously,

*A more detailed description and concrete accounts of the role and nature of the people's uprisings are set forth in later chapters.

suddenly and surely." We had quickly mobilized our main forces from various directions, at the same time ordering our auxiliary forces to concentrate at given points and be ready to closely cooperate with the people's uprisings. One unit taking part in the battle for Hue was ordered to head south for Danang before the action for Hue had ended. The troops that took part in the liberation of Tam Ky were ordered north for the same purpose. Another unit stationed at Thuong Duc was also ordered to advance on Danang. On March 27, our forces started converging on the city, moving by day and by night. At the same time, the political forces inside the city were putting the finishing touches to preparations for a mass uprising.

On the morning of the 28th the attack started with artillery fire directed against the air base, the Danang naval base, the Nuoc Man airport, the Son Tra peninsula (where the main air base and storage depots were situated, W.B.) thus blocking all ways of retreat, including by air or sea.

Our infantry and tanks also started to attack from all directions. The tank-supported infantry advancing from the North took the Hai Van and Lien Chien passes, decimating Marine units guarding them, quickly advanced into the city and pressed on to pierce the Son Tra peninsula. Troops advancing from the South outflanked the Ba Rien and Vinh Dien passes, destroying what was left of the 3rd Infantry division, then advancing quickly towards the south of the city, pushed into Nuoc Man airport, cooperating with local forces and residents to destroy the enemy in the area and then directly attacking the Son Tra peninsula. Troops advancing from the southeast, quickly captured the Ai Nghia base and entered Danang airport.

Supporting the offensive of the liberation armed forces, the people and local defense forces rose up, mastered the situation in various zones, protecting lives and property, urging the puppet troops to lay down their arms and appealing to officers and men to give themselves up.

At 1500 hours on March 29, our forces converging from various directions met in the city center. The offensive and people's uprising at Danang had ended in victory. Over 100,000 puppet troops and the Headquarters of the 1st Army Corps had been completely destroyed. The most powerful military base complex in Central Annam had been destroyed in an attack and uprising that lasted just 32 hours. We seized all arms and military equipment...

The first U.S. Defense Department estimate was that about

300 million dollars worth of military equipment had fallen into VPA hands at Danang, enough to equip three American-size divisions together with at least 200 tanks and 10,000 other military vehicles. Instead of one completely liberated province on March 7, there were thirteen by the end of March, the first 22 days of the campaign. It would have been reasonable to expect the VPA to take a rest, digest and consolidate its gains. That would be to misjudge the genius and dash of Giap, the swiftness with which he could take advantage of new situations and make correct analyses based on peering into the enemy's mind, foreseeing his reactions and weaknesses and the gaps through which his forces could speed on to new victories. According to reliable sources, three months had been allotted for the first phase of the offensive—crushing the enemy in the Central Highlands and the Northern Provinces. If this was completed in a little over three weeks, it was greatly due to the superb morale of the VPA and the inestimable contribution made by the local people's organizations. In summing up that brilliantly successful first phase of the general offensive, while it was still being fused into the second phase, the Giap-Dung account comments:

> After these great victories, in comparing the forces and positions of the enemy with our own, we noted that there had been a very favorable transformation of the situation in our favor. The enemy's forces had been reduced by about one half whereas our forces had rapidly grown.[5] The enemy's defensive positions had been completely destroyed whereas our forces had benefited from new experiences in the new-type offensive actions. The enemy had to withdraw to defend the small part of the territory he controlled in a tactical situation which had already been shattered, full of gaps and weaknesses impossible to repair.

> We, on the contrary, had new bases, new strategic lines to continue to develop, new areas to encircle and attack. Enemy moral had rapidly deteriorated because of the series of defeats, whereas our forces were greatly encouraged by the series of victories. We had made a timely evaluation of the

---

5. As towns and provinces were liberated, young people everywhere volunteered for service in local self-defense guerillas, which permitted the regional forces and some of the local guerilla to be transformed into main force units. Battalions and regiments were rapidly formed including tank and armored car units with armor captured from the enemy—and joined in the headlong advance.

situation and the state of the war had permitted rapid advances. Our military and political forces had defeated those of the enemy. The United States had proved to be powerless and no longer capable of rescuing its puppets. The situation had become 'very ripe' to launch an historic operation —to directly attack Saigon to destroy the puppets and pull off the Great Victory.

Towards the end of March, while the operations in the Central Highlands were still being expanded, we had already decided that the direction of our next attack should be towards Saigon-Gia Dinh. And when the battle of Hue-Danang ended in victory, we decided to start that historic operation and give it the designation 'Ho Chi Minh' . . .

Chapter 2.

Operation Ho Chi Minh

Although the most spectacular actions had been on the Northern Front (First Military Region) and the Central Highlands (Second Military Region) during the 25 days of battles referred to in the previous chapter, this did not indicate that there was not activity occurring elsewhere. In the provinces to the immediate east, north and south of Saigon (Third Military Region), in the Mekong Delta (Fourth Military Region) and around Saigon itself in the Special Defense Sector (a separate command responsible for the in-depth defense of the capital), Captain Le Tan Dat, deputy chief operations officer of the VPA's 4th Army Corps, whose walnut-hued face suggested he was more at home in a jungle hammock than in the fine new headquarters his command had inherited in Saigon, filled in some of these support activities as well as the preparations and launching of "Operation Ho Chi Minh." The 4th Army Corps, he explained, was an all-South unit "composed of elements from various regional uprisings and operations in the Nam Bo (Cochin Chine),[6] regrouped into ever larger units until they reached

---

6. The French divided Vietnam into three administrative regions, from south to north, Cochin Chine, Annam and Tonkin, which the Vietnamese call Nam Bo, Trung Bo and Bac Bo, or Southern, Central and Northern regions, respectively.

Army Corps size." (A textbook Army Corps is an autonomous unit comprised of at least four divisions plus supporting units, W.B.) Its task was to operate in an arc-shaped "expanded battlefront" almost 200 miles in length from west to east, averaging about 60 miles north of Saigon.

"Our first support operations were along Highway 13 (running north from Saigon to Loc Ninh and the Cambodian frontier, W.B.) in Tay Ninh province and along Highway 20 (running northeast from near Bien Hoa to Phan Rang on the coast, W.B.) mainly in Lam Dong province. Between March 20-29 we advanced our front line operations to an average of 50 miles from Saigon, capturing the district center of Dinh Quan in Lam Dong province on March 28 and the provincial capital itself the following day. We then pushed our springboard to within 40 miles of Saigon, infiltrating élite commando units in company and battalion strength into the enemy defenses around the capital. During this period our cadres inside Saigon made contact with our forward units outside."

To keep the Saigon forces busy so that they could not concentrate their attention too much on one spot, Captain Dat said that guerilla and regional forces in the Mekong Delta "rose up and made the enemy keep his nose down." By this time, President Ford had sent the U.S. Army Chief of Staff and former commander of U.S. forces in South Vietnam, General Frederick Weyand, to Saigon to stiffen the capital's defenses. He toured the forward lines with his opposite number, General Nguyen Vinh My, recommending one line for defense in depth, with its western pivot at Phan Rang, about 200 miles northeast of Saigon on the coast, running across to the beginning of the Central Highlands, to block any further advance by VPA forces down Highway 1, towards Saigon and the Mekong Delta. Weyand recommended another line pivoted on Xuan Loc, some 37 miles east of Saigon on Highway 1, only 22 miles from the huge Bien Hoa air base. Xuan Loc was to be held at all costs.

"The fourth fatal error," Prime Minister Huynh Tan Phat explained, "was when General Weyand advised Thieu to defend Xuan Loc at any price and make it the last major outer defense line at the approaches to Saigon. They committed their main force units into defending Xuan Loc, instead of the capital itself."

Things started to go wrong for the Weyand plan almost

immediately when Dalat, the northern anchor of the Phan Rang defense line, was liberated on April 4, despite very tough resistance put up by units composed entirely of officers and officer cadets from the Dalat officers' training school. (The huge naval base at Camranh Bay had fallen the previous day.) To defend Xuan Loc, Thieu had concentrated the 18th Infantry division, seven battalions of Civil Guards and the 3rd Armored division with 500 tanks, armored cars and over 100 pieces of artillery. At the Ben Hoa air base to the West, there was the 3rd Airborne division and a brigade of Marines, and 500 planes were allocated for the defense of Xuan Loc. Defense of the northern approaches to Saigon was entrusted to the 5th division, based at a point about 75 miles north of Saigon, and to the northwest, there was the 25th division, plus eighteen battalions of main force units and Civil Guards, three artillery battalions with fifty artillery pieces, an armored battalion with fifty tanks and armored cars, and what was left of the 22nd division. The 7th and 9th divisions from the Mekong Delta were also held in reserve for the northwestern sector. All in all it was a formidable array of troops and armor, which on the maps must have looked like a semi-circle of steel and concrete blocking all the approaches from which the VPA could be expected to come.

Inside Saigon itself there was the newly formed 3rd Parachutist brigade, a battalion of presidential guards to defend "Independence Palace" and 30,000 field police, specially trained to put down people's uprisings. The crack 1st Airborne division which Thieu had brought down from the north was responsible for the defense of Tan Son Nhut air base, where Thieu had his headquarters.

"To prepare for the final assault," continued Captain Le Tan Dat, "our Armored Corps started moving up from the East. At the same time, our élite 9th division performed a remarkable feat by moving from its position north and northeast of Saigon, through enemy defenses, to take up a position southwest of the capital—the most favorable position for a surprise attack. The first phase of the battle for Saigon started on April 9 when we opened up an artillery barrage against Xuan Loc. Due to the fact that the defense line was very solid, with large numbers of troops involved, we decided to avoid a frontal attack and to outflank it and destroy piecemeal the troops around the perimeter. Between April 9th and 20th, we fired some 200,000 rounds of 120 mm shells into the Xuan Loc defenses so the enemy could neither reinforce nor supply. In response, they flew some 150 bombing missions a day against our positions. They even dropped some of their 7,000 pound 'daisy-cutters' and the latest CBU-55 cluster bombs,[7] but our troops were well dug in and hung on, moving close to their positions by night, moving back in the day-time. On April 18," continued Captain Dat, using a pointer to explain the various positions on a huge military map, "in separate actions we wiped out the 52nd regiment of the 18th division, just to the east of Xuan Loc and inflicted heavy damage on the Parachutists brigade just over 2 miles south of the base which by then was a pile of ruins. On the night of the 20th the enemy tried to break out and flee while we did our best to intercept them. We captured the 18th division commander, General Le Minh Dao, together with 5,500 of his troops, as well as Colonel Phuc, the Xuan Loc provincial chief. Another 3,000 enemy troops had been killed and wounded. Our forces shot down 25 jet fighter-bombers during the action." (This was the only hard-fought battle during the General Offensive up till that point and one of the biggest of the whole war.) Thieu then committed what premier Phat considered his "fifth fatal error."

After we wiped out their positions at Xuan Loc, the opinion of Thieu and his U.S. advisers was that we would exploit this to attack their nearest weak points by way of approaching their strong ones. We had employed this tactic in the past and Thieu used up a lot more troops strengthening these positions on the assumption that we would do it again. In parenthesis this was also an error that they repeat-

---

7. The huge "daisy-cutters" were so named because they were designed to explode just above the ground so the main force of the explosion was horizontal in order to cause the maximum destruction at ground level. The Americans claimed that these monsters were used only for blasting helicopter landing pads out of the jungle. The CBU-55 was the latest, and most horrifying death-dealing device, the Pentagon tried out in Indochina. The CBU was a "mother-bomb" which spewed forth scores of small bombs each of which sprayed a highly inflammable aerosol gas, ignited by a special firing device. The resulting explosion of flame, apart from anything else, consumed all the oxygen in an area of several hundred yards radius, automatically killing every living thing. Paul Léandri, the AFP correspondent shot down by the Saigon police, had aroused the fury of U.S. military in Indochina, for having revealed the use of the CBU-55 when it was first tried out in Cambodia some weeks prior to his death.

edly made, preparing for what we did last time instead of using their imagination to work out what we might do next time. Thieu and the Americans simply did not believe that we would bypass small towns and concentrate on the prize target—Saigon itself. But this is just what we did. The enemy was certain that we would need much time to consolidate our gains and to regroup our forces before daring to attack Saigon. Even after Xuan Loc fell they were sure we could not get into position to attack Saigon before the rainy season gave them some respite to build up their forces and launch counter-attacks to regain some key positions.

To the east, the Phan Rang defense line had crumbled on April 16, when Phan Rang itself fell and the whole headquarters' staff of the 3rd Military Region were killed or captured. All towns for a hundred miles down Highway 1 as far as Phan Thiet were liberated in the days that followed. A remarkable feature of the period preceding the assault on Saigon was the capacity for self-delusion by Thieu, his U.S. advisers and their cronies at the U.S. Embassy. Like Hitler in the final days in his Berlin bunker, they hoped a miracle was going to ward off the inevitable disaster. Thus on April 7, the PRG (Provisional Revolutionary Government) president Nguyen Huu Tho had given an interview to AFP in which he said that Thieu must be ousted "and an administration set up in Saigon which sincerely wants peace, independence, national reconciliation and concord and which will seriously implement the Paris Agreement. "The PRG", he said, "is prepared to talk with such an administration in order to arrive at a prompt solution to the affairs of South Vietnam . . ." A deaf ear was turned to this, under the circumstances, very generous offer. On April 19, the PRG's military delegation in Saigon said a military offensive against the city could be avoided if Thieu stepped down "and all U.S. advisers disguised as civilians left the country." This was also ignored.

On April 21, Thieu finally resigned—but the American military advisers continued to direct the war. Announcing his resignation in a long, emotional speech, Thieu bitterly attacked the United States for "betrayal." He singled out former president Nixon for special vituperation, claiming that there had been "secret commitments" by Nixon in exchange for Thieu agreeing to sign the Paris Agreement. (Later an exchange of letters between Nixon and Thieu was produced to back up the charge.) His main complaint was that the new administration had gone back on Nixon's pledges that the United States would come to his rescue in case he was in military difficulties. He quoted Nixon as saying:

> In the final analysis all accords are but sheets of paper. They will be worthless if they are not implemented and if North Vietnam violates them. Therefore the important thing is what you do after signing the agreement, and what facilities we will make available to you if North Vietnam reneges on, and violates the agreement and renews its attacks against the South. So you should not be concerned about the signing of this agreement ...

Three months earlier, on January 13, Father Tran Tuu Thanh, of the anti-corruption movement, produced a document as evidence that Thieu and his wife received a seven million dollar gift from Nixon as an inducement to sign the Paris Agreement!

On the day of Thieu's resignation, the 71 year-old vice-president Tran Van Huong was sworn in to replace him. This substitution was immediately denounced by the PRG as "maintaining the Thieu government without Thieu." The latter flew off to exile early on the 26th with a long stop-over in Taiwan. In his inaugural speech to a joint session of the National Assembly, also on the 26th, Tran Van Huong pledged that the government "would fight to the death rather than surrender."

"The Ho Chi Minh battle proper got under way at 5:00 P.M. on the 26th," continued Captain Le Tan Dat. "The first phase called for all units to be in their designated positions by the evening of the 29th for a five-pronged assault from all sides. The aim was to crush all defense positions, encircle the enemy forces, split them up and destroy them. In cooperation with the Saigon residents and the crack commando units already inside the city, we were to completely crush the enemy and liberate Saigon. Originally the final assault date was May 1, but the preparations went more smoothly than expected so the date was advanced by two days. The Bien Hoa defense line was an important target but not the main one. However our forces were to attack there to draw enemy forces eastward and facilitate a breakthrough elsewhere. A second task assigned to us was to use our tanks to thrust into the city, occupy the ministry of National Defense (right in the heart of the city, W. B.), the Naval Headquarters and—prize of all prizes—the Presidential Palace. We had also to use part of our force to cut Highway 15, leading southeast to Vungtao (an important pleasure resort and base on the coast, with many stand-by headquarters installations and facilities for large-scale evacuation by sea in case of a threat to Saigon, W.B.).

"Our tactics in the East were to use main force units and massive fire-power to crush the enemy defense line. From the North, we had to capture intact the vast military storage depot at Go Vap, less than two miles from Saigon. To do this our infantry and main force units would have to thrust deeply into the enemy rear, encircling the 5th division but not attacking it. Had we stopped to fight a battle there we would have taken losses and slowed up achieving our main battle aims. Once we had carried out the encirclement, we could hand over the task of maintaining it to local forces while we pushed on to our jump-off positions for the 29th.

"The task of the prong advancing from the Northwest was to attack Tan Son Nhut airport and capture Thieu's General Staff Headquarters. The Western prong was to use its tank forces and in close cooperation with the local masses, to capture the 25th division headquarters at Dung Du—the former headquarters of the U.S. 25th "Tropical Lightning" division. From the Southwest, the task was to outflank the enemy and get as close to Saigon as possible.

"On April 27th, we launched assaults on the defense line east of Bien Hoa and along Highway 15, waging many fierce battles here, as this was considered the main gateway to Saigon. As anticipated we drew enemy strength away from areas where our strongest punches would be delivered. There were furious tank battles and artillery duels with enemy planes whirling overhead all the time, diving to bomb and strafe. We were attacking the strongest ramparts of the enemy defense system. At Ho Nai, just over two miles east of Bien Hoa, we had to launch three assaults before resistance was crushed. At the headquarters of the Army Motorized Units School at Nuoc Trong, the enemy launched five fierce counter-attacks. Tanks and armored cars were burning all over the place. They had the advantage of air power, we had the advantage of superior morale and local forces who knew the terrain and were expert in handling shoulder-fired anti-tank missiles. The battle raged all that day and the next when we launched an assault on Bien Hoa itself, although in this phase of the operation we were outnumbered three to one. Again there were very fierce battles, tanks firing at each other at point-blank range. Our guerillas were very effective here. The battle for Bien Hoa raged for seven hours without any let-up, but at the end of that time we were masters of the air base and provincial capital. That same evening, our pilots using captured American planes, bombed Tan Son Nhut airport, destroying several enemy planes and causing other damage. At the same time, units of our Northwestern prong moved artillery close enough to bring the airport under artillery and mortar fire. With these two major air bases out of action, the enemy Air Force was transferred to Can Tho. All the prongs had done well. On the massive Eastern front, the Armored Vehicles Depot had been taken, also Baria—a few miles northwest of Vungtao."

An immediate consequence of the bombing and shelling of Tan Son Nhut was the start of the panic exodus from Saigon. President Ford ordered the immediate evacuation of all Americans and this was the signal for a "who can pay most" scramble for places aboard U.S. helicopters, by then the only means of getting out. Among the first Vietnamese to clamber aboard one of those helicopters taking off from the roof of the U.S. Embassy was former vice-president, Air Force-Marshal Nguyen Cao Ky. Two days earlier he had scornfully castigated the "cowards who are leaving with the Americans." On the 29th, after the VPA had halted the shelling at Tan Son Nhut, two big American C-130 transports tried to land, but had to abandon the attempt because of what were described as "panic-stricken crowds on the runways." There was plenty of panic but the key element here, as at Danang earlier, was a well-planned effort by local people's organizations to use the method of occupying the runways to prevent planes landing or taking off. They were quite up to "generating panic" when occasion demanded!

On April 28, Tran Van Huong had resigned as president in favor of General Duong Van "Big" Minh. The latter accepted the post despite urgent warnings from PRG personalities who wanted to spare him the humiliation of becoming an "enemy" even for a few days. A close relative was flown specially from Paris to warn him. Blocked at Bangkok by the fall of Tan Son Nhut, he contacted "Big" Minh by phone urging him not to accept such a doomed post. In vain! Minh's inaugural speech showed the lack of realism that still reigned in Saigon, even amongst the relatively enlightened. It seems that even the bombing and shelling of Tan Son Nhut was seen as an isolated act—probably because it was halted once the job was done—and there was little notion of the speed and might of the forces rapidly closing in on the city.

"We must obtain a ceasefire agreement, the sooner the better," said President-for-three-days Duong Van Minh, "and negotiate a political solution for South Veitnam within the framework of the Paris Agreement, to end the war and to restore peace in a spirit of national reconciliation and concord. The government which I am leading is a government of national reconciliation and concord . . ."

"While the main force units had been waging these extremely tough battles to the east and around Bien Hoa," Captain Dat went on, "our commando units, plus some local forces paid a heavy price to secure three main bridges across the Dong Nai river, on Highway 1. Our units fought throughout the 28th and 29th, beating off seven determined counter-attacks, before we could secure them. Our troops and the local forces fought with exemplary heroism. Once these bridges were in our hands, the enemy was cut off from his forward headquarters; his communications and supplies disrupted. On the evening of the 29th, the northern prong attacked the Go Vap supply complex and cut Highway 13, blocking an attempt by the 5th Division to move back into Saigon. Our commando units in the meantime had secretly opened two breaches in the Tan Son Nhut defenses and early on the morning of the 30th, our forces occupied the airfield and all installations, including Thieu's former general staff headquarters. Part of the forces which had outflanked the 5th division wheeled back and launched a surprise attack, virtually wiping it out in a short and savage battle. The survivors surrendered at 10 a.m. on the 30th, the divisional commander, General Le Minh Vy, committing suicide. At 9 a.m. the same morning the assault started against the 25th division, with the support of the heroic Cu Chi guerillas and regional forces. The division quickly disintegrated. Many fled and we captured some 5,000, including the acting divisional commander."

To the west and southwest, elements of the 4th Army Corps had manouevred into position in the rear of the main defense line and, helped by tank-supported infantry, approached very close to the city on the night of the 29th. From the east, other main force units, strongly supported by local self-defense guerillas, had seized control of a section of the Dong Nai river from the Cat Lai naval base about 9 miles east of the capital almost right up to the Naval headquarters on the Saigon water front. In the approach from the east there had been two major battles, apart from those to seize the bridges over the Dong Nai —at the big Ha Tien cement factory, 12 miles east of Saigon and at a major cross-roads 8 miles southeast of the capital.

Major General Di Thien Tich, commander of the 9th division, a youngish looking officer for such a post and a calm, reflective man who reminded me a little of Vo Nguyen Giap by his measured, analytical way of presenting things, explained the part his division played in the actual assault on Saigon. It had been given the seemingly impossible task of moving from positions northeast of Saigon to seize jump-off positions in the southwest, infiltrating armor and artillery through the heart of the enemy defense system and be in position by the night of the 29th, for a pre-dawn assault the following morning. How they managed this is a saga in itself which will be dealt with later.

"Although we had been allotted three battalions of T.54 tanks and armored cars, a regiment of field artillery and another of anti-aircraft artillery," said General Di Thien Tich, "the problem was that we had to get across the wide Vam Co river and cross a dozen miles of swamps to get into the right spot at the right time. Our primary task was to make a two-pronged attack into Saigon's southern suburbs and make straight for the headquarters of the Saigon-Gia Dinh Special Defense Sector. It was not sure how much of our armor and artillery we could get into position in time so we thought we would have to rely—as usual—mainly on our infantry and shoulder-carried weapons, in the use of which our troops are very expert. We avoided making frontal attacks on the enemy's outer defenses along the Vam Co river, because the element of timing was crucial. We had to coordinate our assault on the capital with people's uprisings in the 5th, 6th, 7th, 10th and 11th precincts and partly support those in the 1st, 2nd and 13th. In the latter three they would also have support from some other units. Everything depended on the secrecy with which we could get into position so we could use the vital element of surprise. Once we launched the assault, we counted on high speed and continuity of movement to give the enemy no respite; to catch him off-balance and keep him off-balance.

"By dawn of the 29th, all the infantry had turned up and

were concentrated at the rendezvous point, but all our armor and artillery was still on the other side of the Vam Co river. We had had some narrow escapes from being discovered. On the night of the 28th, one of our units had to over-run an enemy post to prevent the destruction of a bridge, vital to getting our heavy weapons across. But, as had been agreed, local guerillas were blowing up posts all over the place that night, so the enemy attached no special importance to our action. On the night of the 28th-29th, our Hoa Lu regiment[8] also had to destroy the puppet battalion No. 327 which was guarding the Sang bridge in the western outskirts of Saigon. Our troops seized this bridge and thus we were able to get part of the armor and artillery across before dawn. Some armored cars got bogged down in the swamp and we had to destroy them, but we pushed on with what we had. Thanks to good discipline, secrecy was kept and although the enemy finally woke up to the fact that 'something was going on,' they believed it was the movement of regional troops only.

"We were able to achieve complete surprise when we attacked at 5:00 a.m. on the 30th, throwing in everything we had; infantry, artillery and armor in concentrated blows at all positions in our way. Within one hour the Binh Gia regiment had destroyed enemy positions at the five-way Van Lom crossroads; Hoa Lu had liberated the Ba Hom crossroads and a battalion of Binh Gia had raced ahead to Ba Queo (a major intersection in the western suburbs, overlooked by the city's most modern hospital, W. B.). After breaching the heavy defenses at a whole series of crossroads and intersections we could press straight on towards the inner defenses. Our forces were still virtually intact, although all our tanks and armored cars had still not caught up with the vanguard infantry. People were now out in the streets, cheering us on, urging the enemy to surrender, waving NLF flags at our men.

"At the Bay Hien intersection (where seven streets meet just a little over one mile from the heart of Saigon, W. B.) where the Binh Gia regiment arrived about 7 a.m., the enemy resisted very fiercely. Planes joined in, bombing and strafing our forces. The battle lasted over 40 minutes during which we took

---

8. Each of the three regiments of the 9th division is named after a battle in which it particularly distinguished itself. The 1st is the Binh Gia, the 2nd, the Dong Xoai and the 3rd, the Hoa Lu.

our heaviest losses—over 40 killed and wounded. At one point there was an hour-long battle in which Binh Gia was attacked by two 'Special Forces' battalions and another battalion of regular infantry. The enemy was desperately trying to keep Highway 10 open to bring in reinforcements. Hoa Lu came to the rescue and the battalion of regular troops surrendered, the other two battalions making off to surrender later on . . ."

The divisions operations' officer, Captain Bui Huy, a short, slight man who spoke in staccato volleys interrupted to say: "I was at the battle at the Bay Hien intersection. At a critical stage 20 enemy tanks joined in, but the people were out in mass by then. They just encircled those tanks, clambered all over them, telling the crews they were going to die uselessly. The crews couldn't even aim their guns. So they gave up—surrendered. The local residents started to look after our wounded immediately, although there were bullets flying in all directions."

"Binh Gia was also held up briefly by a brigade of paratroopers," continued General Di Thien Tich, "but here again the people played a very important role, calling on the para's to surrender, pointing out that they would only kill and be killed for nothing. That ended rather smoothly and all three regiments were able to advance again. After the Ba Hom battle, Hoa Lu swung around, crossed the river and took over the Phu Lam radio-telecommunications center, handing it to local forces to maintain security. From then on the whole action converged on the Special Defense headquarters. Hoa Lu recrossed the river and split into two prongs advancing from the south, Binh Gia and Dong Xoai from the northwest. All strongpoints on the way had been taken over by the local people's forces. NLF flags were flying everywhere. By 10:15 a.m., Binh Gia had reached the headquarters. Enemy paratroopers launched a sharp counter-attack. The two prongs of Hoa Lu arrived and joined in the battle. Under these combined blows and with the people mixing in, the Paratroopers went to pieces. By 10:30 a.m. Binh Gia had taken over the Saigon-Gia Dinh Special Defense headquarters, capturing the entire leadership, starting with their commander, General Lam Van Phat, then raced off, closely followed by Dong Xoai, to the Presidential Palace. But by the time they got there at 11:40 a.m. the NLF flag was already flying from the flagpole. Other friendly units had got there earlier."

I asked how General Lam Van Phat actually surrendered. As commander of the Saigon defenses, he was obviously one of the most important, if not *the* most important of the five military zone commanders.

"When the Binh Gia regiment reached the main gates of his headquarters,' replied General Tich, "Phat ordered all-out resistance. But Binh Gia charged straight in, smashing down the gates. They were fired on from all directions in what was quite a brisk fire-fight which lasted ten or fifteen minutes before the two prongs of Hoa Lu appeared on the scene and Phat realized the game was up. He ordered his troops to lay down their arms. Comrades rushed in with a flag and hoisted it over the headquarters building and all was over except to pick up the weapons."

Asked how he assessed the victory, including the "Long March" of his own division, after they had set up their first units (armed mainly with hoes and dummy rifles), General Tich replied:

"It was because of the far-sighted leadership of the Lao Dong party for over 30 years that we were always able to have a correct line appropriate to local conditions. We were all so completely determined to win and never lost sight of this even under the most difficult circumstances. Wherever they were: in the Tigers Cages at Poulo Condor, chained to their cells in other prisons, awaiting execution—our comrades never doubted eventual victory. They worked for this every living moment and even every dying moment. Our division symbolized this total determination to 'fight and win.' That is why we were able to overcome all difficulties. The coordination with other units up to, and especially during, the final battle was excellent. The people's uprisings, their support at every moment it was needed, were also vital elements in what we can really call our Final Victory."

The sixth "fatal error" of Thieu and his Pentagon advisers was defined by Prime Minister Huynh Tan Phat as follows:

> Even when the Saigon Command realized we had switched towards Saigon, they thought we would first eliminate all the defensive positions on the outer approaches in a classical, textbook manner; digging in, waiting for all units to be on the starting lines, before daring to attack the city itself. In fact, while some were still consolidating the encirclement with the aid of local forces, others attacked right into the heart of the city itself, aiming straight towards the Presidential Palace, taking the enemy entirely by surprise at the speed and audacity of it all.

President Duong Van Minh surrendered at the top of the steps of the Presidential Palace to a high-ranking VPA officer and was immediately escorted to the TV station to read a surrender statement and order a formal ceasefire. Half an hour before the first tank came charging through the palace gates, he had broadcast a statement ordering the Saigon troops to cease fighting; to remain calm and in the positions they were holding, requesting at the same time, "the fraternal soldiers of the PRG to cease hosilities." He said he was awaiting the arrival of PRG representatives "to discuss the formal handing over of power in an orderly manner so as to avoid the useless shedding of our people's blood." To my question as to what was the 7th and last "fatal error" the Americans and their former "man in Saigon" had made, Prime Minister Huynh Tan Phat replied:

> The Americans played the "Big" Minh card far too late. If he had been used earlier, it would have facilitated some diplomatic manoeuvres which could have created complications for us. But when they finally brought themselves around to getting rid of Thieu, they wasted a whole week in fooling around with Huong! They played the "Big" Minh card just in time for him to offer unconditional surrender.

If such errors had not been made, would it have made any difference, I asked.

Prime Minister Phat's eyes twinkled and he gave one of his rich smiles: "Not in the long run. It would have prolonged their agony for a while. Once the Americans had made that first error in supporting or encouraging Thieu to turn his back on the Paris Agreement, their fate was sealed. We were determined never to be tricked again. We knew we would win, but did not expect the end to come so rapidly and so totally."

So it ended! Fifty-five days and nights of battle and movement that military historians—not to mention operational officers and tacticians—will discuss for decades. The statistical results of the battle for Saigon alone, as provided by General Di Thien Tich, speak for the magnitude of the forces involved and the dimensions of the victory of the revolutionary forces.

CASUALTIES SUFFERED BY THE ARVN FORCES

Destroyed
   11 infantry divisions
    8 independent regiments
 216 battalions of Civil Guards and regional troops

	12	armored regiments
Over	800	tanks and armored cars
	35	artillery battalions
Over	700	artillery pieces
	3	air divisions
	1,000	planes
	1,200	naval vessels, river patrol boats etc.

Of

680,000	ARVN troops engaged
21,000	killed and wounded
231,000	captured or surrendered

Captured War Booty

About	1,000	planes
About	1,000	naval vessels
	6,500	military vehicles of all types
	660	artillery pieces
	275,000	weapons of all types, excluding artillery

General Di Thien Tich said that from May 10 onwards, officers and troops of the former ARVN were told to register and that by the date of our meeting (August 16, 1975), 592,000 had registered in the Saigon-Gia Dinh Sector, including 23 generals, 6,198 senior officers (from majors to full colonels) and 39,000 junior officers. Not all of those who registered would have taken part in the battle for Saigon, nor would all those who had taken part necessarily register in the Saigon-Gia Dinh Sector.

Chapter 3.

The East Today, The West Tomorrow

Among the three guide-lines for military-political units laid down by Ho Chi Minh at the time of the formation of Vo Nguyen Giap's famous 34-man Tran Hung Dao platoon in December 1944—the embryo of today's Vietnam Peoples Army—was the following:

> Concerning tactics, practice guerilla methods: secrecy, speed, initiative (today in the East, tomorrow in the West); appear and disappear by surprise, without leaving a trace . . .

For guerillas moving on foot, this was quite possible and it drove the French, and later the Americans, out of their minds to try to cope with an enemy "which is everywhere and at the same time nowhere" as a young U.S. Senator from Massachusetts, John Kennedy, remarked in April 1954, when advising the French to get out of Indochina! That such tactics could be employed by units with modern weapons, including tanks and artillery, probably never entered Ho Chi Minh's mind in times when transport was exclusively on strips of automobile tires with crossed thongs that later became famous as "Ho Chi Minh sandals." In any case "Uncle" Ho's precepts remained as guidelines whenever they could be applied, also the first of the three guidelines which stated: "the political activity . . . is more important than the military activity . . ." As Giap only had 17 rifles, 14 flint-locks, two blunderbusses and a pistol, his military activities were going to be limited anyway!

> "President Ho paid great attention to secrecy," Giap was to write later. "It was imperative to preserve absolute secrecy, to conceal our forces well, disorient the enemy. It is essential that the enemy under-estimate our strength, that he completely ignores our activities . . . When we received our first mission, the President wrote us twice again to recommend: 'you must maintain secrecy' . . ." (Ho sent this to Giap on a bit of cigarette paper slipped into a packet of cigarettes.)

General Di Thien Tich, must have had all this very much in mind when 31 years later, he received, almost literally "East today, West tomorrow" instructions with the knowledge that only by maintaining absolute secrecy under almost impossible conditions could he carry out the task.

It was on April 27, when the general got his marching orders, to transfer the whole division—tanks, armored cars, artillery and all—from an area about 70 kms northeast from Saigon to the Duc Hua area about 20 kms southwest of the capital and to be there by the night of the 29th, ready for action before dawn next day.

"For maximum security," said General Tich, "we broke up into battalion and company-sized units, heading towards the Vam Co river, marching by night at maximum speed. For a start we left the armor and artillery behind. We hid by day on the 28th in the jungle, marched again all night. Hiding up by day on the 29th was difficult because it was open country. But our men were very disciplined, covering themselves with grass and straw, and lay in the furrows of ploughed land. Plenty of peasants saw us. They just winked or grinned and otherwise pretended they hadn't seen us. There were no betrayals. Crossing the very wide Vam Co was a problem; also the fact that we had to weave our way through 25 to 30 miles of strong enemy defenses. Another very big obstacle was crossing the 12 mile-wide Bien Loc swamp. But it had been arranged that there would be lots of guerilla activity in the areas through which we had to pass. Also we had the codes and names of enemy officers in the various posts, so we hooked our field telephones on their lines, assuring that everything was 'all quiet' in the places where we wanted to cross the river, or to infiltrate through a group of their block-houses. At that stage the rank and file puppet troops and junior officers were not looking for much trouble anyway. At some of the river crossings we left small groups behind to help the armor and artillery units following along behind. Local guerillas led us to the best spots to get the heavy weapons across the swamp. Once we got into the Duc Hua area, things were easier. We knew the terrain, the people knew us, so there were no real problems. We had opened the way into Saigon via this route during the 1968 Têt offensive. We were the vanguard unit to open the breach so that the others could follow us on. One of the difficulties then was that we didn't know Saigon well—we were constantly getting lost. This time everything was well organized. There was coordination of action between the people's organizations and ours. We had guides who knew the short cuts to our targets.

"We were better organized too—but so was the enemy. In the area we had to traverse, he had 12 battalions of main force units, 6 battalions of armored cars, 10 companies of Field Police plus the 5th parachute brigade stationed south of Tan Son Nhut airport which we had to skirt. We had to cross a military sub-sector (a district center heavily defended in depth, especially in the Saigon perimeter areas, W.B.), a main defense line with inter-connected posts, barracks, pillboxes all over the place. In general the enemy was reeling from our heavy blows but he was still very powerful. There were plenty of stubborn, very cruel and desperate unit commanders who thought they were fighting for their lives and certainly *were* fighting for their fortunes.

"Among the decisive factors in our favor was the high morale of our men and the heroic support of the local people. We urged them to rise up and encircle enemy pillboxes, barracks and other positions: to do their best to keep the puppets inside their positions and barracks while we weaved our way through. And they did this nobly. Once when our Third (Hoa Lu) regiment ran into some troubles, the people rose up and seized four enemy posts surrounding them . . ."

The people's role in the capture of Saigon is also stressed in the account given by Generals Vo Nguyen Giap and Van Tien Dung:

The population inside and outside the city rose up to seize power in numerous hamlets, welcoming our troops as they advanced into the city, guiding them, feeding them, seeking to support their actions, calling on enemy soldiers to lay down their arms and surrender . . .

I asked General Tich about casualties in his division, for the whole "Operation Ho Chi Minh."

"Considering what was accomplished—very light," he said, "mainly during the Battle of Saigon. We took a few accidental casualties from 'interdiction fire'[9] during our forced march, but the main losses were in the various battles for the crossroads after entering the Saigon outskirts. We had about 50 killed in those actions. We were outnumbered, the positions were very strongly defended. The enemy used the maximum means at his disposal. If we had not quickly dominated the situation by throwing everything we had into the battles while at the same time continuing to advance with great speed, our losses would have been much higher. The second place where we took casualties after we had won the battles for the crossroads, was when our units were racing down the broad Le Van Duyet avenue towards the Saigon-Gia Dinh Special Defense Headquarters. The enemy had a clear field of fire for their artillery and machine-guns and could use their planes in long bombing and strafing runs. We had 50 killed and wounded along Le Van Duyet avenue, bringing our total losses in killed and wounded from the time we set out on April 27 to less than two hundred."

"What were the most difficult moments for the 9th division?" I asked. General Tinh misunderstood the question, which I had meant in relation to the campaign.

"The most difficult period was in 1962-1963," he replied. "Our equipment and military technique were very low. We didn't have real arms, only dummy rifles, hoes and all sorts of rudimentary weapons. We started to produce some clumsy grenades and mines, enough for the type of weapons then being used against us. Then the enemy started using helicopters which could spot hide-outs and movements from the air and amphibian tanks which could swim across to some of our safest base areas. This caught us off-balance for a time. We learned to make some primitive anti-tank mines from unexploded bombs and shells and hit back. But the difficulties of 1962-1963 were very great and overcome only by a disciplined spirit of struggle.

---

9. A haphazard cross-firing system introduced by the Americans to sweep at regular intervals at night, all points of the compass around the Saigon posts to "interdict" any nocturnal movement."

"The Binh Gia battle in early 1965 was a great morale-booster for us. By then we had expanded from companies, to battalions and finally into a regiment. Using our own anti-tank and anti-helicopter weapons, we wiped out four battalions of Paratroops, Rangers and Marines, and an armored car battalion, mainly in broad daylight, despite their monopoly of air-power. It was a great victory not only for our unit, but for the whole of the South. After that we knew we could take on tanks, armored cars and helicopters. It was because of that victory that our first regiment was given the name of Binh Gia."[10]

Following my second visit to the Liberated Zones for two months at the end of 1964 and beginning of 1965, I had written about the rapid growth and expansion of units I had encountered during my first visit a year previously. This was even more notable during my third and fourth visits in 1966, by which time the Binh Gia regiment had been grouped—in September 1965—with two others to form a division in order to be able to cope with the sort of problems caused by the direct commitment of U.S. combat troops six months earlier. Later, from afar, I smiled when I read reports of a "North Vietnamese division" operating in just those areas in Tay Ninh, Binh Duong, Phuoc Long where I knew what was later to be known as NLF 9th Division was operating. I described at the time the "split and growth" method by which the NLF in the South was quickly building up an impressive army, the leadership of which was quite confident it could defeat the U.S.A.—even if the latter put in a million men. In fact, the sober estimate of the NLF leadership, even in 1964, was that, taking into account America's global commitments, it was doubtful that more than half a million troops could be put into the field. I can do no better than indulge in a little self-plagiarism and repeat what I wrote at the time:[11]

---

10. It was the battle of Binh Gia, at the turn of the year 1964-1965—which I observed from a safe vantage point insisted on by my NLF hosts, always worried that a foreign friend might become a casualty—which spelled the defeat of "Special War" in which the United States supplied everything but the actual cannon-fodder. It was the crushing defeat of the best units that Saigon could put into the field, that decided the United States to commit its own combat troops and promote "Special War" to "Limited War."

11. The following extracts are from Wilfred Burchett, *Vietnam Will Win* New York: Guardian Publishers, 1968, pp. 24-26. Articles on the same subject were published in the *Guardian* from 1965 onwards.

After the first sparks of spontaneous resistance in widely separated areas of the country had led to a decision to launch generalized armed resistance, armed groups of differing size and quality sprang into being almost simultaneously all over the country. From these initial groups the 'growth and split' process developed on a country-wide scale right from the beginning. These were not just a single unit as Giap had in 1944 but hundreds of platoons, although many were armed only with hoes, knives and other rudimentary weapons.

During one of my visits to the liberated areas in late 1964, I asked Le Van Huong, chief of staff of a liberation army regiment, to explain how it had been built up to its present size. "Soon after the Front issued its call for an armed uprising and the formation of regular, full-time forces," he explained, "two platoons were formed in our district. I was in charge of one and Thuong Chien, the regiment's political officer, was in charge of the other. We met and agreed to expand each of our platoons (around 30 men) into a company (a hundred men). It took quite a while to do this, not for lack of recruits but for lack of arms. Even when we started to expand, we had only about 10 firearms for each platoon. Sometimes a platoon member would lend his weapon to a comrade and the latter would come back with two weapons, returning the one he had borrowed. During the first months when we made attacks, for every man with a weapon there was always one unarmed man ready to snatch a rifle from the enemy or from our own dead and wounded. When we had two under-strength companies, we fused them as nucleus for a battalion. With the bigger unit, we could increase the scale of the attacks, which in the beginning were almost exclusively to get arms. When we had appreciably increased our stock of weapons, we armed a third incomplete company and, with a fourth company of reserves for whom we had no arms at all, we formed our first battalion.

Later on, to form a second battalion, we took our first company away from the first battalion and used this as a nucleus for a second battalion. But growth this time was very slow, so we detached some cadres from the first battalion and incorporated some regional troops and called this the second battalion.[12] In fact it was only at company strength, but as

---

12. The NLF forces, as those later in Cambodia, were of three categories: part-time self-defense guerillas for the protection of villages; regional

it was partly formed from regional troops, we gave it a fairly free hand. It started its own recruiting campaign among the young people of the region and fairly soon it was expanded and we really had a second battalion. Then we pooled the two battalions and called ourselves a regiment. We took 10 cadres from the first and second battalions and incorporated the reserve companies, for whom we had gradually been securing arms, to form a third battalion, which grew much quicker than the first two.

When we started operating as a regiment, we had plenty of problems. Enemy regiments, even battalions, had far greater fire-power. Although by the time we called ourselves a regiment every man had a weapon, these were mainly an odd assortment of rifles and a few light machine-guns. The NLF sent us a few heavier weapons and other supplies (from their headquarters' stocks), but we were supposed to be as self-supporting as possible. We decided to try to add a medium-weapons support platoon to each company with medium machine guns and 40mm to 60mm mortars, and a heavy-weapons company to each battalion with heavy machine-guns, 81mm mortars and bazookas. This meant concentrating attention on capturing these type of weapons. Each company was to try to get similar rifles, American carbines at that time, otherwise we would have problems with standardizing munitions. By and large, we have achieved standardization of equipment and have built up our medium and heavy-support units. Our firepower up to company level is now at least equal to that of the Saigon troops (our discussion took place before U.S. troops were directly committed in South Vietnam). Only at battalion level do they have the advantage of artillery, and can call in air support . . .

"We have the advantage that every man in our unit is a combatant," interjected (political officer) Thuong Chien. "The local population bring us food, right up to the battle lines; they evacuate our wounded and help us carry captured equipment back from the battlefield . . ."

. . . I inspected the arms of several of the support companies and platoons. There were medium and heavy machine-guns, mortars and bazookas, all of U.S. manufacture. At that time, apart from a few old rifles and light machine-guns

---

forces—full-time troops who operated within specific region areas; and the regular army, which conducted mobile warfare and whose activities were not limited to defined regions.

of French make, everything one saw—webbing belts and water canteens and even flourbag "knapsacks"—along the jungle trails and at the base camps was "Made in U.S.A." exclusively . . .

The regiment I was describing was named "Binh Gia" following the battle of that name. Later it was to fuse with two other regiments that had been formed in the same "growth and split" fashion to become the redoutable élite 9th Division, one of the most battle-hardened and excellent fighting forces to exist anywhere. Every weapon in those days had its own history, which the owner was proud to relate. In the days of General Westmoreland, when the fables of "body counts" as a means of measuring his doubtful military successes began to wear a bit thin (the computers discovering that he had wiped out the entire able-bodied population of South Vietnam several times), "success" was measured by the number of "individual and crew-served weapons" abandoned by the NLF on the battlefield. NLF commanders laughed at this, pointing out that every battlefield was considered as a "hot market place" where one could exchange "old for new", often discarding even useable weapons in favor of those needed to standardize a unit's equipment. (In the early days, the Diem government once held an exhibition, to boost the morale of their troops, of guerilla equipment found on the battlefield. Everything from hoes and bicycle chains to primitive bombards and flintlock rifles was displayed to show how miserably the guerillas were equipped and no soldier worth his name should have any qualms about doing battle with them! What was not explained was that in most cases hoes, bicycle chains, and flintlocks had been "exchanged" for rifles and pistols, and the fearsome bombards for hand grenades!)

General Di Thien Tich took up the saga of his division from the point at which I had last encountered it as a yet unnamed regiment.

"A couple of months after the division was formed," he explained, "the U.S. Expeditionary Corps in November 1965 launched a big operation to try to break the backbone of our main force units, and to intrude deeply into our base areas. They tried to force the dispersal of our regular units by driving us into the border areas to force us to return to small-scale guerilla warfare. Our division, together with other reinforcing regiments from the Mekong Delta, totally defeated this enemy attack. Among the outstanding battles was that of Bau Bang, in which we wiped out over 2,400 troops of the U.S. 1st Infantry division, knocking out 8 tanks and 12 artillery pieces. For our first real contact with U.S. forces, this was a considerable victory."

Ten days after the Bau Bang battle, I had been at an advanced NLF headquarters base in a Michelin rubber plantation with President Nguyen Huu Tho while another major battle with elements of the 9th division was raging at Dau Tieng, a few miles distant. Bicycle-borne couriers arrived every ten minutes or so with battle reports, supplemented by others that came through a battered field telephone. President Tho laughed uproariously when I showed him some American press reports on the Bau Bang battle. On successive days, U.S. communiqués upgraded their own losses from "light" to "moderate" which meant casualties of somewhere between 15 to 40 percent of the force engaged, while claiming to have inflicted "heavy" casualties on the enemy, mainly "two hundred killed by air and artillery strikes". As Nguyen Huu Tho and his staff officer, Nguyen Van Chau explained it, two infantry battalions, two tank squadrons and an artillery company from the U.S. 1st (Big Brother) division, had set out from their base headquarters at Lai Khe to make a sweep into what was effectively one of the NLF's main base areas. After moving cautiously up Highway 13, they camped for the night in a rubber plantation at Bau Bang.

In a typical application of "Uncle" Ho's instructions about "secrecy, sped, initiative . . . appear and disappear by surprise . . .", the NLF units made a swift night march, spent some time locating all the American units and struck half an hour before dawn. Nguyen Huu Tho's account of what happened, as I noted it down in a dugout under Michelin's broad-leafed rubber trees, was as follows:

> The order to attack was given and the Americans were taken completely by surprise. Within the first minutes, their command post and communications center were wiped out and this added to their confusion and panic. At the same time another of our units attacked the U.S. artillery positions at Lai Khe, silencing the guns there. An American reinforcing unit set out from Lai Khe when the shooting at Bau Bang was heard, but the greater part turned back, presumably because they heard our mortars firing at Lai Khe and noticed there was no returning fire from their own artillery.

> Within half an hour, the greater part of the units at Bau

Bang were destroyed. They had 36 tanks there, and another three arrived with that part of the reinforcing unit which continued from Lai Khe. The survivors from our first assault scrambled aboard those tanks and tried to flee, but our men rushed the tanks and in close-in fighting with machineguns, bazookas, grenades and satchel charges, they wiped out 37 on the spot. Two that escaped were destroyed by one of our ambush units set up for the heavy reinforcements we had expected from Lai Khe. All ten artillery pieces were destroyed before they could fire a shot, and before the sun was up, virtually the whole American task force was out of action. We estimate their total casualties were around 2,000.

Because we destroyed the communications center within the first few minutes, the divisional headquarters seemed to have no idea what happened. Planes were late on the scene and the artillery which was supposed to support this unit—apart from that at Bau Bang which had been destroyed—started firing only when the action was over.

Around 8:00 a.m. and not 7:00 a.m., as their accounts say, fighter-bombers came over and started circling. After a while they seem to have concluded that their own dead and wounded lying around the battlefield were our troops, hiding in the grass and undergrowth. They had no ground-air radio contact because they had nothing operational left on the ground. Our troops were marching off with all their communications equipment. They started bombing the battlefield, bombing their own dead and wounded. Then their artillery joined in. The battle that 'raged all day' according to their communiqué never took place, except that between their own planes and artillery and their own dead and wounded. It was not until late in the afternoon that two puppet battalions entered the area to collect what was left of the two battalions . . .[13]

What they found was presumably the reason for the amended communiqué which described U.S. losses as "medium" instead of "light."

"After the Bau Bang defeat and another at Dau Tieng soon after, the Americans changed to penetration tactics," continued General Tich, "intended to wipe out our Central Committee headquarters; to smash our main force units and blow up our

---

13. *Vietnam Will Win*, pp. 63-64.

storage depots. They succeeded in killing a lot of peasants and burning down a lot of villages, but otherwise achieved nothing. But this was also armed reconnaissance to pave the way for operation "Junction city", [14] the biggest U.S. offensive of the war. With the experience gained in the 1965-1966 dry season, we were convinced we could beat back the worst the Americans could do in 1966-1967. Our division, together with regional forces and local self-defense guerillas, defeated this operation in which elements of six U.S. divisions were employed. In 55 days (the figure seems fatal in recent Vietnamese history! W. B.) of almost continuous battle, we wiped out 12,155 U.S. troops, destroyed 820 armored vehicles and knocked down 72 planes and helicopters. Our headquarters area, bases and supply depots remained intact. The U.S. troops burned all houses, destroyed all stocks of rice found in the villages, sunk fishing boats, smashed all farm implements, wiped out anything that could be used for production in a 'kill all, burn all, destroy all' rampage which only increased the hatred everyone felt towards them. They put out fantastic figures of our losses (later it was admitted that not only were old people and babies, but also buffalo and pigs included in the "body count" statistics, W. B.) to cover up their own failures. It was during this operation that the battle of Dong Xoai took place on March 10, 1967—on that one day our second regiment knocked out by surprise attack over 500 G.I.'s, about 100 armored vehicles and 12 artillery pieces. It was this battle that earned it the name Dong Xoai regiment. A week later the same regiment, with similar tactics, destroyed a battalion of U.S. armored vehicles. Three days later, our whole division manoeuvred into position and gave the Americans the shock of their lives when we smashed our way directly into the U.S. 25th "Lightning" division headquarters at Duong Du, where we wiped out a battalion each of infantry, armored cars and artillery. On March 31, the Binh Gia regiment destroyed 1 battalion and 2 companies, 795 G.I.'s altogether, of the 1st Infantry division at Bau Ba Dung . . ."

---

14. "Junction City" was mounted in Tay Ninh Province in February-April, 1975, with the maximum use of air-borne troops and was aimed at first sealing off the whole area where it was assumed (correctly) that the NLF had its headquarters and supply bases; geometrically dividing up the sealed-off area into squares, through which units would methodically destroy everything in the way human beings or military supplies. Progress as usual was measured by "body count" statistics.

In other words, the 9th division in these March actions was applying the third part of the classic axiom of People's War: "When the enemy attacks—withdraw; when the enemy tires—harrass; when the enemy withdraws—attack." Junction City folded up altogether after that—General Westmoreland claimed that the enemy had avoided "destruction" by slipping across the border into the "Cambodian sanctuaries." I was based in Phnom Penh at that time, and with other journalists made frequent visits to the frontier areas and, while we saw plenty of evidence of U.S. air activity, billowing clouds of red-tinged smoke as villages went up in flames, we never saw any sign of "Vietcong sanctuaries." Nor did members of the International Control Commission, despite assiduous efforts by the Canadian delegates, when they were frequently called to investigate the bombing of Cambodian villages allegedly due to "hot pursuit" missions by U.S. pilots, or to "unclearly marked boundaries"—a pretext that always infuriated Prince Sihanouk.

So the saga of the 9th division went on. General Tich spoke of its role in the 1968 Tết offensive in penetrating into Saigon; in attacking in the rear of U.S. and South Vietnamese troops invading Cambodia in April-May, 1970, and in the South Laos invasion the following year, at which time General Tich said: "We stepped up our activities and did our best to crush any attempts to expand the war, forcing Saigon units which had been sent into Cambodia to scuttle back across the frontier again, by launching attacks against their home bases."

In the "Spring Offensive" of 1972, the 3rd regiment destroyed an entire American armored regiment at a place called Hoa Lu and so received the name it now bears. After the Paris Agreement, the 9th "bent over backwards" not to respond to provocations, but when the Saigon "land-grabbing" operations got too flagrant and too near the sensitive base areas in Tay Ninh, they resisted. In a major battle at Khiem Hanh on September 29 and 30, sparked off when Saigon troops attacked a PRG enclave, the division inflicted a heavy defeat on Thieu's 3rd Army Corps. Saigon tried to cover up, but finally admitted that one battalion had been wiped out. General Di Thien Tich said the "enemy used the heaviest concentration of artillery fire until that time, but our troops got in close, 'grabbed the enemy by the belts' to neutralize their superior fire-power and wiped out over 10,000 of them."

It was interesting to learn that the 9th had played the major role in the decisive battle to capture Phuoc Long province, especially in the liberation of the capital, Binh Long. Western press reports, mainly based on Saigon briefings, claimed this was done by the "North Vietnamese 7th division".

There was nothing in the sober, factual account of General Di Thien Tich's account of the birth, childhood, adolescence and growth to full manhood of the 9th division to conflict with its motto of "Unity and Modesty" and its main operational slogan of "Annihilate the Enemy". If one day, like the regiments, it is also given a name, "Ho Chi Minh" division would seem to be appropriate, so closely did this unit model itself upon the military precepts of "Uncle" Ho, which were also those of Vo Nguyen Giap.

Chapter 4.

The Flag Offensive

An American contingency plan was that if the worst came to the almost unmentionable worst, there would be a regroupment of forces at Can Tho, the unofficial capital of the Mekong Delta. From there, at least the rich Mekong Delta would be held while forces would be regrouped, re-equipped and built up for a counter-offensive. Saigon, at least, could be retaken and, together with the Mekong Delta, a rump state with well over half the population and 80 percent of the known riches and established industry could be developed and made prosperous—a powerful magnet for the population of the impoverished rest of a partitioned South Vietnam. The Can Tho air base had been expanded to this end; the Air Force headquarters and as many planes as possible had been transferred there following the loss of the Bien Hoa and Tan Son Nhut air bases.

But they ran into one of those contradictions which American leaders are so adept at producing. In order to squeeze a few hundred million or so extra dollars out of a reluctant Congress, President Ford conjured up the most gruesome picture of what was going to happen to those who had collaborated with the United States, with the "free world," in the event of a "Communist take-over". How many Americans he convinced is hard to say—certainly not a majority of Congressmen, who turned stony faces and deaf ears to his pleas. But the "blood bath" image was presented so persuasively that the Saigon military hierarchy were practically standing on each other's shoulders to clamber aboard helicopters and follow the example of Nguyen Van Thieu, Nguyen Cao Ky and others to flee to wherever they had long since exported their ill-gotten dollar gains. Ford, Kissinger and Schlesinger had been so eloquent that quite a few other generals committed suicide rather than face the fate which these three top U.S. leaders had said would most assuredly and inevitably be theirs!

Objectively speaking, there seemed no reason why a stand could not have been in the 4th Military Region, virtually untouched by the main drive of the general offensive. There were still three intact divisions there: the 7th, 9th and 21st infantry divisions with supporting armored and artillery units, Civil Guards and other paramilitary units, plus plenty of reserve manpower. The Mekong Delta has a population of over nine million. Good communications had been developed, including a network of air bases. So why did it fold up within 24 hours of the collapse of Saigon? I went to have a long look at Can Tho and another of the main Delta cities, My Tho. (Together with Ben Tre these three capitals of provinces which bear the same names are renowned for their revolutionary ardor and heroism in both resistance wars.)

Highway 4, which leads southwest from Saigon through the heart of the Delta to its southernmost point at Ca Mau, is a modern, four-lane highway. As one approached important bridges there were lighter-colored, freshly sanded patches of asphalt bridging gaps ten to thirty feet wide—right across the road—which had obviously gone right down to the ricefield mud. A dozen such, spaced over half a mile, were regular features at the approach to every major bridge. Where such stretches started—or ended—there were usually burned out hulks of tanks, trucks and armored cars on the side of the road. Concrete telegraph and telephone poles on either side in such sections of the highway had collapsed into the fields, wires waving in the wind from the last of those still standing. Every now and again there was the carcass of a helicopter or fighter-bomber sticking up awkwardly out of the fields. Nothing could look more monstrously out of place among the rice stubble. Pillboxes with gaping holes in their walls and bridge spans propped up on criss-crossed railway sleepers testified to the uninterrupted battle which went on along Highway 4. The even color of the freshly "bandaged" wounds, testified to the probability—later confirmed—that most of those roads over which our Can Tho-bound car rolled were inflicted during "Operation Ho Chi Minh."

It is a fine highway, however, and it occurred to me how the Pentagon chiefs must have regretted not being able to roll up Highway 4 and other similar "carpets" and have them shipped back to the U.S.! Such highways were part of the valuable infra-structure that was inevitably left behind. They were not built to serve the needs of the people but merely to move troops more efficiently from one point to another to suppress them. Speeding over its smooth surface, I could not but think of Harriman's remark: "When our military move into any part of the world they want the most and best of everything they can get." Highway 4, could be written off as an investment in the sacred cause of "saving American lives"!

To get to Can Tho city, we traversed Long An, My Tho and Vinh Long provinces, vast plains stretching as far as the eye could see, crossing two broad, parallel arms of the Mekong on powerful ferries, spacious and speedy, each capable of carrying 8 to 10 big trucks—a veritable fleet of them at each crossing. They represented more of the body of military infra-structure. On the west bank of the second crossing lay Can Tho, a fine, well laid-out city of broad avenues and overcrowded streets. Over 300,000 of the province's 630,000 population were concentrated here, a tribute to the success of the "accelerated urbanization" program of using B-52s to empty the sea in which the guerilla fish swam!

My first visit was to the city's second defense perimeter, a periphery road which ran along the Mekong for over two miles then swung around to encircle the city, an impressive network of bunkers and fire-points at every crossroads. Just where the perimeter road left the river and swung to the right on its oval-shaped course, there were six burned-out hulks of M-113 amphibious tanks. They had been deployed to prevent the VPA forces from crossing the river from what was recognized as PRG territory which started from the opposite bank. The 21st Infantry division and an armored regiment had been deployed to guard the perimeter road. What they had overlooked, it seemed, was the existence of self-defense guerillas inside the perimeter. It looked a peaceful-enough corner. Coconut palms and clumps of giant bamboo towered over banana and paw paw trees. A little old woman sweeping up leaves outside the only hut in sight said that on the night of the 29th, some "local lads" advised her to move well back from the road for a few hours, which she did. "Then there were some tremendous 'bang bangs'," she said, "and almost immediately a big column of black smoke going straight up into the air. After some smaller 'bang bangs' had stopped, I came home, very surprised to see these things burning away at my front door."

A guide from the CanTho PRG headquarters explained that there had been 12 armored cars, four more of which had been destroyed a bit further along the road, two making it back to safety. It had been a short, sharp engagement. Mines laid on the road blew up the first vehicle, the rest were picked off with bazookas fired at less than 20 yards. There were no losses by the local guerillas and a river crossing point was assured. The city was taken over virtually without bloodshed.

To find out how, I spoke with Nguyen Thi Muoi Be, chairwoman of the An Nghiep Peoples Revolutionary Committee (An Nghiep being one of the city's twelve wards). Slim and tall, elegantly dressed in a sable-colored jacket and wide, black trousers and surprisingly young for her position—and even more so for what she had done—with a dimpled, mischievous smile she was very self-possessed and treated with deference by her fellow Committee members. "I'll start," she said, "by giving you a run-down on An Nghiep before and during Liberation. There are 2,789 households with 19,032 residents—a bit below the average for the other wards. They are Buddhists and Catholics, but also many from the Cao Dai and Hoa Hao religious sects. The puppets had one military police station defended by a platoon of Civil Guards; one ordinary police station; the No. 4 Transport and Supply depot, defended by over one hundred regular troops. There were many 'Civil Guard' watch-towers and various repressive street organizations. Altogether there were 650 'Civil Guards', all well-armed. An Nghiep is quite close to the 4th Military Region headquarters, responsible for operations throughout the Delta, so police vigilance here was more severe than in other parts.

"One of the main characteristics is that An Nghiep is a working class area and the police were very zealous in pulling people up to demand their papers—especially in the couple of weeks prior to Liberation. They knew something was moving under the surface but they couldn't put their fingers on it. The authorities were very sensitive to the atmosphere here because Can Tho was supposed to be the reserve capital if Saigon fell and it was known that the An Nghiep people were very much for the revolution. Security measures were doubled and trebled so it was quite difficult to make contacts for preparatory work.

"On April 10, I received instructions to enter the city from my base in the countryside and help prepare for the general uprising. My job was to contact sympathizers, stimulate the people in general—but my first contacts had to be with those whom we were sure could keep revolutionary secrets. I had instructions from a higher echelon to inform all the secret revolutionary bases inside the city to prepare for an uprising. From these bases, at the appropriate moment, the word would be spread out to the broad masses. During preliminary discussions before I left, we had worked out specific tasks for every participant, including when and where I would operate. Cloth had to be acquired to make flags and banners; stocks of paper to prepare leaflets. By April 28, the preliminary tasks were completed—cloth and paper acquired and distributed into safe hands. On the 28th we heard that 'Big' Minh had taken over as president and wanted to negotiate a peaceful settlement, so we decided to go ahead and prepare the flags, banners and leaflets. Then I received word from higher-up to be prepared at any moment to launch the political struggle. On the night of April 28-29 we roneoed the leaflets. At that time our revolutionary nucleus consisted of just 15 patriots. Added to these we had four underground militia—two rather sheepish lads in blue overalls, who stepped forward and saluted—and 40 patriotic 'Civil Guards,' ready to come over to our side when we gave the word. There were three types of leaflets: (1) Calling on the people to rise up and seize power, and on the puppets to surrender. (2) Setting out the 10 points of leniency towards puppet troops. (3) The 10 points of discipline for VPA troops (about not touching a needle or thread of the people, etc. W. B.).

"Very early on the morning of the 30th, we started distributing leaflets. Then at 10:15 a.m. we heard 'Big' Minh's radio appeal for the puppet troops to cease fighting. People were overjoyed at this and poured out into the streets, and up went our flags and banners. Recruits and conscripts at the No. 4 Transport and Supply depot broke out and headed for home. Soldiers in great numbers, including many officers, asked for our leaflets. Up till 9:00 a.m. we had distributed them secretly, sticking them up on the walls and trees, but after that we gave them out openly. People poured out into the streets in ever greater numbers, hugging each other and those handing out leaflets, especially as they saw our flags flying all over the place. Puppet soldiers started getting into civilian clothes and throwing away their uniforms. One of the first flags we put up on official buildings was at the Transport and Supply depot, where a very polite officer asked for the honor of actually fixing the flag to the flagpole. Then we hoisted them up over the Military Police and Civilian Police headquarters. In An Nghiep, an atmosphere of fraternization continued all day as people got ready to welcome the liberation troops. Our flags and banners were everywhere . . ."

Nguyen Ha Vang of the Lao Dong party's city committee, greying, with a sombre, lined face said: "In An Nghiep things went smoothly because our comrade Be worked very well and it is a working class area. It wasn't the same everywhere. When we went to occupy the radio station at 3:00 p.m. the Region commander, General Nguyen Van Nam, realizing that we had practically no arms and that our armed forces had not arrived, ordered his troops to repress us and to defend the station—or if the situation got too difficult—to blow it up. It was clear he was taking no notice of orders from Saigon. But the colonel in charge refused to order his troops to attack. Instead he commandeered a motor boat and set off down the Mekong (in this he was following the example of the U.S. Consul-General, W.B.). General Nam ordered planes to take off and sink it, entrusting this task to a real butcher, Colonel Tran Huu Tien. Planes took off, but we still don't know if they sunk the boat— all sorts of boats were heading down to the sea by then where U.S. warships were waiting to pick them up. Colonel Tien was notorious for having had 300 patriots beheaded in a single week at the Vi Thanh concentration camp in 1969, and it was just this butcher who General Nam had appointed city commander, at noon on April 30. It was clear that Nam still thought the war was to be continued from the new capital of Can Tho, and he was apparently expecting plane-loads of headquarters officers and reinforcements at any moment.

"Colonel Tien ordered a company of his troops to reoccupy the radio station which we had taken over. When they arrived they saw our flags everywhere. Leaflets were showered down on them; they threw down their arms and went home. By 3:00

p.m. our forces had still not arrived but by now we were broadcasting appeals for people to rise up and seize power everywhere and get ready to welcome the liberation troops. There were flags and banners all over the place but General Nam was behaving as if nothing had changed.

"Some of our underground cadres had been working for months on Nam's personal bodyguard unit. As the afternoon wore on, Nam suddenly discovered that his aide-de-camp and the deputy commander of the bodyguard unit had stolen his personal helicopter and fled. By that time big crowds had gathered in his headquarters compound, shouting slogans and demanding his surrender. He strode out on to the balcony in a towering rage, pistol in hand, demanding that they disperse. When no one took any notice, he emptied his pistol—except for one bullet—into the crowd, strode back into his office and fired the last bullet into his head. When butcher Tien heard of this, knowing the game was up, he did the same. These two had so many crimes on their consciences that they could not believe our policy of leniency could apply to them. Abandoned by those they considered their most faithful protectors—the hundred or so U.S. military advisers who had already fled—and by their paid lackeys, hated and despised by the people, these two arch-criminals could simply not face the future.

"Later that night, our regular armed forces started arriving. They had been held up by some battles along Highway 4 and also by the good work done by our road destruction units to halt enemy movements. At the entrance to the city they were held up for nearly two hours by the tens of thousands of people who completely filled the streets, with everyone wanting to offer fruit and flowers and make welcoming speeches. . . . "

If some generals and senior officers suicided—and there were quite a few cases—it was because their consciences were heavy with guilt, their hands stained with the blood of tens of thousands of patriots, something which the dire prophecies of Ford, Kissinger and Schlesinger did not permit them to forget. They could envisage nothing but the firing squad at best, and they simply could not face risking the sort of punishment they had been meting out daily to those, whom in their hearts they knew were the finest, most selfless and courageous patriots. With the primitive ideology they had to absorb to attain such high ranks, revenge would be an automatic reflex. It was natural for them to see themselves being submitted to the same barbarous tortures they had been inflicting on *their* captives—with a bullet in the head or the guillotine for most of those who survived the attentions of the torture squads.

One need not have a particularly lurid imagination to picture what would have happened if the leadership of the PRG had fallen into such hands; or what would have happened if the Saigon army had succeeded in occupying Hanoi and Haiphong! The hundreds of My Lai's in South Vietnam, not to mention what happened when the counterparts of the Thieu's, Nam's and Tien's took over in Indonesia and Chile, are example enough!

I asked what had happened at the Can Tho air base, upon which U.S.-Saigon hopes for continuing the war had largely been founded. It was Nguyen Ha Vang who replied:

In general the enemy tried to cling to Can Tho at all costs, which is why they stationed two divisions around the city. The top Saigon brass hoped they could withdraw to here and stage a counter attack to recapture Saigon. The presence of units of the U.S. 7th Fleet, with thousands of Marines on board, cruising up and down our coast, helped to strengthen this illusion throughout April 30 and for the next few days. Rumors, spread by the enemy's psychological warfare agents, had it that two generals who had left Saigon were now aboard U.S. Aircraft carriers and would be flown into Can Tho at any moment to reconstitute a new headquarters and organize a counter-offensive. On the afternoon of the 30th, after we had established firm control over the radio station and stabilized the general situation, we mobilized a huge crowd of people and marched—unarmed —to the air base, occupying all installations, putting up our flags and taking over the whole base. Confronted with this display of mass strength, the base commander surrendered to us. Later, when our main force units arrived, they sent a regiment to take over.

Answering my question as to whether there had been any resistance at all, Nguyen Ha Vang replied:

At first we took over installations solely by our political forces, but some counter-revolutionary elements, seeing we had no armed forces, started raising their heads. There were some isolated acts of resistance on that first day, but these were quickly crushed. What was decisive was that we had the radio station. Through our broadcasts everyone got the idea that we were really in power. By the time the main force units entered the city, late on the night of the 30th, there was no resistance. But had it not been for the political takeover earlier, there certainly would have been heavy fighting. As it was, the city and all its installations were taken over intact with no destruction at all.

At Binh Duong hamlet, part of Long Tuyen village in the outskirts, one could get some idea of the extent of the repression —especially severe in any of the old revolutionary base areas. In a modest house set in a coconut grove a dozen yards from the broad, calmly flowing Mekong, a meeting had been arranged with some of the local resistance activists. From thumbnail sketches of some of the members of the Long Tuyen Peoples Revolutionary Committee emerged a picture of the dangers and heroism of those who kept a flicker of revolutionary flame alight under the most impossible circumstances. Vo An Bao, the chairman, short and bullet-headed, had lived in a coffin-shaped hole in the ground outside Binh Duong hamlet for years, prior to April 30, 1975. He had lost one eye through police beatings. Dang Thi Hiep, of the hamlet Liberation Women's Association, had just returned from five years in the notorious prison of Poulo Condor. Of the three children of the owner of the house, Nguyen Van Khoa, two had died in concentration camps and the third had regrouped to the North with the VPA, after the 1954 Geneva Agreement. Vo Thi Phuong, a frail, gentle-faced woman, with her hair gathered in the traditional chignon of the Delta women, who headed the Long Tuyen Liberation Women's Association, had lost 21 members of her family in the two resistance struggles. Her husband had been one of those who had to propel himself to freedom with his hands, his legs having become atrophied after several years in the "Tiger Cages" of Poulo Condor. Duong Thi Hiep, with a serene, serious face and shoulder-length bobbed hair was still on leave from revolutionary activities after prison torture and traumatic experiences in which she had been partly buried alive. It was still an effort for her to speak in anything more than a whisper.

Vo An Bao gave a brief report. "Long Tuyen village is seven miles long by less than four wide, with 2,425 houses and a total population of 35,575. The village suffered terribly from repression. One of the most savage criminals in all South Vietnam, the Hoa Hao colonel, Le Quang, was in charge of this area for a long time. His speciality was disemboweling revolutionaries and eating their livers with his henchmen. Once he hailed eight people passing in a boat. As far as we know they had nothing to do with revolutionary activities. He arrested them as they came to the shore, killed them and disemboweled them on the river bank. Later he did the same thing with thirty guerillas he had managed to capture, laying their opened bodies out on the road. Relatives coming to weep over them were immediately arrested. He was one of Ngo Dinh Diem's chief henchmen. In the end, he was captured and executed . . ." (A tiny toothless woman had slipped in, dabbing at her eyes as Vo An Bao spoke. It turned out that she had lost all five sons, either arrested and killed or fallen in combat.)

"The fate of our village," continued Vo An Bao, "can be measured by the fluctuating statistics of (Lao Dong) party membership. In 1963-1964, there were 75 members—in 1965 it had dropped to 10—the rest had been killed. We started to rebuild, but based on living outside the hamlets, quite literally underground, in holes in the ground. In 1967 our underground organization was attacked. Eight were arrested and killed. We built up again, but the enemy managed to infiltrate our organization and eleven more were arrested and killed. At the time of Liberation there were only two of us left, plus two sympathizers. Of the 75 members in 1963-1965, I am the only survivor."

I had noticed that every house in the hamlet—as well as others passed on the way to Binh Duong—were surrounded by barbed wire fences, some of them completely enclosed in a sort of spider-web arrangement that covered the roof as well.

"Security was such that you could scarcely breathe," said Vo An Bao, when I asked about the barbed wire. "Villagers have got so used to it that they use it now as trellises for vines and climbing flowers. There were 8 platoons of Civil Guards, manning 11 posts in Long Tuyen village. There was a 30-member platoon of so-called 'secret agents' at a crossroads, controlling everyone's movements. A 120-member company of Security troops permanently patrolled the main road to prevent any contact between the villagers themselves or between them and outsiders. Two companies of Civil Guards were stationed at a curve in the main road from where they could check traffic in both directions for long stretches. Their main job was to prevent the approach of any of our regional or main-force units. In addition there were 7,000 'self-defense' guards, 1,000 of whom were considered 'trusties' or shock troops who could be called upon to do anything. There was also one 12-member civilian committee for each of the six hamlets, to provide an added check on any suspicious activities. These operated in three-hamlet inter-groups to report on any movements between the hamlets. The control came down to every home. A list of those who lived in each house, with a photograph of every person listed, had to be produced any time the police demanded. If a police check turned up someone not on the list, he was immediately arrested. The head of a four-family group was also held responsible for such 'violations.' And if anyone on the list was absent without some valid and easily controllable reason, the head of that family and of the four-family group was arrested.

"Each house had to have a kerosene lamp burning over the gate at night, so that neighbors could spot anyone moving in or out, and a gong or bell to sound the alarm in such a case. Alongside the front door was a board with small discs corresponding to the number of inmates, and colored according to their security rating. If there were any revolutionary activities, those with the worst ratings were automatically arrested. Apart from all this, each family had to have a sort of blackboard at the entrance on which they were supposed to compete in writing the most insulting denunciation of 'communists' and revolutionaries in general."

The obvious question to Vo An Bao, in view of all this, was how it was possible to carry out any revolutionary activity at all?

"Four of us revolutionary cadres lived in underground trenches, never moving out in daytime," he replied. "We depended for food on children who would wander into the woods, pretending to search for herbs and roots, and would leave us food. On one occasion when a security sweep was under way, I couldn't move for three days and the children couldn't bring me food. When it was all over and I tried to get out, my legs and one good eye failed me. But then the children arrived with some extra food and after a day or two I was alright again. We moved out only after 10:00 p.m. to maintain contacts, keep up morale, and when some action was coming up, to allot trusted sympathizers special tasks. The greatest luxury in those days was occasionally to be able to lie up in the shelter of some comrade's house for a day or two. On the night of the 28th, all our contacts were busy making flags, from cloth gradually stocked from the beginning of the month. The following night, our regional forces came together and we attacked the Ong Duong post—the key one controlling Binh Duong hamlet. We wiped it out, captured over 70 firearms and hoisted the NLF flag over the post and nearby bridge, early the following morning. People could hardly believe their eyes. Our cadres appealed through megaphones for them to rise up and take over the administration. They burst out from the barbed wire by the thousands in a general uprising, seizing military posts and puppet buildings. The hamlet chief, a cruel, bloodthirsty tyrant if ever there was one, resisted, and I personally shot him dead. By 10:00 p.m. on the 30th, we had seized all offices of the traitor administration and its defense forces in all six hamlets of Long Tuyen. Our flags were proudly flying everywhere. It was only at midnight that our first main force units arrived at Binh Duong. They didn't stop but pressed on to Can Tho. The killing of the hamlet chief and our flags everywhere were the symbols that the black night of the puppet régime had really ended and a bright new day had dawned for all of us."

Chapter 5.

Heroes and Heroines

What constantly emerged in discussions with those who initiated the "people's uprisings" part of the "general offensive" was that it needed only a tiny handful of dedicated persons to act as the detonators for tremendous explosions of mass activity. The Saigon régime, and its American experts on security and the most sophisticated Gestapo-like police methods, had prepared the terrain for this. Unendurable repression had made the South Vietnamese people as ripe for generalized uprising as a long dry summer prepares grass and undergrowth for hurricane-force brush fires. No greater offense to human dignity could be imagined than the life-style imposed on Binh Duong and tens of thousands of other hamlets. But they looked fine on the American HES (Hamlet Evaluation System) charts. As one American enthusiast was to tell me: "We only have to push a button for any province, any district, any hamlet and we know exactly within a decimal point what the security situation is!" Doubtless Binh Duong figured as 100 percent secure. Journalists could be taken to the spot, read the anti-communist hate boards and report the ferocious hatred the Binh Duong villagers felt towards the "Vietcong". It is only by understanding the real situation that the importance of the flags can be grasped. The flag was a beacon of hope and the Thieu government had made it even more so.

Immediately after the Paris Agreement, Thieu decreed the death penalty for anyone found with an NLF flag, and the bombing or shelling of any hamlet which displayed it. People were ordered to take summary action and execute anyone with an NLF flag without even bothering to hand them over to the authorities. In the PRG-controlled, and contested zones, there was no ban on the display of the Saigon flag because "national reconciliation" was the order of the day. But for the puppet commmanders to see the NLF flags all over the place, surrounding their bastions of power, was like the sounding of the death knell.

For every four men, women, children and babies in Long Tuyen, there was one permanent armed agent of repression, with regular troops in reserve for any situation that the local repressive organs could not handle. The proportion was not much less in the rest of the villages of South Vietnam. Under such conditions—when even exchanging the time of day with one's neighbor could send you to jail and automatically to the torture squads, because arrest was synonymous with interrogation under torture—it needed exceptional heroism to carry on revolutionary activities. That heroism, itself was often born of unspeakable repression. This was the case, for instance, of Duong Thi Hiep, the sad-faced young woman mentioned in the previous chapter, part of the group from Binh Duong hamlet. When I asked about her activities, she related the following:

"Before 1968, I was just a housewife. During the Têt uprising, my husband was killed on the battlefield so I asked to work in his place. My younger sister, Nam Thanh, also carried out revolutionary work and she was arrested about that time. She died in prison a year later after having been terribly tortured by a notorious brute called Sau Khanh. I asked the local NLF committee if I could have the task of executing him—and it was so agreed. I was also given the task of collecting money for the revolution from various merchants and small manufacturers. At that time I had four children of my own, plus the two of my sister, whom I had adopted. In order to get inside the police post and close enough to kill Sau Khanh, I disguised myself as a peddler, at first selling cakes and later on, embroidery. But about that time Khanh, who knew that everyone hated him, hired a very vigilant bodyguard named Nam Luong and it was impossible to get past him. So I never did get a chance to avenge my sister's death and rid the world of a very evil tyrant.

"In 1971, when I was collecting contributions, the owner of one of the enterprises who gave regularly not only failed to contribute but he denounced me to the police. I was arrested and tortured many, many times, usually beaten with clubs until I fell unconscious. When I came to there were questions and then more beatings. They always wanted to know what I did with the money I collected. I pretended it was for myself and the six children. They never got anything else out of me and after six months they let me go. As I had lost my legal status and the local police would always be on my tracks, I went to Soc Trang (about 80 miles to the Southwest, W.B.) where I had relatives but was otherwise unknown. By chance, I met the chief of one of the military posts, a Major Loi, who soon after our first meeting tried to get me to marry him. I refused. At our last meeting in his office, he again asked and I again refused. He got furious, called in an aide and ordered him to bury me alive.[15] I was escorted outside the city with a burial squad. A grave was dug and I was thrown into it, a board laid across my body and soldiers started shovelling in the dirt. I kept pleading for my life because of the children. The officer agreed that if I could raise 100,000 piastres (about 2,500 U.S. dollars at the time) quickly, he would let me escape. One of the shovellers took a message to my children for my relatives while I lay there half-buried. By some miracle my relatives got the money together, so I was let go. But it was impossible to return to Soc Trang. It was a moment when there were police checks every day. There were amphibious tanks and patrol boats everywhere. How to get a job and feed my children? I sent a message begging my relatives to look after them for a while; I cut my hair short and returned to Can Tho and, as I had got terribly thin, I hoped no one would recognize me, setting myself up as a street-vendor.

"Captain Bao, head of the Long Tuyen security guards, was constantly searching for me because I had failed to report as I was supposed to after being freed from jail. Because I was physically and mentally weakened by what I had been through, I was given leave from political work until I recovered my

---

15. Although Duong Thi Hiep did not mention this, offers of marriage from security officers were often used as a test of the political affiliations of young women. If they refused an apparently "good match," it was assumed this was because they had a husband or fiance engaged in revolutionary work.

strength. So I was unable to play any part in the people's uprisings at the end of April," she whispered almost apologetically.

"What about the children?" I asked. Her face lit up in a wan smile. "Three of my sons have grown up and are doing revolutionary work in Long Tuyen. A fourth is at school. The most difficult period was when I had to leave the children with my relatives. With the enemy all over the place I couldn't do otherwise. Now they are with me. I can look after them and my comrades look after me."

I asked Vo Thi Phuong to say something about herself and her husband who had returned from Poulo Condor. With a triangular, poetic face, long slim fingers and fragile wrists, it was difficult to imagine her as the tempered, veteran revolutionary that someone whispered to me she was.

"Among the fourteen members of my family killed in the second resistance," she said, "was my elder brother, who was secretary of the Lao Dong party committee in the 'black' period mentioned by Comrade Vo An Bao. I was in the same party cell as Bao in 1960, working together with Comrade Tu Hong, who later became my husband. In 1966, Tu Hong was arrested and after being held in various prisons on the mainland, he was sentenced to 15 years and sent to Poulo Condor, where he spent several years in the 'tiger cages.'[16] He returned after the Paris Agreement, incapacitated from the waist down. Now he can take a few steps with great difficulty—but he is doing revolutionary work again."

"At the time my husband was arrested," continued Vo Thi

---

16. On July 2, 1970, the first independent report about conditions at the Poulo Condor island penitentiary came when two U.S. Congressmen, Augustus Hawkins, Democrat from California and William Anderson, Democrat from Tennessee, were guided there by Don Luce, who had resigned some years previously from an American-sponsored International Volunteer Service in South Vietnam in protest at its activities. The congressmen reported finding about 500 prisoners, including 150 women, in small concrete "tiger cages" under conditions which amounted to "the most shocking treatment of human beings" either of them had ever seen. The cages were five feet by nine feet and windowless, each containing five prisoners. None of the prisoners could stand, "having lost the use of their legs either from malnutrition, or paralysis from lack of exercise." Buckets of lime stood on iron grills above the cages—the only source of light—which the prisoners said were thrown over them if they asked for food or water. Because Don Luce was fluent in Vietnamese the Congressmen could converse with the prisoners.

Phuong, "I was pregnant. The police were looking for me everywhere and I had to be on the move. In 1968 I was arrested, but the only thing they had in their records against me was that I had been wounded in January 1961, when they had opened fire on a women's demonstration. I admitted nothing, despite a good beating. A relative offered to put up a bond to guarantee my future 'good behavior,' so I was released and I returned to Long Tuyen to help organize the struggle against the extension of the Can Tho air base . . ." (It had been explained to me in Can Tho that a major political struggle had developed in 1968 and again in 1974 to prevent extensions to the air base which, in 1974, entailed the evacuation of some 10,000 peasants from their ricelands. This was part of the preparations to make Can Tho a fall-back capital and military headquarters.)

"We organized women to lie down in long lines in front of the bulldozers," Vo Thi Phuong explained. "It was a long and protracted struggle which took up all our time." Vo An Bao added that the women threatened the troops guarding the project that they would be killed if they continued to take part in an action to rob the peasants of their land. "Vo Thi Phuong," he said, "headed a band of women armed with jungle knives which several times ambushed puppet patrols protecting the work, killing some of them so the warnings would have greater effect. At one point they dropped hand grenades simultaneously into all the stone crushers and the work had to be suspended for 4 months. On another occasion, when bulldozers were sent to level hundreds of acres of ricefields, the peasants—mainly the women organized by Vo Thi Phuong—lay down in every direction and simply blocked them from moving. Four civilian contractors, after repeated warnings, were shot down by self-defense guerillas hiding up to their necks in a nearby canal. The air base never did get extended the way the Americans wanted it because of the mass struggle."

"We did our best in the frontline, even under the worst conditions, to keep the struggle alive," concluded Vo Thi Phuong. "My husband never ceased his revolutionary activities even in Poulo Condor. At one point the police discovered the close relations between us and even falsified some documents about this. I was placed under close surveillance and the party leadership told me to cease political work for a period. Then came the Paris Agreement and I had an incapacitated husband to look after. Now I'm happy to have resumed work as a responsible cadre in the Liberation Women's organization."

"And the baby?" I asked. "Did the baby survive?" The reply was accompanied by a rich smile. "Yes—he was a very healthy boy baby—now 9 years and very strong and healthy. We are very happy that he will grow up in a unified and peaceful Vietnam and thus justify the sacrifices of so many of his uncles and aunts."

"Why did you join the Revolution?" I put the question to 30 year old Nguyen Linh, a cadre from the cultural and propaganda section of the Can Tho People's Revolutionary Committee who—fluent in French and fair in English—accompanied me on my various visits.

"For a start, because my parents were revolutionaries," he replied. "They contributed their fair share during both resistance wars. My father took part in an uprising against the French at Soc Trang in 1945, although he was a civil servant in the French administration. My father and mother were both members of the Lao Dong party. I started as a militant through anti-American student activities at Can Tho university, was denounced by a traitor and as I couldn't continue my studies I left for the Liberated Zones. For most of the time I worked with a cultural and propaganda group, helping also to edit an NLF paper, moving around on the various battlefronts. I took part in all the big campaigns in the Delta, but especially those in the U Minh forest[17] where the enemy waged very fierce campaigns to wipe out our long-standing bases there. It remained solid till the end despite the enemy's repeated: 'Eliminate all Vietcong bases' campaigns."

Nguyen Linh was one of the very few cadres I met who had never been arrested. I asked what were his most difficult moments.

"When the puppets launched a vast campaign with 40,000 troops in the U Minh area. The campaign lasted on and off for

---

17. The famous U Minh forest of giant mangroves covered some 100,000 acres in the southernmost tip of the Ca Mau Peninsula. By selective pruning and burning, a very high quality charcoal was obtained which was a valuable source of fuel for Saigon and was also exported to Hongkong and Singapore. Because it was a traditional revolutionary base in both resistance wars, it was subject to intensive chemical warfare and the centuries-old forests have been practically wiped out. The ecology of the region has been changed. As far as the eye can see there are only blackened stumps left from the napalm bombings, interspersed with knee-high wild grass. The general opinion of scientists at the time of my visit to Saigon was that it was useless to try to replant the forests One idea was that the whole area could be turned over to crocodile farming.

over three years. Our cultural group also took to rifles at that time and our editorial office even managed to knock down a helicopter. We had to be constantly on the move, fighting our way out of one encirclement after the other. We were completely cut off from other areas and for ammunition had to depend on what we captured from the enemy."

"Weren't there problems of food and water?"

"None. Although the water is originally salty, it gets filtered through the mangrove roots and is drinkable or was. Now the whole area is silted up and you have to dig for water. There were always plenty of oysters and other shellfish—and ordinary fish. But the Americans and puppets did a terrible job on the forests. They repeatedly sprayed them with defoliation chemicals. When all the leaves were stripped off and everything dry as timber, they napalmed the whole area. At least two-thirds of the trees were burned out. For some periods we were encircled for months at a time and had to reinforce our fish diet with wild vegetables and roots. The local people—mostly charcoal-burners—were wonderful, but they suffered great difficulties. They were accustomed to exchanging their charcoal for rice and other basic food supplies, but this ended when all roads were blocked by the puppets. At first they said: 'As long as there are leaves left in the forest, we won't capitulate. After a time there were no leaves left—and later no forest, but still they didn't capitulate. They lived off wild roots and shellfish as we did—and never complained."

Heroism was not restricted only to fighting and active political work. In My Tho, for instance, where the repression was just as severe as at Can Tho, with seemingly no space for cadres to breathe (let alone move around and function), I asked Muoi Ha, a smiling, very youngish-looking veteran[18] and member of the city's Military Management Committee, how it was possible for cadres to function the way they did. How did he, for instance, manage to survive, in view of the total nature of police control of residence, movement and contacts. "We were protected by the people," he said, and by way of illustration

---

18. I was astonished to learn that Muoi Ha had commanded the action at Ap Bac, on January 2, 1963. It was one of the great test battles of the war in which the Saigon forces—with U.S. advisers—used 3,000 men, plus air power, heli-borne troops and M-113 amphibious tanks against 300 guerillas. They suffered a shattering defeat, losing 400 killed and wounded, five helicopters and eight 113's, for 13 guerillas killed and 15 wounded.

took me to My Tho's most ancient and beautiful Vinh Trang pagoda. Introducing me to the Bonze Superior, Thich Tri Long, clad in the brown robes of a Buddhist monk, with a serene face radiating human goodness, Muoi Ha said:

"In addition to practicing his religion, Thich Tri Long has always supported our revolution; that against the French as well as that against the Americans. He hid cadres in the roof of the pagoda, fed them, protected them and thus risked his life to render great service to the revolution."

An NLF flag was flying over the pagoda entrance and an imitation bronze embossed head of Ho Chi Minh had been placed in front of the altar.

"As Bonze Superior of the Vinh Trang pagoda," Thich Tri Long said gravely, "I welcome a friend who has come from afar to visit this historic spot. Yes, our pagoda supported the Vietminh in their struggle against the French colonialists. We hid them in the roof and in cupboards and provided their daily food. After the French were defeated at Dien Bien Phu and the Geneva Agreements were signed, we led a peaceful life here for a time. But when the Americans wanted to install Ngo Dinh Diem as president, our bonzes were forced to go and vote for Diem against Bao Dai. We organized voters to deface Diem's portrait at the polling booths as a mark of protest. Once Diem was elected, he often sent his agents here to disturb our religious rites. Several of our bonzes and bonzesses burned themselves to death to protest his actions. We resisted the Diem dictatorship by such means as were open to us.

"Many young people tried to avoid being conscripted into the puppet army so they came here to serve as bonzes. At one time, we sheltered as many as 90 of them, from 15 to 20 years of age. The puppet administration sent troops to press-gang even our bonzes into bearing arms to kill their compatriots. We also resisted this as best we could. As the Liberated Zone expanded, most of the young men who had taken shelter with us went there, some of them joining the NLF forces. We sheltered and fed NLF cadres, as we had those of the Vietminh. I have been at the pagoda since I was 7 years of age and the former Bonze Superior was my uncle, who helped shelter the Vietminh cadres."

"Was it not a very dangerous activity?" I asked. He smiled —a beautiful, placid smile.

"The Thieu police, like the Diem police, constantly suspected the pagoda was connected with the revolution. They often came to search but found nothing. They even suspected that our religious services were in favor of the revolution. Perhaps sometimes they were. The majority of Buddhists wholeheartedly support the revolution. Revolutionaries work for a happier life, for the prosperity of the nation. Most Buddhists, including the bonzes, support such aims. Buddhism teaches that we should achieve a just society, equality among men, happiness for all, no corruption or selfishness. The revolutionaries also support such precepts and that is why we support them. For this, when the police came, I was always at peace with my inner self and accepted the ever-present dangers as my modest contribution."

Muoi Ha took me to a house in one of the city's main shopping areas, No. 123 Nguyen Tri Phuong street in the Chien Thanh residential block of the 5th precinct. The owner, Le Tam Lien, was a 52 year old school teacher. Between the panelled ceiling and the roof was a space just two feet high where two cadres could be hidden. The trap-door panel, indistinguishable from the others, could be immovably fixed from above by those who had to use it. A two days' supply of food and water was constantly replenished. Muoi Ha had hidden there several times. Le Tam Lien had been arrested in 1967 and 1969 on suspicion, but despite careful searches of his house, nothing was found. More importantly, in a large underground shelter in the same building, a VPA commando unit set up its headquarters and, on the night of April 29, surged forth to launch a devastating attack on an armored column moving in to reinforce the city's defenses. Half a dozen M-113s were knocked out, the rest —including 20 truckloads of troops—surrendered. The cellar had served for a similar purpose during the 1968 Tết offensive. In another innocent-looking house, also in the 5th precinct, opposite a smouldering garbage dump, the wiry, little owner, Nguyen Duc Hien, showed us the regular shelter everyone was obliged to have "in case of a 'Vietcong' attack,' but also a secret opening from that to a deeper and more spacious one. "There was usually such a stench in the legal shelter," said Le Tam Lien with a laugh, "that no security nark ever dared enter it. They usually held their nostrils with one hand and manipulated a flashlight with the other to check there was no one there." (Similarly, Nguyen Thi Moui Be, in Can Tho, had taken me to the house where she and another cadre had been duplicating leaflets on the night of April 29, when there was a police raid.

All "legal" residents lined up on the front porch, as required, with their identity cards, while Nguyen Thi Muoi Be and her assistant, duplicating machine, paper and all, disappeared into the "legal" shelter, pushing a specially prepared mess of stinking fish and rotting fruit towards the shelter entrance. The police, in fact, were satisfied with the line-up and did not enter the house.) Stench as a police deterrent was one of the many secrets of the revolution and it was a symbol of the completeness of the April 30 victory that such secrets, which otherwise cadres would have guarded with their lives, could now be revealed.

"Every Lao Dong central committee member" explained Muoi Ha, as we left Le Tam Lien's hospitable residence—long since purged of its protective stench—"had at least ten such hiding places in which he or she could seek refuge at any time, depending in what part of town they found themselves during a crisis. That is what we mean when we say we were protected by the people. There were cases when the owners of such shelters were arrested, tortured—in some cases to death—without betraying the secrets of the revolution. Our people understood very well the necessity of protecting the cadres."

The heroes and heroines were at every hand, in different walks of life, engaged in the most diverse activities. At a village near Can Tho, we found an 83 year old Chinese resident, who used to leave little notes about the movement of puppet troops, stuck under the bark of trees for NLF liaison officers to collect. Twice his house—isolated from others in the village—was bombed to bits because he was suspected of "doing something;" twice he rebuilt and never ceased writing his precious little notes and tucking them into trees in a pre-arranged system of rotation. Old Quach Kim, with his white, wispy Ho Chi Minh-type beard, his 49 grandchildren and over 30 great grand-children, knew well that he would be shot out of hand if a single note had been found and traced to him. But it is one of the special aspects of the Vietnamese revolution that there were people of all ages, races, religions and social backgrounds, ready to risk their lives for what they believed was right.

These were realities that the Pentagon computers were incapable of assimilating. Doubtless Quach Kim's hamlet also figured among the 100 percent "secure." But what American investigator could ever peer into the heads of a Quach Kim, a Thich Tri Long, and millions of others and find out what they really thought.

As examples of collective heroism, one could take almost any hamlet or village in the whole of the South. One could take Tân Hôi, for instance, neighboring on Ap Bac, a mile back from Highway 4, in My Tho province. Members of the Provisional Revolutionary Committee, the Lao Dong party and Women's Liberation Associated, flanked by self-defense guerillas—almost exclusively women—were lined up to greet the visitor from afar. Lean-faced men, round-faced women, but all very tough and with the imprint of suffering and determination on their faces. They escorted us into a former barracks—now the Provisional Revolutionary Headquarters—into which the sunlight was streaming through bullet holes of various calibres. Vo Van Tha, with a lean, lined face like others of his age, introduced himself as president of the local Lao Dong committee and proceeded to give a brief account of revolutionary activities since the region rose up against the French in November 1940. (It was these uprisings in My Tho and Ben Tre provinces that gave birth to the yellow-starred red flag of the Democratic Republic of Vietnam which revolutionaries felt was restored to its birthplace by the northern section of the VPA in the March-April general offensive.)

"Our village," explained Vo Van Tha, "holds a strategic position, so close to Highway 4, and the enemy used all means to subdue it. Bombing, shelling, herding us into 'strategic hamlets,' destroying our crops and fruit trees with poisonous chemicals. During 1969-1971, the puppets destroyed our homes seven times and seven times we rebuilt them. They destroyed and we rebuilt. They destroyed again, we rebuilt again. They came with M-113's to destroy the ricefields and orchards. We replanted, practicing the 'three clings' policy. 'Peasants cling to the land, Lao Dong party clings to the peasants; guerillas cling to the enemy.'

"Of our total of a few more than 5,000 inhabitants, 900 from our village had been wiped out in the few years prior to April 30. Whole families were killed in the bombings and shellings. These were usually followed by 'mopping up' operations. When houses were destroyed we set up temporary lean-to's with corrugated iron sheeting while we gathered bamboo and rice straw for thatch for more permanent ones, but we clung to the land and cultivated it well. We hit back with our two platoons of guerillas, 25 in one, 27 in the other. The main activity was laying ambushes and keeping the enemy away by passive defense measures. From captured American mines or unexploded bombs and shells, we removed the powder and replaced it in plastic containers that their mine detectors couldn't discover. These we laid on lateral roads and they were so effective that in later years the Americans and puppets did not dare leave the main highway. Everyone took part in the resistance. Special groups of children had the task of bringing all unexploded bombs and shells to our 'captured weapons' group in charge of repairing captured weapons, making mines and devising the best use of any weapons that came into our hands. A 12 year old boy, Tien Van Bong, who had lost both hands in a bombing, avenged himself by using the stumps of his wrists to hurl a hand grenade into the rear of an open truck, killing a puppet lieutenant and several soldiers. A 70 year old peasant, Nguyen Van Bay, studied the habits of one enemy patrol and set a mine which blew up a General Motors truck full of troops. We farmed well, the cultivated area was never reduced. From 1960 on, we never missed making a good contribution of rice to the regular armed forces. But while we tilled and harvested the fields our thoughts were always on how to deal bigger and better blows against the enemy."

Vo Van Tha led us to a small fortress, fifty yards away, formerly garrisoned by a company of troops whose barracks and mess-hall had been the building where we were meeting. A building of similar size some 20 yards away had been for locking up peasant families if one of their members had been caught in revolutionary activities. The fortress was the pivotal center of a whole system of small ones, spaced about 500 yards apart, dominating the area east of the nearby district center of Cai Lay and overlooked Tân Hôi village about 200 yards distant. The outer walls covered in barbed wire, it was disposed around a watchtower made of logs cemented together, surrounded by a reinforced concrete perimeter with regular firing points. Inside the perimeter were cell-like sleeping quarters and storage depots —all below ground level. The perimeter and dividing walls were now a collapsed mass of rubble. What had happened? For reply, Vo Van Tha escorted me to a point 150 yards distant where a small team was standing around a grenade launcher, a model unique in the history of armaments. It was a catapult, consisting of an A-shaped bamboo frame over two meters high and multi-colored thongs made from tens of thousands of ordinary rubber bands—the sort you can buy in any stationery shop, pleated together in links, each about three inches long. With a typical Vietnamese artistic touch, each link, of about two hundred bands, was the same color: red, orange, blue, green etc.

At a command from Le Quang Thanh, the committee man for military affairs, a group of four young men stepped forward, saluted smartly, and under Thanh's expert guidance set up the frame pointed towards the fort. When the legs were adjusted to Thanh's satisfaction, especially the inward-pointing struts that were to take the stress, the first of the four young men grasped a rubber pouch attached to the thongs, the second grabbed the waist of the first, the third and fourth grabbing the waists in front of them and they leaned backwards, each link stretching to a length of at least a foot. Thanh sighted over their heads, tapped a shoulder here and there until the alignment was what he wanted, then placed an unripe guava in the pouch and gave a quiet order. Everyone let go and the guava went whizzing away at tremendous speed to land a few yards to the right of the fort's perimeter. A slight adjustment of one of the legs and this time, once the young men had leaned back to achieve maximum tension, a tennis ball-sized hand grenade was placed in the pouch. Away it went at Thanh's command, to explode "bang" in the middle of the fort.

"By adding a couple of men, we can increase the range up to 300 yards," said Le Quang Thanh. Another grenade was fired with the same accuracy. "The great merit," he explained, "is that there is no noise of departure, no indication of from what direction it comes. We usually precede an assault on a fort by a grenade bombardment from three sides which enables our forces to approach from the fourth side. The garrison obviously thinks the grenades are hand-thrown and start firing down at close range around the perimeter which enables us to get very close." The rubber-band grenade launcher was Tân Hôi's own contribution to the world's weapon systems and Le Quang Thanh said that most villages had invented some sort of weaponry, but that it had been difficult to get together and exchange experiences.

Back at the meeting room, Le Van Tha explained how the villagers had "risen up and seized power." "A week before April 30," he said, "we had received instructions from district headquarters to prepare a three-aspect attack—military, political and propagandist—on the four military posts in our area. That meant, propaganda among enemy troops; political action by mass demonstrations; and direct military assault if the enemy refused to surrender. These were Tân Hôi, the biggest which you have just seen, Cau Duc and posts No's 33 and 34.

"At 9:00 a.m. on the 30th, about 400 people staged demonstrations around each of the posts, singing, dancing and getting in ever closer to prevent the soldiers firing on our troops in case a direct assault was necessary. This went on till around 3:00 p.m., when the garrisons started firing at the crowd and threw a few hand grenades. Then we brought up the wives and mothers of the soldiers in the posts. They went right up into the front row and urged their men to down their arms and come out. Hundreds of family members, including children and mothers with babies in their arms, stood right in the front line so the troops and officers could see them. But the commanding officers were very obstinate; they had committed so many crimes that they were probably worried about their own skins. We read out over the megaphones the NLF's ten-point lenient policy towards the puppet troops. The only reply was a few shots directed at the megaphones.

"The climax of political struggle came when some 1,500 people with torches and kerosene lamps completely encircled the Tân Hôi post, getting in very close, calling on the garrison to surrender, but still without results. Suddenly at 9:00 p.m., they opened up a gap through which our armed forces could pass to launch a first attack. For several hours we attacked the outer defenses, blowing gaps through the barbed wire and breaching the outer walls with our grenade-launchers. The crowd had moved back by then, but kept up the propaganda barrage through the megaphones. We continued the attack until 4:00 a.m., when the puppets sent word that they wanted a respite to prepare their surrender. We halted the attack but our forces remained in their positions. At 6:00 a.m., they started coming out of Tân Hôi with a white flag and from the other three posts a few minutes later. Within half an hour, they had all laid down their arms; except for seven of the worst of them from Tân Hôi, who managed to slip away during the night and have still not been rounded up. We captured 75 weapons, including mortars and 12.7 mm machine-guns. We used two or three grenade launchers against each post, and they blew the insides to bits."

This sort of action went on in most villages in My Tho and Can Tho provinces and almost certainly throughout the Mekong Delta. It was not a question of an automatic laying down of arms, according to instructions from Saigon, although following "Big" Minh's surrender declaration, the chief of general staff of Saigon's armed forces on the morning of the 30th, had also issued orders that all military units were to surrender to the nearest VPA or PRG units. The manner in which the military reacted from the 4th Military Region commander, General Nguyen Van Nam, down to the post commander in Tân Hòi, shows that the military had had prior instructions, which they considered still valid, to hang on to the Mekong Delta, regardless of what happened in Saigon and the rest of the country. The plan was thwarted by the thousand-fold multiplication of the actions as described above and in the previous chapter.

Chapter 6.

My Tho

One of the most vivid memories of my first trip to the Liberated Zones, at the turn of the year 1963-1964, was a meeting with Huynh Tan Phat and members of the NLF's Saigon-Gia Dinh committee, of which Huynh Tan Phat was chairman, among his many other functions. At the time, I wrote about it as follows:

> A trim, smiling man with twinkling eyes and a thin line of moustache, dressed as if he had stepped straight out of his Saigon office, came into the peasant's hut where my hammock had been slung for the night. I had slept late, and had been musing at the constant roar of planes and helicopters which seemed neither to grow nearer nor to recede into the distance. It had just been explained that they were warming up their motors at Saigon's Tan Son Nhut airport.

> "Welcome to Saigon" said the smiling man in French of a Parisian quality, both hands stretched out in greeting. 'Meet the members of our Committee.' There were 12 altogether, out of 16 members of the Executive Committee of the Liberation Front's Saigon-Gia Dinh branch (Gia Dinh is Saigon's province). The smiling man was Huynh Tan Phat, a well-known Saigon architect. Apart from heading the Saigon-Gia Dinh Committee, he is one of the outstanding national leaders of the Liberation Front, as the Secretary-General of its Central Committee and head of the Democratic

party, one of the three political parties affiliated to the NLF. Like so many of the Front's leaders, he had temporarily abandoned his profession and city comforts for the hard, dangerous life of the liberation struggle. I knew that his wife was serving a life sentence (for revolutionary activity).[19]

Among the Committee members, as Huynh Tan Phat presented them, were two journalists, a writer, a musician, two peasants, a factory worker, a representative of Saigon youth whose profession I did not note, a housewife, student and, of course, Huynh Tan Phat himself . . .

"We have to live closely integrated with the enemy," explained Huynh Tan Phat, with a marvelously humorous twinkle that rarely leaves his eyes. "They think, for instance, that this hamlet is theirs. In fact it's ours. People often come out from Saigon and have no idea that they are in one of our liberated areas. We don't bother them, never ask them for papers unless we smell an agent. In that case we would have been warned in advance.

Our territory and the enemy's is closely interlocked, especially here so near Saigon. But you only come up against the enemy if you run right into an enemy post or get within the sights of his artillery or machine guns. We have a policy called 'corking up' enemy posts, meaning that they are surrounded by our guerillas day and night and the garrison can only move out with our permission."

He produced a map to illustrate the situation. He showed me the hamlet in Binh Chanh district, where I had spent the first hours of the Year of the Dragon and I was astonished to note that I had spent the night and most of next day a few hundred yards from a post. "Actually that post no longer exists," he said and put a cross through it. "It was taken out a couple of months ago. For months previous to that, it was encircled day and night; the garrison had to ask

---

19. By chance, a little over a year later, I met Madame Huynh Tan Phat just after she had been released from jail due to a partial amnesty. She was trudging back along a jungle trail to a headquarters and had not yet seen her husband. As I had seen him a few days earlier, she was eager for news. I described his vigor and dynamic optimism. "Ah," she said, in a voice full of pride, "but he always thinks he's much younger than he is." She also survived the intervening years and they are united under more comfortable circumstances in the prime minister's residence in Saigon! Other prison inmates told me of her heroic comportment during eight years of jail.

our guerillas for permission to visit the market, or draw water for cooking from the Kinh Xang canal right alongside. They feared an attack at any moment so they have abandoned it." The post had been held by a company of Saigon troops and it was 4 miles from Saigon. More alarming, however, seemed the situation in the immediate vicinity of the hamlet where we were meeting...

Posts—with no crosses through them—were all around, two of them at a distance of 1,000 and 1,500 yards respectively. And suddenly, there started a tremendous noise of exploding artillery and mortar shells, heavy machine-gun fire, the roaring of diving planes and the dull crack of napalm bombs. It was very difficult to hear Huynh Tan Phat's voice and even more to accept his calm assurances that the enemy could never move out. "Yes", he said, "it does look rather frightening on a map. We seem to be completely encircled by enemy posts but, in fact, it is they who are encircled by us. The garrisons can't move out except in big, combined operations with Saigon's mobile reserves."

When a pause was proposed, I asked about the noise of what seemed to be a very fierce battle in our immediate vicinity, but of which no notice was taken. "Didn't anyone tell you about that?" asked Huynh Tan Phat, with an apologetic smile. "That's the U.S. Parachutist Training Center at Trung Hoa, a couple of miles from here. They can't train their conscripts in parachute jumping any more because too many used to fall into our areas, some of them purposely. Now they give them infantry training under simulated battle conditions. It goes on nearly every morning; someone should have warned you..."[20]

My mind went back to that very convincing explanation of an otherwise inexplicable state of affairs, 12 years later, when I looked at the situation in My Tho as it was on the eve of April 30. A lively city of 120,000, My Tho is situated on a loop of the Mekong, separated from the main body of that mighty brown river by a narrow island. On a military map, it looked as if the entire area surrounding the city up to the Mekong had a bad rash of measles; each tiny point represented pillboxes, hundreds of them spaced in depth between 500 and 1,000 yards apart in a broad arc, more and more concentrated as they ap-

---

20. Wilfred G. Burchett, *VIETNAM—Inside Story of the Guerilla War*, New York: International Publishers, March 1965, pp. 33-35.

proached the city outskirts. "Yes, it looks hopeless," said Muoi Ha, of the city's Military Management Committee, "unless you knew that all those pillboxes were surrounded by our guerillas from positions about 50 yards away." We were standing at a point a dozen yards from Provincial Road No. 24, in My Phong village, just two and a half miles from the center of the city. A hundred yards back from a small group of shops that lined the road, were the tall masts of a U.S. Special Forces headquarters. This was intended as the second fall-back U.S. military headquarters in case Saigon fell and also the first fall-back position at Vung Tau. Between the shops and the radio masts, in a small copse of coconut and banana palms, was the PRG headquarters for directing actions in My Tho city!

"In the weeks prior to April 30," explained Muoi Ha, "our forces gradually tightened their encirclement of the city, elements of our 'special units' were infiltrated inside the city itself. We carried out full dress rehearsals, usually against enemy positions, to build up experience for the real job.

"While the attack on Saigon was being developed in the early hours of the 30th, our forces headed straight for the center of My Tho from two sides, securing precincts 2 and 3 in the east and 5 and 6 in the west, then continuing on towards the heart of the city. We had to divert part of our forces when 20 helicopters flew in from Saigon to a helicopter landing field in the western outskirts. When they saw our forces there, they tried to take off, but we rushed them and captured them all intact. This ended a place for the general evacuation of helicopters from Saigon. By 10:00 a.m., we had occupied many enemy installations and were operating in the center of the city. Between 10:00 a.m. and 2:00 p.m. however, there was considerable resistance; despite instructions from Saigon the enemy was still holding out in the center with heavy firing coming from the police headquarters. At 3:00 p.m. our regional troops started coming in, and, reinforced an hour later by some of our 'special force' units, they stormed the police headquarters and a secondary school which the puppets had transformed into one of their military strongpoints. Between 5:00 p.m. and 6:00 p.m., we organized a show of force, parading what troops and weapons we had, with considerable mass support. The puppets started laying down their arms all over the place. Some naval units fired a few shells, then retreated down the Mekong towards the sea. My Tho was liberated except for a few heavily-defended installations which would have been costly to take by assault. These were encircled, however, and their surrender was only a matter of time. While the action inside My Tho city was going on, the guerilla units which had been surrounding the posts, started taking them over, mainly by persuasion, but where that failed by armed action."

We went to the headquarters of the hated Rural Pacification Corps. If ever a unit had a "guilt complex" for its barbarous methods in putting down the peasants, it was the Rural Pacification Corps—the special fief of American general John Vann, whose death in a plane crash was described as the equivalent of "a loss of two divisions." After repeated demands by flag-waving civilians to surrender had been refused by the company defending the headquarters, a VPA "Special Forces" platoon, in puppet uniforms, marched straight up to the front gate —flanked by double rows of electrified barbed wire—shot the sentry, smashed down the gates and charged straight into the headquarters' buildings, firing as they went. The puppets fled in dismay, throwing down their weapons as they went. "It was an interesting experiment with a small shock force against an enemy far superior in numbers," said Muoi Ha. What was also interesting was that the combat position from which the attack was launched was just about 200 yards from the Rural Pacification Headquarters and the whole action, as all others that day, was directed from the coconut grove command post about half a mile away.

Later, at a meeting with some other members of the Military Management Committee[21] and representatives of some other revolutionary and mass organizations, Moui Ha spoke of some of the difficulties that had had to be overcome along the hard road to victory. Recalling that in the years between 1954-1960 the U.S.-Diem régime considered repression in My Tho as a "model experiment in Communist suppression," Muoi Ho said:

"We had losses but the revolutionary leadership and bases in the villages were preserved. We, sitting here tonight, were very specifically targets of the 'Denounce Communists' cam-

---

21. In most places liberated as the general offensive swept south, Peoples Revolutionary Committees were installed as the chief administrative organs. But in Saigon and a few other big provincial cities where there were large numbers of former Saigon troops still around and public security could be a major problem, administrative functions were temporarily assumed by Military Management Committees.

paign. It was aimed at eliminating people like us. But within a year of that campaign ending, we had totally shattered enemy control in My Tho province. We were in the vanguard of standing up to U.S. 'Special War,'[22] by defeating in the Ap Bac battle the helicopter and amphibious tank tactics which were intended as the backbone of 'Special War' techniques.

"Within one year of that victory", continued Muoi Ha, "we re-deployed our forces and distintegrated the network of 'stategic hamlets,' liberating 75 percent of the rural area in My Tho province, including some district capitals. These were the 'golden days' of our offensive operations of that period. The demonstration at Ap Bac that proved that they could no longer count on helicopter tactics to impose their policies had a very demoralizing effect on the enemy.

"Highway 4 has always been a bone of contention between us and the enemy" continued Muoi Ha, "especially what we call the 'Binh-Duc belt' of five villages starting only 6 miles from My Tho in the direction of Saigon. 1967 was the year in which guerilla warfare was most developed in that area. In one night, for instance, we cut Highway 4 in thirty different sectors. Enemy transport was completely halted for over a fortnight. Our guerillas stayed on the spot to prevent repair work, wrecking 80 enemy vehicles during that time and helping ourselves to large stocks of military supplies. The Americans were obliged to use helicopters to drop stones for repair work and we shot down several of them. They decided to impose their control once and for all and launched 'Operation Colorado', using three of their own and two puppet divisions in a drive to control and 'pacify' Highway 4. We chose our time, then suddenly struck and wiped out two U.S. battalions which scared them considerably. As they advanced, the Americans set up networks of posts and pillboxes, detailing a brigade of their own troops to garrison these—but we never left them in peace. Elements of the U.S. 9th division occupied the five villages of the 'Binh-Duc' belt, but our guerillas kept these units encircled, including their batteries of 75's, 105's and even 180 mm artillery pieces. For two years,

22. "Special War," together with "Limited War", which meant the commitment of U.S. combat troops, and "Global, Nuclear War" were the three types of war which the U.S. should be prepared to fight, according to General Maxwell D. Taylor, special military adviser to President Kennedy. In "Special War" the U.S. would provide everything—except ground combat troops.

the Americans occupied these villages, but during that period we put out of action 18,000 U.S. troops. It became too expensive for them and in 1969, they withdrew."

Muoi Ha went on to explain that the period between 1969-1972, when Nixon's policy of Vietnamization of the war was being introduced, was a period of a great intensification of the machinery of repression. As many as 25 military and police posts were set up to control a single village; "to control everything, including how much rice and fruit each household produced and where it went, to make sure nothing was left over for the guerillas." It was the period when the Americans started to use B-52s against villages suspected of "Vietcong" sympathies, and the introduction of artillery "interdiction" fire, according to computerized time-tables. "Because our peasants got used to diving for cover at the first sound of firing, the Americans used supersonic shells which exploded before you heard the firing," said Muoi Ha. "This went on regularly from 7:00 p.m. until 5:00 a.m. We had to sleep underground, but the difficulty in the Delta is that you strike water at a few inches, so we had to build surface shelters, hidden in various mounds or terraces between ricefields. Despite this nightly firing, there was surprisingly little loss of life. Occasionally people got caught in a cluster of exploding shells and they were killed or wounded. But just as the cadres adjusted their movements to the fairly regular pattern of fire, so the peasants adjusted the rhythm of cultivating their fields in between the barrages. They knew when to alternate between fields and shelters."

Helicopter gunships were introduced to keep people off the fields in daytime. "There were often groups of them hovering over the fields, shooting down anyone working in the fields or moving along the roads. Peasants changed their traditional black or brown clothes to white, because the U.S. pretext for shooting at anyone in the traditional brown or black was that he or she must be 'Vietcong.' When anyone dressed in white was killed or wounded, there were big protest demonstrations."

I asked about the B-52 bombings. From afar, the use of these giant bombers against the densely populated Delta villages, where there was no possibility of deep shelters, seemed the ultimate horror, short of nuclear bombs.

"Actually the results were far short of the intentions," replied Muoi Ha." Delta houses are usually on slightly raised platforms of tightly rammed earth so it was possible to have shelters. The B-52's almost always bombed at night. Sentries fired warning shots as soon as they heard the 'swoosh' of bombs coming down. The B-52's fly so high that it takes quite a while for their bombs to come down—long enough for people to dive into shelters. Despite the density of population the losses were small and in My Tho, the revolutionary nucleus remained virtually intact despite the B-52s and helicopter gunships. Local guerillas remained in place, at most 200 meters from enemy posts and usually much closer. Cadres also settled in alongside the enemy posts—not to direct activities there—but because these were the safest bases from which to operate. By 'clinging to the belts' of the enemy, we encircled them. They couldn't move out. On the maps it looked as if we were encircled—the truth was the opposite.

"If any post got too zealous in its 'pacification' activities, we killed a few of the garrison—officers if possible—just to let them know we were around. In the hamlets, with every house wrapped up in barbed wire and every movement watched, it was like being in prison; in our encirclement trenches and dugouts, a few score yards from the enemy, we were free! The enemy hated this. It was they who were in prison and it got on their nerves. Sometimes they sent someone to negotiate with us to leave them alone. 'Just go home.' But nothing doing. We organized demonstrations within a thousand or two yards from their posts. They rarely fired on them because of our good propaganda work. There were always cadres up front with megaphones. If shots were fired: 'What! Would you shoot at your own mothers and sisters?' would come across to them. This was one of the aspects of 'Vietnamization' that Nixon hadn't thought of. When Americans occupied the posts this type of propaganda was impossible. But Vietnamese singing nostalgic folk songs, dancing traditional folk dances in which most of the garrison members would have loved to join; everything evoked national and family sentiments; memories of peaceful village life that could be again, which demoralized the puppets isolated in their posts. Of course, had we relied exclusively on sentimental appeals this would not have been enough. But we had the force to back up our appeals and reproaches with punishment. There were main force units at provincial, district—and in many cases—village levels. It had to be this way, with the nearest forests over a hundred miles distant. Impossible to retreat there when things got tough. In any case, we were pledged to the second of the 'three clings.' The Party clings to the people. So we remained right under the noses of the enemy, pulling those noses when necessary.

"Despite their terror tactics and repeated 'pacification' campaigns, it was always the revolutionary forces that held the initiative; that took the offensive. It must be difficult for you who know us, and even more so for friends abroad who do not," continued Muoi Ha, "to imagine how guerillas could exist and function so close to the enemy. There's nothing miraculous about it—it's because we literally do cling to the people and the people cling to us. Because of the great revolutionary traditions in this area, even those who worked in the enemy-controlled towns and villages remained true revolutionaries. That is why at the climax of the 1972 spring offensive we liberated 25 of My Tho's 92 villages and dissolved just over one hundred 'strategic hamlets.' This was only possible because of the active cooperation of the villagers. We had long ago come to the conclusion that, regardless of difficulties, the people are always capable of mastering the situation."

As an example he cited the fact that at one point 200,000 peasants—about one third of the population of My Tho province—were in 'strategic hamlets' and another 50,000 had sought refuge from the B-52's in My Tho city, officially classified as "refugees from 'Vietcong' terror," but in both cases they became the "most loyal supporters of revolutionary struggle. How could they feel any loyalty to a régime which sent B-52 bombers to exterminate their villages?" asked Moui Ha. The B-52 raids ended with the signature of the Paris Agreement, hailed with great enthusiasm throughout the Delta, according to Muoi Ha.

"It seemed wonderful," he continued, "but our joy was short-lived. Thieu immediately sent two divisions of troops for 'pacification' and land-grabbing operations. Our cadres had rigid instructions to respect the ceasefire and not to respond to provocations. We gritted our teeth and some cadres wept with rage, when Thieu's troops started reoccupying the 25 villages we had liberated in 1972, arresting many patriots suspected of supporting the revolution. Those first few months were terrible, but we never fired a shot—not even in self-defense.

"Then came the PRG decision to resist further advances—which we did—quickly followed by another to retake lost territory. We started by re-liberating the 25 villages, thereby inflicting very heavy losses on the enemy. After this we got word to prepare for the Ho Chi Minh campaign and our morale soared sky-high."

Muoi Ha and his comrades were assigned three main tasks. The traditional one in all major military efforts—to neutralize Highway 4 and block the movement of supplies preventing enemy units from concentrating or moving towards Saigon! Get as many of their own troops as could be spared as close to Saigon as possible to take part in the assault on the capital! Immediately, the assault on Saigon was launched, to seize power in My Tho as rapidly as possible! No small assignment! One that called for hurling everything available into what was obviously designed as the "final battle." "In fulfilling the first two tasks," continued Muoi Ha, "we occupied a 35 mile stretch of road between Cai Lay and Tan Huong (district centers about equidistant to the west and to the east of My Tho, W. B.). Our main force and regional units manoeuvred into position alongside the road to support our guerillas who proceeded to cut wide gaps across the highway and to plant mines on the approaches to the sections where the highway-cutting operations were going on. When the enemy came to try to repair the gaps, we engaged them in what turned out to be very hot battles. We fired at them from prepared ground positions; they returned the fire with their artillery and bombed us with their aviation. Due to our superior morale and experience, our forces came off best and the Highway was kept out of action from My Tho onwards throughout the battle of Saigon. Some of our troops also moved up to join the 9th division in its push on the capital.

"As for the third task. We intended to seize My Tho as soon as we heard the battle for Saigon had started. One main force regiment, three battalions of regional forces and some platoons of self-defense guerillas were ear-marked for this operation. (Most of the local guerillas were assigned to deal with the various posts they had been encircling, W. B.) But it so happened that when Saigon was being liberated, our main force regiment was still 30 miles away from My Tho on Highway 4 and our regional forces were still in place to prevent repair work. (Muoi Ha did not specify, but it seems that this was because the assault on Saigon had been advanced by two days at the last moment and some provincial party headquarters could not be warned in time, W. B.). However, we decided to carry out our task using only local guerillas plus mass uprisings, to seize the city. That is why, by the time our regional and main force units arrived, the job was practically done." The main force units, which were motorized—as at Can Tho—were held up by the excellence of the highway destruction and did not start entering the city until about 10:00 p.m. With this display of the kind of force they understood, those Saigon units which had still been holding out, surrendered. "15,000 puppet troops, including front line regulars, simply disintegrated," said Moui Ha, concluding the account of the liberation of My Tho. "We then declared three days of official celebrations, in which the puppet troops and including many of their officers enthusiastically participated. Even for the officers, whatever their inner thoughts, it meant the fighting and dying was over."

How did the troops react to the change in régime during the first few weeks? How did the officers behave? How were the social and economic consequences of so many decades of war and occupation and puppet rule coped with? These were some of the obvious questions I raised with the representatives of the various revolutionary organizations in discussions which lasted into the small hours of the morning. It appeared that there were no problems with the rank and file troops and junior officers. Most of the troops were from peasant or workers families, either press-ganged into the army or forced into it for urgent economic reasons. The rich paid large sums for substitutes for their sons in the call-up, sometimes to poor families which had an available son, sometimes to puppet officials to find the substitutes. A 42 year old woman told us how she scraped together the equivalent of over 3,000 U.S. dollars so that her husband would not be taken. He was called up anyway, but he crippled both his legs, and only thus avoided service. One of her neighbors had injected chemicals into her son's eyes which badly affected his eyesight. He was conscripted and died in action soon afterwards—she was arrested and died in jail. A majority of the junior officers, according to Van Nghia, also of the Military Management Committee, were enthusiastic about the end of the war.

"After seven-day reorientation courses," he said, "the junior officers grasp the historic importance of the victory. They feel proud to be Vietnamese and the victors over such a mighty force as U.S. imperialism. At the same time their class feelings are aroused against those Vietnamese forces which were behind the puppets. For a long time they had seen the venal, corrupt nature of the puppet leaders, including most of their own divisional commanders. Even some of the senior officers—those who have retained a sense of patriotism—are relieved at the collapse of the puppet régime. But there are also some 'no-hopers,' highranking officers, hopelessly corrupted by super-privileges and a luxurious life. No reorientation or remoulding courses can change their outlook. They may be detained for quite a while unless they radically change their attitude."

To my question as to whether the young people in the cities had become unduly and permanently influenced by the long period of American occupation and everything that went with that and which was left behind, the consensus was that the young and old alike in the cities had been attracted to U.S. styles of eating, drinking and dressing, "not to mention vices such as pornography, drug addiction and prostitution" as a member of the Liberation Woman's Association expressed it. "But," she added, to the approving nods of the others, "the influence of revolutionary traditions on the young people is also profound. They are proud of the 30 years of struggle of their parents and other elders whom they respect. There is this good influence alongside the other and we are certain it is the former which will predominate." Muoi Ha added: "We have taken no administrative measures at all, but the indecent and extravagant style of dressing has disappeared; women don't spend long hours on elaborate hair-dos and having their fingernails painted. People just felt it was out of place with the national traditions which we revolutionaries defend. Lots of things that went against our traditions and morality simply disappeared overnight. We brought with us performances based on our traditional culture but with revolutionary new songs and dances, which were favorably received. Life was transformed from within, without outside pressures. The terrain was favorable because most people had had their fill of the U.S. 'way of life' as they saw it on the streets, on TV and in cinemas. People quite naturally turned their backs on the culture of the vanquished and turned to that of the victors, which was their own."

Some administrative measures had been taken against night clubs, drugs and prostitution. The cadre from the Liberation Women's Association said there had been about 1,000 prostitutes in My Tho, but "amongst them are many good, decent young women who were forced into it against their will. One young woman came forward," she said, "to explain that she was an orphan, sold to a Chinese family at the age of 14, then resold to a night club where she was forced into prostitution. She married a puppet sergeant to escape this but he turned out to be a hooligan who wanted to enrich himself by her continuing as a prostitute. She left him to work in a restaurant where she met an American who 'married' her as she thought. She had three children by him, then he left for the U.S.A. and she never heard from him again. No provision had been made for the children. She had no way of supporting them, no one to turn to, so she went back to prostitution. 'When our city was liberated,' she told us, 'I felt I also had been liberated; I can now end my shameful life as a prostitute.' There are many similar cases. Our attitude is to cure them of disease, which they almost all had, teach them careers and find jobs for them. We are also trying to reform the hooligans, pickpockets and drug addicts and train them for useful jobs."

Muoi Ha said that the number of criminal types was proportionately quite small, and that only those who refused to give themselves up would be punished, while the others would be re-educated. The aim was to return them all to productive life and not punish for past misdeeds, which, it was considered, were the consequences of the abnormal society in which they had grown up. This approach had given good results. The daily average of twenty to thirty robberies, brawls, rapes etc. until April 30 had fallen to four or five. For the month of July there had been only 15 cases of theft, the smallest on record: "There are still a few gangster types at large," said Muoi Ha, "but we have a three-point approach to problems of social order and security: (1) Educating the masses as to the historic importance of the people's victory. (2) Generate contempt of the old régime by denouncing the crimes it committed and the hardships imposed on people's daily life and (3) Entrust the masses with the task of exposing the gangsters or those who strive to undermine the revolution. Some 300 gangsters were rounded up by this method and we can say that security is no longer a problem. Everyone realizes that our method is re-education and not the firing squad which is why even family members will approach us about relatives whom they have been unable to persuade to change their ways."

Among social-economic problems in the first few weeks were some 30-40,000 unemployed; 16,000 soldiers' families unprovided for; a proportion of the 50,000 of those who had been bombed out of their villages, about 15,000 poverty-stricken people on the starvation line. "As stop-gap measures to ward off starvation," said Muoi Ha, "we called for contributions from the wealthy. In a very short time, we collected the equivalent of about 300,000 dollars which enabled us to distribute free emergency rations. We encouraged everyone to return to their village and urged small manufacturers to start producing and help ease the unemployment problem. We guaranteed raw materials and markets, and they responded well. We encouraged the expansion of existing factories and the starting up of new ones, sometimes based on pooling the skills of artisans in small industrial cooperatives. The basic thing is to get 40,000 people back on to the land in what we call the 'new economic zones' where many unemployed and demobbed soldiers are now going. We have provided building materials and encouraged the setting up of carpenters' cooperatives to repair existing houses in the countryside and build new ones. We can say that since Liberation, people's lives are relatively stabilized; there are certainly nothing like the difficulties of three months ago." As a final summing-up, Muoi Ha said: "Well, it's not much, but that's how things are. People are aware of the great changes taking place, the difficulties also, but they clearly see the real possibilities for a radiant future for the whole country. One can feel the trend towards national concord and unity. There has been no assassination of our cadres, nor economic sabotage. A few gangsters who committed robberies disguised as our troops to discredit the revolution were soon rounded up by the people, and our prestige was never higher. Basing ourselves as usual on the people we look forward to the future with great confidence."

It was difficult not to agree that such confidence, shared not only by this small band of dedicated cadres, but by every person with whom I spoke in this old revolutionary area, was justified. Compared to the incredibly difficult and painful route they had traversed, the way ahead was comparatively plain sailing.

Chapter 7.

Cu Chi

When one studied the press accounts of the general offensive, there were elements that were inexplicable if one rejected the factor of the people's uprisings. The speed, for instance, with which events transpired; the fact that well over half the provincial capitals fell while the VPA main force units were miles or days away; the fact that the fall of a provincial capital was in every case synonymous with the fall of an entire province. World public opinion had lived on the myth that was carefully cultivated by the propaganda of Washington and Saigon—that because Thieu controlled all the provincial capitals and almost all of the district centers, he controlled 95 percent of the country. Had the real situation come to light—that the provincial and district capitals were Saigon-controlled islets in a sea of PRG-controlled territory—the billion dollar flow would quickly have dried up. Was the true situation known in Washington? There is plenty of evidence that Americans in charge in Saigon did their best to prevent it being known by such phoney devices as the HES (Hamlet Evaluation System) and even by the holding of one-man elections. These never intended to give the people any electoral choice but to present a high voter turnout (the percentage of voter registration to voting population), representing the proportion of the population under Saigon's control. That this was an exercise in self-delusion was well known to Americans on the spot. In order to have a legal existence—and the NLF encouraged all their cadres and supporters to have legal existence—one had to have an identity card. Proof of real "legality" was that it bore a stamp which proved you had voted in the previous elections. Not to have such a stamp meant immediate arrest.

What Thieu had was a facade of control maintained by an unprecedentedly powerful machine of repression. But the waves of organized resistance lapped right up to the walls of what seemed to be bastions of Saigon power and seeped under those walls to erode at the centers of power within. The result was a situation on a nation-wide scale which amounted to a perfect example of the classical final phase of People's War—the cities encircled by the countryside. It was also the type of situation, pushed to its highest point, in which Vo Nguyen Gap delighted —catching the enemy in the contradiction between concentration and dispersal of his forces. It was the situation he always tried to bring about in a tactical way before launching a battle. But this time he had it in a strategic sense. The contradiction between Thieu's dispersal of forces to hold territory and concentration of forces to defend key points and launch offensive operations. Thieu tried to solve this by concentrating his main units to defend big towns and bases and handling his dispersal problem by using Civil Guards and so-called village "self-defense" units to police the territory he wanted to hold. But the "self-defense" units were also peasants and working people who, when the time came for real choice, went over to the people, arms and all.

"You may wonder how we could use 'Civil Guards' as our own self-defense units", Nguyen Thi Muoi Be had said in Can Tho. "These are mostly lads of 15 or 16 who had no choice once they were called up. The rich had money to bribe higher officers to secure exemption for their sons. So those who did this were mainly poor people, sons of peasants or peasants themselves who had fled to the city to avoid the bombings. They were the sort who were really waiting for the victory of the revolution. It was easy to approach them and win them over. They were the most enthusiastic in welcoming our regular forces."

Giap, if we assume he was in overall command of the general offensive and people's uprisings, had an army in place all over South Vietnam: around every base, town and city. It was only a question of pressing the right button at the right time and these forces would spring into action. It would not be like the Têt offensive, when a single button was pressed and there were simultaneous uprisings and attacks. This time there were numerous buttons to be pressed consecutively when main force units, including the tanks and heavy artillery which he could send from the North, were ready to support the local peoples organizations and their armed forces in dealing with the enemy's force units. But, as the examples of Can Tho and My Tho showed, even the local people's forces were able to deal with those of the enemy's main force units which were pinned down, in defense of fixed positions.

For propaganda purposes, the Western press took their cue from the Americans and Thieu in Saigon and presented what happened as an invasion of the South by the North. (The savagery with which the AFP correspondent, Paul Léandri, was shot down, was because he dared to poke a hole through this theory right at the beginning. Thieu's propagandists saw their whole case being destroyed if he was allowed to continue!) No invading army could have swept on and wheeled about, jumping two or three hundred miles in a day, then rushing back for another hundred or so, as the time-table of the fall of the provincial capitals seem to indicate. What happened was that forces that had been in place for many years were activated in a certain sequence which permitted the most rapid and logical advance towards the main target—the heart of the enemy's military and administrative power. Everywhere I checked, I found that local organs (and this started with the Lao Dong party committee) were given word well in advance to get organized. As the decisive moment approached for action, they were told be ready to spring into action at a specific stage in the development of the offensive. For Can Tho and My Tho and other Mekong Delta centers, this meant the moment the assault on Saigon had started.

The essential and almost incredible thing is that throughout three decades of terrible repression which got steadily worse as the Americans replaced the French, and the all-out fascist methods of Vietnamization which replaced those of Americans, revolutionary organizations were still in place, ready to leap into action at the right signal. Cu Chi, a district which adjoins the northern outskirts of Saigon was a good example. I had been there during my previous visits to the Liberated Zones and it was there that I had first met Huynh Tan Phat. I was pleasantly surprised to find the same Lao Dong party secretary, Ba Bo, whom I had met on previous visits, starting 11 years earlier, still in charge, a little grayer, but his leathery face as cheerful as usual. He recalled my previous visits, assured me that "we all survived" and was kind enough to say that what I had written of my previous visits had "greatly encouraged us."

How *had* they managed to survive was obviously my first question. Cu Chi, one of six districts which make up Gia Dinh province, was a most advanced and exposed position. As a well-known revolutionary base area, the Americans had made very special efforts to "empty the sea." Following ten days of intensive "search and destroy" operations at the beginning of 1966, they had headquartered the 25th Infantry division alongside the district center. In the month that followed, the divisional command claimed to have fired 180,000 shells into Cu Chi district and to have continued at the same tempo throughout the year. I had written about Cu Chi after my first visit and how their armed forces had been built up from arms captured in a night attack against a post at Phu My Hung, 9 miles from Saigon, with one single "Mother Carbine," lots of wooden dummy carbines and plenty of bluff, backed up by exploding bamboo tubes stuffed with bicycle carbide and calls to surrender over megaphones, between the terrifying explosions of the bamboo tubes.[23]

An American journalist who read my account of Cu Chi, said with a grin: "You'll never get back into Cu Chi now that the 25th division is there. And if you did get back you'd never recognize the place. The first remark was incorrect, the second correct. I did get back for my third visit, in 1966. It was certainly difficult to recognize! Later, I wrote:

> Of the prosperous bamboo-surrounded villages I had seen during my first visit to Cu Chi nearly three years previously, not a trace remained; not a hamlet, not a house (in the usual sense of the term), not a tree, not a buffalo. Where there had been lush stretches of rice, magnificent fields of cabbages, turnips and pineapples, there were only overlapping craters. Earlier that year in North Vietnam, I had seen fields of sweet potatoes and corn "rise to their feet." Actually these were camouflaged self-defense units during manoeuvres in one case and school-children with green-leaf camouflage getting to their feet after an air raid in another.

23. VIETNAM—Inside Story of the Guerilla War, pp. 109-111.

But at Cu Chi I saw the soil itself standing up after the passage of a flight of helicopters. Stark naked men who rose up from the mud to haul and push plows and wield hoes and drop back into the mud when the helicopters returned...

I spoke with one gaunt, naked cultivator. He was not embarrassed and he did not need to be. The gray mud, caked over his body removed any impression of nudity. He was a statue in living clay, part of the soil come to life in human form.

"My people have always been here," he said. "My father, my father's father and his father as long as we can count back. Their bones lie here, even if the Yankee devils have torn up their tombstones with their bombs and shells and tanks. I will live and fight here and if I die from Yankee shells or bombs, at least my bones will remain on the same bit of soil as those of my ancestors."

"After the 25th division set up its headquarters at Dung Du (a couple of miles south of Cu Chi, W.B.), the Party changed its tactics," said Ba Bo "reassessing our forces and tasks. It was decided to split up to carry out three distinct tasks. Cultivation to feed ourselves; protection of the people by establishing armed units in their residential areas; hang on, to find weaknesses in the enemy's posture and continue to attack. We also decided on three-way tactics. Military, political and propagandist. We would concentrate on guerilla warfare, stepping up the production of our own weapons (they already had efficient arsenals for making grenades and mines and repairing small arms at the time of my first visit, W.B.), mainly for destroying tanks and other military vehicles. The Americans were very afraid of such guerilla activities, especially the destruction of tanks and ambushes of patrols. You can see everywhere the debris of tanks and armored cars that we destroyed in those days, the late 1960's.

"We developed what we called the 'Iron Triangle', based on the villages of Xom Moi, Tranh Lam; Nguyen Duc and Phuoc Vinh An. It was here that the greatest number of tanks were destroyed with great regularity. This was part of the general development of the war. The 'Iron Triangle' became an area very difficult for the enemy to penetrate. The Americans had no idea how to tackle this situation at first. It was direct military confrontation, with our small forces taking the initiative, finding the correct tactic for every occasion. It was so effective that the population also started to take part. We came to the conclusion that to fight against the Americans was not all that difficult, except that in daytime operations they always outnumbered us in infantry and obviously had a monopoly on tanks, artillery and air support. One of their offensives against us lasted a full month, but because of our tunnel systems, we were able to block both ends of the operation and keep hitting them in the middle. (Cu Chi is famous for its extensive tunnel systems, in one of which I had to take shelter during an unexpected battle during my first visit, W.B.) At Tranh Lam, for instance, we caught them between two sections of our tunnel systems, inflicting heavy losses. . ."

As Ba Bo described it, the methods used were one of the most perfect applications of the "grasshoppers versus elephants" concept, with the Americans lunging and plunging around, not even knowing half the time what was stinging them, nor from where it came. Actions usually lasted only ten or fifteen minutes, the guerillas then fading out. They were operating from zig-zagging slit trenches with frequent entries and exits into deep tunnel systems. It was obviously highly frustrating for the Americans, who could take heavy losses within a few minutes without sighting the enemy. "There were cases," said Ba Bo, "when we saw them sit down and weep at half a patrol wiped out without a single one of our men having been sighted." Later the whole "Iron Triangle" area was raked with heavy artillery day and night, forcing Ba Bo and his men to withdraw with their armed forces to rear bases. U.S. units followed them, trying to penetrate the base areas and hunt them down. "We used tunnel systems instead of slit trenches," continued Ba Bo, "with holes big enough for one man to pop out, fire at his target and pop down again before the Americans knew what hit them." The Americans also tried changing their tactics, armored cars preceding infantry, infantry with mine detectors followed by armored cars to protect them. It was a constant battle of military wits, with the Americans usually one move behind. "Whatever order of advance was used," Ba Bo said, "we constantly hit them by brief bursts of fire from behind or from the flanks, forcing their armored vehicles on to a course that would bring them amongst our mines."

Anti-tanks methods were improved. Because of heavy losses, the Americans switched from the light M-113 amphibious tanks to the 48-ton Shermans. Ba Bo and his men accordingly doubled the explosive charge in their mines from 10 to 20 kgs, supplemented by unexploded bombs. Anti-personnel traps were developed, grenades hung in trees with fine nylon threads in the grass to detonate a whole series of such booby traps. "Sometimes we electrically exploded anti-tank mines against the first and last tank in a convoy then opened up on the rest with bazookas," explained one of Ba Bo's anti-tank warfare experts.

By the time of the 1968 Tet offensive, the NLF had two battalions of regular troops in Cu Chi district, four autonomous companies of regional troops and one or two platoons of self-defense guerillas in every village. Contacts had been made with some of the Vietnamese-English language interpreters with the Americans and signs began to appear everywhere: "Minefields ... Turn Back" with the usual death heads for emphasis. "Why Fight and Die on Vietnamese Soil?" and many other variants of the same theme, an aspect of psychological warfare at which the Vietnamese are singularly proficient. "The warnings about the mines had a great effect," said Ba Bo, "because there really were mines where the signs indicated. It got to the point where troops of the 25th could not turn their heads without seeing a slogan of some sort. Their first impulse was to smash them down, but after one or two exploded they treated them with more respect."

Village women were used to work on the Saigon troops who followed in the wake of all U.S. operations, warning that they "had seen 'Vietcong' planting mines and traps in the direction they were taking." Usually the women had taken a hand in the planting! But the Saigon troops were half-grateful for the warnings which they promptly passed on to equally half-grateful U.S. troops. The column would often change direction, to one more favorable for the guerillas to launch a lightning attack.

The Cu Chi forces obviously played their part in the Tết offensive and immediately afterwards ran into great trouble—the U.S.-Saigon Command having decided to get rid of them once and for all. A vast chessboard type of operation was launched, spearheaded by tanks and armored cars followed up by U.S. parachutists who were landed on one square after another until every last corner of the "Iron Triangle" had been processed. Behind the parachuted troops were Vietnamese "Special Force" units whose job it was to mop up and permanently secure the terrain once it was cleared. Ba Bo admitted that this was a period of heavy losses because the new tactics had caught them by surprise. The attack was pushed right into their rear base area and once the armed forces had been pushed back a massive assault on vegetation was launched to rob the guerillas of any cover or any possibility of raising food.[24]

"It was one of the most iniquitous of U.S. policies," said Hai Quang, another cadre whom I had met on my previous visit, a quiet man, with a lined, thoughtful face, whom one could never imagine getting ruffled in any situation. Later he escorted me through many thousands of acres to illustrate what he meant. "When repeated air-spraying of chemical defoliants proved not to be one hundred percent effective," he said, "they used giant bulldozers to uproot and crush everything that lived and grew. 1969 was the peak year in this war against nature. Rubber plantations, citrus and other orchards, coconut and banana palms, bamboo clumps—everything was bulldozed out of existence. Once that was done, planes flew over to sow seeds of what we call 'American grass'. (A reedy type of grass, as I later saw it, 6 to 8 feet tall with tufty heads of seeds, W.B.) In 1970, after the first sowing was sufficiently dry, scores of thousands of gallons of gasoline were dumped and then set ablaze by napalm bombing. We suppose the idea was to lure our armed forces back to establish bases in the tall grass and then burn us alive."

The period immediately after the vegetation-destroying operation was a very difficult one, Ba Bo explained. The headquarters group was forced to disperse, lying up in very secret shelters by day and emerging by night. After the military sweep and bull-dozing part of the operation was over, the headquarters group returned to their forward base area. "As it was stripped of everything," said Ba Bo, "the enemy was certain nobody could exist without being immediately spotted. But all of us here today (there were ten cadres, W.B.) and a few more were there, tucked away in groups of two and threes. We found a few clumps of vegetation that had been overlooked and decided to use those places as bases and start up guerilla warfare again."

They found the former hamlets deserted; in some, every single person had been killed while others had been abandoned because the houses had been burned and there was no possibility

---

24. Forty-three percent of South Vietnam's plantations and orchards (13,000 square kilometers) and forty-four percent of the forests (25,000 square kilometers) were wiped out through chemical warfare and mechanical means such as the use of giant bulldozers and tanks.

of starting up cultivation again. There had also been heavy military losses. By regrouping the survivors of the two original regular battalions, they had one district battalion. "It seemed hopeless—1969 had been a year of heavy losses," said Ba Bo, "but we started the work of rebuilding. By 1971-1972, a few people had come back, and we reconstituted one or two units, each with three fire-arms, for each hamlet, with sometimes as many as 15 fire-arms for a village."

In the 1972 "spring offensive," Cu Chi was allotted the task of seizing a section of Highway 14, which they did, and from then on build up their forces again fairly rapidly, "continuing," as Ba Bo expressed it, "to seize the initiative again on the three fronts in military, political and propaganda affairs." They encouraged some 3,000 villagers to return to their original villages, helping them rebuild their homes, plant fruit trees and start cultivating rice and vegetable plots again. By that time the Americans had started pulling out and Thieu's forces started building military posts to consolidate those abandoned by the Americans. The guerilla forces in the meantime had been built up to their former strength.

"Then came the Paris Agreement, on which most of us had set great hopes," continued Ba Bo. "But we also recalled how we had been deceived by the Geneva Agreement, 19 years earlier. We remained very vigilant, but we also had the strictest instructions to obey the Agreement which we intended to do. We had just two hours of peace after the cease fire was supposed to go into effect. The first thing was that the enemy pushed in to An Nhan Tay village, which was in our territory, and started building military posts there. From there they started land-grabbing operations; destroying by bulldozers all of the houses rebuilt by the 3,000 villagers who had come back, together with all their fruits trees and crops. They managed to force 2,000 of them into 'strategic hamlets', destroying all their property—the rest managed to flee. They pushed further and further into our territory, building military posts as they went. After some months, it was clear that they were heading for our main base area at Duong Minh Chau. This we had to prevent. So we struck back, first of all recapturing An Nhan Tay and the Bo Can post which the puppets had established there.

"The enemy then started setting up a lot of posts along the Highway a sort of no-man's land which separated our territory from that controlled by Saigon. Again the aim was to push people off the land. Even families of puppet troops, as well as those of the revolutionaries were arrested for resisting this."

By this time, there had been the PRG's two orders of the day, of October and November 1973, freeing the Cu Chi partisans from the previous restrictions. They made maximum use of the Paris Agreement as a propaganda document. Everybody in the Liberated Areas was well aware of the contents. There had been special study courses on it, and some cadres could practically recite it by heart. Saigon treated it, as they had the 1954 Geneva Agreement, as a subversive document. But now that the Americans had gone, the propaganda teams could be reactivated, with the old tricks of using the relatives of those manning the posts to urge their sons, brothers and husbands to stop the fighting. They had done this before and often very effectively, but now they had a trump card in the Paris Agreement. Continuing to kill and be killed was a clear violation of the Agreement and of the rights of everyone in the armed forces. A campaign was developed, urging the Saigon garrisons to petition the Thieu regime to make the contents of the Agreement available. The effectiveness of such propaganda was all the greater because the Saigon troops knew only too well that all military initiatives came from their side.

Once they got the "green light"—in November 1973—to re-take territory, the Cu Chi forces went over to the offensive, wiping out 47 posts in November-December alone. One guerilla unit crept up on a force of 57 troops protecting a bull-dozing operation against houses and fruit trees, wiping out the lot. "That one action," said Nam Thuan, member of the district party committee, "ended such operations in that area." In another battle a 43-man company of Security Police was wiped out without loss. "This was all part of the preparation for the Spring General Offensive" said Nam Thuan. "Because of the victories in November-December, morale was very high, and everyone wanted to join the armed forces, if possible the vanguard units. Our instructions were to make things as hot as possible for the enemy and at the end of March we were told to be ready to help liberate Saigon. We divided our forces into two prongs. One to liberate the Phu Hoa zone on Highway 15 to facilitate the advance of the VPA main force units towards the capital; the other to capture the Cu Chi district headquarters. It is difficult to describe the intense enthusiasm with which everybody set about this. We knew that this time we were going to deliver the death blow to the whole system from which we had all suffered so greatly. On the 28th, we wiped out two more posts which could have been bothersome for what we planned for the following day.

"We captured Phu Hoa at 11:00 a.m. on the 29th and by 2:00 p.m., the NLF flag was flying over the Cu Chi headquarters. At Phu Hoa we captured 17 puppets, including their commander, Brig. General Ly Thong Ba; the garrison fled, but we pursued them in captured armored cars and trucks, encircling the main part about half a mile from Cu Chi and accepting the surrender of the military commander of the Cu Chi region and 297 of the garrison. We immediately started a propaganda campaign calling on all the others to surrender, and on the night of the 29th we all met here (in the former Cu Chi military headquarters) to celebrate our historic victory. But it had to be a very short celebration. We still had big things to do—organize our forces including intelligence and medical services. We put our most battle-hardened units together, the two battalions, regional companies and self-defense platoons—and we had a regiment. We had drivers and gunners who could handle the armored cars captured at the Cu Chi headquarters. We quickly formed a new battalion of local forces to take over security duties, including the protection of all public buildings we had seized on the 30th to prevent sabotage, while we raced on towards Saigon. Our task, a special reward for the accomplishments of the Cu Chi guerillas over the years, was to plant the NLF flag on the Gia Dinh Provincial Defense Headquarters.

"We set out at dawn, shooting up all enemy forces we found on the way to Gia Dinh. Our new regiment knocked out quite a few tanks and destroyed between 30 and 40 armored cars (both sides of the road between Cu Chi and Gia Dinh were still littered with wrecks of tanks and armored cars, many of them deeply embedded in the rice fields as they left the highway in a panicky and hopeless escape attempt, W.B.) thus opening the way for the regular VPA forces approaching Saigon from this direction. We captured quite a few armored cars, immediately putting our men aboard and heading towards Gia Dinh, where we unfurled our flag before the surrender declaration was made in Saigon. Once power was consolidated in Cu Chi we ordered enemy officers and troops to register, the number so doing amounting to 16,000..."

And thus there was a "happy ending" to the unimaginably fierce struggle which swayed back and forth across the once flourishing orchards and fertile fields of heroic Cu Chi.

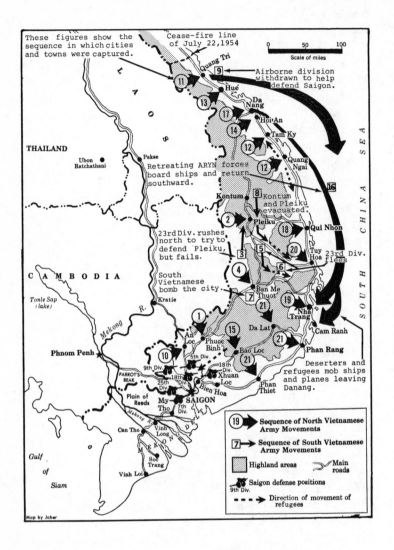

These figures show the sequence in which cities and towns were captured.

Cease-fire line of July 22,1954

Scale of miles
0   50   100

Airborne division withdrawn to help defend Saigon.

THAILAND

Ubon Ratchathani

Pakse

Retreating ARVN forces board ships and return southward.

Kontum and Pleiku evacuated.

23rd Div. rushes north to try to defend Pleiku, but fails.

South Vietnamese bomb the city.

CAMBODIA

Tonle Sap (lake)

23rd Div. flees

Phnom Penh

Deserters and refugees mob ships and planes leaving Danang.

Gulf of Siam

19 → Sequence of North Vietnamese Army Movements

7 → Sequence of South Vietnamese Army Movements

Highland areas

Main roads

Saigon defense positions

- - -→ Direction of movement of refugees

Map by Jaber

LAOS

SOUTH CHINA SEA

Quang Tri
Hué
Da Nang
Hoi An
Tam Ky
Quang Ngai
Qui Nhon
Tuy Hoa
Cam Ranh
Phan Rang
Phan Thiet

Kontum
Pleiku
Ban Me Thuot
Da Lat
Nha Trang
Bao Loc

Kratie
Mekong R.

An Loc
Phuoc Binh
9th Div.
PARROT'S BEAK
25th Div.
18th Div.
Xuan Loc
Bien Hoa
SAIGON
My Tho
7th Div.
5th Div.

Plain of Reeds

Can Tho
Vinh Long
Soc Trang
Vinh Loi

Part II

Events Leading Up to the Fall

Chapter 8.

A Spurned Olive Branch

January 28, 1967, was an occasion of which all journalists dream—an exclusive interview with the right man, on the right spot, on the most burning question of the day, one that was the main focus of international diplomatic activities.

Hanoi was the place, Foreign Minister Nguyen Duy Trinh the man, peace or continuing war in Vietnam the issue. As for the timing, it was just twelve days before there was to be a four-day truce, to celebrate Têt, the Vietnamese lunar New Year. It was a time of intensive diplomatic activity, with initiatives from the Pope and UN Secretary General U Thant; with Polish and Italian diplomats negotiating in Saigon; French and North Vietnamese diplomats in contact in Paris; American and Soviet diplomats in Moscow on the eve of Prime Minister Alexei Kosygin's visit to London to confer with Prime Minister Harold Wilson as—amongst other things—his Co-Chairman of the 1954 Geneva Conference on Indochina. Amateur American peace-seekers were also in Hanoi—all activities aimed at trying to move the confrontation in Vietnam from battlefield to conference table.

Pushed by public opinion at home and abroad to get the war ended, President Johnson and his Secretary of State, Dean Rusk, had made repeated statements that one or the other of them was "ready to go any place any time" if there was the slightest chance for a negotiated peace and that the U.S. bombings of the North which had started systematically in February 1965 would be halted if there were the slightest sign, "private or public, official or non-official" that Hanoi was ready for the conference table. In response to one of U Thant's repeated remarks that a halt to the bombings would create the proper atmosphere for talks, the U.S. delegate to the United Nations, Arthur Goldberg, had said on the last day of 1966, that the United States was "ready to order a prior end to all bombing of North Vietnam, the moment there is an assurance, private or otherwise, that there would be a reciprocal response towards peace from North Vietnam . . . "

A short, stocky man with a very stubborn face, foreign minister Nguyen Duy Trinh devoted most of his replies to my written questions to hammering the United States for having launched the air war of destruction against the North, stressing the firm determination of his people and government never to yield to force. The real message came in his reply to my last question:

> "The United States has spoken of the need for dialogue or contact between itself and the DRV. Would you comment on this?"

> "The United States has made such statements, but in its deeds it has shown the utmost obduracy and perfidy and continues the escalation, stepping up and expanding the aggressive war. If it really wants talks, it must first unconditionally halt the bombing raids and all other acts of war against the DRV. It is only after the unconditional cessation of U.S. bombing and all other acts of war against the DRV that there could be talks between the DRV and the United States."

This was interpreted in diplomatic circles around the world that Hanoi had given President Johnson the clear signal he said he was awaiting. To make it quite clear, Mai Van Bo, head of the North Vietnamese diplomatic mission in Paris, informed Pierre Etiene Manac'h, who then headed the Asian Department of the French Foreign Office, that his government wanted Washington to understand that the Nguyen Duy Trinh interview was very important and that talks could really follow an unconditional end to the bombings. Manac'h, one of France's most brilliant diplomats, relayed the message to John Dean, first secretary at the U.S. Embassy, in the presence of Senator Robert Kennedy, then on a fact-finding tour in Europe. A few days later, Premier Kosygin was due to arrive in London, and it was clear that Vietnam would be a primary subject of discussion. The world awaited with considerable interest President Johnson's response.

At a dinner with Nguyen Duy Trinh following the interview, I found him very skeptical as to any immediate results. To my off-the-record question as to why the DRV (Democratic Republic of Vietnam) had not used a thirty five day bombing pause starting at the Têt celebrations the previous year to make such a gesture, he replied that the Americans would have interpreted that as a weakness—

> We couldn't stand up to the bombings. They would have hit us harder. And a year ago, to be quite frank, we were not quite sure how we were going to cope. A year ago we were still moving our essential industries underground, decentralizing the economy. While we were certain that we would survive, there were many unknown factors and difficulties. Now we know we can cope. The industries we dispersed are producing. We can repair roads and bridges faster than the Americans can destroy them. Our people are more united than ever. We can maintain and even increase food production; we can keep transport moving and can fulfill our role as the great rear base for the struggle in the south. We understand quite well the risk we have taken in proposing talks. Washington is certain to interpret this as a sign of weakness. Double, treble the dose, they think, and we crack. That is their mentality. They interpret any gesture of ours in favor of peace as a sign that we are at our last 'gasp' and so they should strike harder. It is difficult to explain this to a lot of our friends. The fact that we have made this gesture today is only possible because we are strong and completely confident of our ability to carry on despite the worst the U.S. imperialists can do.

The interview was perhaps the most explicit, but not the only gesture that Hanoi made at that time. Ten days earlier, President Ho Chi Minh had received the well known American pacifist, Rev. A. J. Muste, together with Rabbi Abraham Feinberg of Toronto and the former Church of England Bishop of Johannesburg, Dr. Ambrose Reeves. Addressing himself to Rev. Muste, President Ho Chi Minh said:

President Johnson has stated that he will talk to anyone, anywhere, and at any time, about peace. I invite President Johnson to be our guest, sitting just where you are now. Let him come with his wife, his daughters, his doctor, and his cook, but let him not come with a gun on his hip. Let him not bring his admirals and his generals. I pledge on my honor as an old revolutionary that Mr. Johnson will have complete security.

As soon as they returned from seeing the President, Rev. Muste told me what had been said and asked whether he could possibly have been joking. I replied that Johnson only had to take the invitation at face value and see. But however we wanted to interpret it, this was the clearest and most sincere appeal to get a dialogue started, and that President Ho was not one to joke about such a serious matter. At about the same time, there were two distinguished U.S. editors in Hanoi, Harry S. Ashmore, who had won an unprecedented double Pulitzer Prize by his reporting on the racist horrors at Little Rock, Arkansas, and William C. Baggs, editor of the *Miami News,* both of them leading lights in the Center for the Study of Democratic Institutions. They were received by President Ho and were impressed by the conciliatory mood in Hanoi, relaying their views to President Johnson via Undersecretary of State, Nicholas Katzenbach. Harrison Salisbury, assistant managing-editor of the New York Times, was also in Hanoi that fateful January and in a four and a half hour interview with premier Pham Van Dong, became convinced that the DRV leadership was ready for negotiations, but that the American military was not:

> "I was told while I was still in Hanoi," he later wrote, "by someone who had recently been in Saigon, that the American military establishment there would not accept negotiations at this time, no matter what Hanoi did. 'They think they have Hanoi in the run,' said this man. 'They are not going to quit now. They want to pour it on. If it poured on hard enough, there won't be any Hanoi to bother with.'
>
> I don't know if that accurately reflected the thinking of the American military establishment in Saigon, but I encountered this line in Washington in some quarters on my return..."[25]

---

25. Harrison Salisbury, *Behind the Lines—Hanoi* New York: Bantam Books, 1967, p 210.

President Johnson's reaction to all this was astonishingly close to that predicted by Nguyen Duy Trinh. At a TV press conference on February 2, the President backed away from all his previous proposals and called for "reciprocity" in exchange for a bombing halt, something which he knew in advance was unacceptable to Hanoi. He spoke of "mutual steps" of de-escalation, but the point was that Hanoi was not bombing the United States—it was the U.S. that was bombing North Vietnam. Johnson said he hoped for "some new steps" from Hanoi:

"In all candor", he said, "I must say that I am not aware of any serious effort that the other side has made, in my judgment, to bring the fighting to a stop and to stop the war."

In other words, halting the bombings so that talks could start was not on, although this had been precisely the U.S. position, repeated time and again, in the months that preceded the Nguyen Duy Trinh interview. A few hours after the Johnson press conference, I sent the following dispatch from Hanoi to the Tokyo daily, *Yomiuri*—which appeared in its Japanese and English editions:

For the moment, Hanoi is confident that it has demonstrated its good will and is still hoping, despite Johnson's press conference remarks that Washington will show some modicum of good will ...

Hanoi's statement on talks was made to test the sincerity of Washington's frequent expressions of a desire for peace through negotiations. Hanoi feels it has opened the door with Nguyen Duy Trinh's statement and that it is up to Washington to make the next move.

If Washington is ready to stick to his (Johnson's) earlier pronouncements, he must definitely halt the bombardments, start the talks and see what steps are possible next ...[26]

I warned that it would be a "major blunder" if Washington interpreted the gesture as a sign of weakness but that Hanoi "is prepared for a hawk-like reaction ..."

On February 6, Premier Kosygin arrived in London and in his first discussion with Wilson, he stressed the importance of the Nguyen Duy Trinh interview, correcting the absurd hairsplitting semantics argument of the State department that the

---

26. *Yomiuri Shimbun*, Tokyo, February 3, 1967.

foreign minister had said that talks "could," and not necessarily "would," start if the bombings were halted. Talks "would" start said Kosygin.

In his book[27], Harold Wilson describes how Kosygin, in their first private talk "directed the conversation straight to Vietnam":

> I set out the position as we saw it, bringing Mr. Kosygin up to date on the latest Washington position and the state of opinion in the United States. I referred to an interview given in Hanoi on 28 January to an Australian journalist, Mr. Wilfred Burchett, and confirmed as authentic by the DRV party journal . . .

> Basing himself on public statements, and particularly the Burchett interview I had cited, he (Kosygin) could see similar phrases in public utterances by President Johnson and Mr. Dean Rusk. Warming to his subject, he said that if we, he and I, could take together the North Vietnamese (the DRV Foreign Minister's statement in the press interview) as a basis and say to the President—together or separately, privately or publicly in the communiqué or in a special message—that the statement was an acceptable basis for discussion, then this was the best move for us to take, leading to bilateral talks. He specifically agreed that because of Têt the present time was, the most appropriate one. He said— and this again was new—that our task was to advise and to assist the U.S. and the DRV to meet and discuss their problems at the negotiating table . . .

A formula was agreed upon, under which the North Vietnamese would give a secret assurance that if the bombings stopped, no new troops would be introduced into South Vietnam and the Americans would stop reinforcing their forces in the South. The U.S. agreed and a letter was prepared, authenticated by the U.S. Embassy and, stated Mr. Wilson: "I was assured that there had been the fullest consultation with the State Department at top level." Mr. Wilson quotes the U. S. Ambassador to London, David Bruce—later briefly to head the U.S. Delegation to the Vietnam Peace talks—as being most enthusiastic:

> "Prime minister" he said, "I think you've made it. This is going to be the biggest diplomatic coup of this century."

---

27. Harold Wilson, *The Labour Government; 1964-70. A Personal Record* Penguin Books, pp. 444-6.

Then at about 10 p.m. (Feb. 9th) the telephone rang. It was the White House—Walt Rostow had tried to phone Michael Palliser who had gone home with flu, and had been told to ring Downing Street. The gist of his message was that on the President's instructions our text had been redrafted. A new text would come over the White House-Downing Street teleprinter starting now, and should be the one to be used with the Russians ...

The new text stated that the U.S. would order a bombing halt "as soon as they were assured that infiltration from North Vietnam to South Vietnam *had stopped*." There were other changes too, such as public instead of secret assurances by Hanoi, the whole amounting to what Harold Wilson saw as:

> ... a total reversal of the policy the U.S. had put forward for transmission to the Soviet prime minister ...

Of possible explanations, he wrote:

> One, which I was reluctant to believe, was that the White House had taken me—and hence Mr. Kosygin—for a ride. Two, the most likely, that the Washington hawks had staged a successful takeover ...

That was the end of the "biggest diplomatic coup of this century" and the next day Wilson was complaining to Johnson that he must realize "what a hell of a situation I am in for on my last day of talks with Kosygin." The bombing pause on which such hopes had been set lasted just as long as the Wilson-Kosygin meeting. By the time Kosygin was on his way home, U.S. bombers were over North Vietnam again and hopes for peace were once more blasted to bits. All that Wilson and Kosygin got was the customary snub reserved for all those who—no matter how high their status—tried to take the Vietnam war away from the Pentagon.

If all this is mentioned in some detail, it is only to underline that at every stage of the Indochina conflict—going all the way back to Dien Bien Phu—the United States could have had an infinitely better settlement from its viewpoint than the rat-like desertion of sinking ships that took place in Phnom Penh and Saigon in April 1975 and in Vientiane a month later. It is obvious —from his book—that Harold Wilson was smarting from wounded pride even years later and it is hard to imagine that Alexei Kosygin felt any less hurt. They had fallen into the trap

which snapped tight on many distinguished U.S. diplomats—
that of believing that U.S. policies were those which were pub-
licly proclaimed by U.S. presidents and secretaries of state—
when half the time these were soporifics to calm public opinion
at home and abroad. That the Wilsons and Kosygins, or Fan-
fanis in Italy and De Gaulles in France earnestly worked away
to produce solutions which they were convinced were those the
White House wanted, was the least of the worries of the John-
sons, Nixons and Fords. The bombings had been halted for
just five days—too impossibly short for any serious diplomatic
follow-up of the Nguyen Duy Trinh opening. The tonnage
was steadily increased until within six months, it was running at
about twice the figure at the time of my interview with the
foreign minister.

In the meantime the State Department pundits were still fob-
bing off peace-seekers with the "uncertainties" of the "could"
instead of "would" formula on talks possibilities. In the summer of 1967, I returned to Hanoi and asked Nguyen Duy Trinh
whether it was worthwhile doing another interview and correcting the mood of the verb. "No," he said with his typical
stubborn smile, "they still think they can break us with their
bombs. So let them do their worst. Only when they see that
their bombs can never break us is it worthwhile having another
try. That may take many more months."

In July 1967, while I was passing through Paris on my way
to cover an OLAS (Organization of Latin American States)
conference in Havana, I had an urgent request for a meeting
with d'Astier de la Vigerie, editor of L'Evènement, a Paris
monthly to which I contributed regularly. He was not only a
most responsible editor, but had also been a former French resistance leader, a left-wing Gaullist and popular and original TV
commentator. A man with a passionate, burning quality which I
admired—a man of action and integrity. In somewhat mysteri-
ous terms he convinced me of the vital importance—but he was
pledged not to reveal why—of getting two Frenchmen to Hanoi. One of them, a high official in the UN Food and Agriculture
Organization in Rome, Raymond Aubrac, was an old friend of
Ho Chi Minh's. The other, Herbert Marcovich, was a micro-
biologist connected with the Pasteur Institute in Paris. The success or failure of their enterprise depended on their presence in
in Hanoi between certain specific dates, a mission, d'Astier assured me, of a nature that could be helpful to the Vietnam-

ese. I pressed for details but drew a blank. Either I trusted d'Astier's judgment or not! It was far too close to the only dates possible for the visit, to obtain a visa through normal channels. If everything worked perfectly, there was just a chance of their catching the International Control Commission (ICC) liaison plane in Phnom Penh, spending four days in Hanoi, and returning in time to keep their exact time schedule. In view of Prof. Marcovich's connection with the Pasteur Institute, I guessed that it had something to do with chemical warfare which the United States was waging very intensively. I sent a telegram to my old friend, the late DRV minister of Public Health, Dr. Pham Ngoc Thach, explaining simply that Raymond Aubrac and his friend Herbert Marcovich from the Pasteur Institute urgently needed visas for Hanoi and that only if they could pick them up in Phnom Penh on a specified date could the visit take place.

Professor Marcovich came to see me and I explained the formalities for getting a seat on the ICC plane in Phnom Penh—then left for Havana, hoping for the best.

To the astonishment of all concerned—myself included—everything worked smoothly. Their visas were awaiting them in Phnom Penh and they caught the regular Friday (July 21, 1967) ICC flight to Hanoi. Marcovich visited the local Pasteur Institute while Aubrac was received, for old times' sake, by President Ho Chi Minh. To the astonishment of the latter, Aubrac suddenly pulled out of his pocket what later became known as the San Antonio formula,[28] seeking Ho Chi Minh's reactions to this. Little did I know that behind all the mystery and speed was a certain Dr. Henry Kissinger, then director of the Defense Studies program at Harvard University and a National Security Advisor to the White House. Kissinger had become friendly with Marcovich at a Pugwash scientists conference in Poland in September 1966 [29]. Through Marcovich, he learned that Aubrac, a Harvard graduate, was a friend of Ho Chi Minh and conceived the idea of using the two to re-establish some con-

---

28. The San Antonio formula was so named after a speech by President Johnson at San Antonio, Texas, at a medal-presenting ceremony, in which he stated that the bombings could stop if this "would lead promptly to productive discussions" and that North Vietnam "would not take advantage of a bombing halt or limitation."

29. The Pugwash conference (named after the site of the first of these, about 60 miles north of Halifax in Southeast Canada) was conceived by

tact with Hanoi, broken by Johnson's abrupt rejection of the Nguyen Duy Trinh offer, and the subsequent escalation of the bombings. The dates and shortness of the visit were later explained as dictated because Kissinger promised Hanoi would not be bombed during those dates. Despite being taken completely by surprise, Ho Chi Minh produced a reaction which Marcovich and Aubrac considered eminently favorable. In Paris, a beaming Kissinger congratulated them on the excellent results of their "historic mission"—begging them however not to reveal that the visit had been "arranged by Burchett"—flying back to Washington to brief President Johnson on what Kissinger seemed to consider a diplomatic coup. Within a few days it was indicated that the State Department was also delighted. Aubrac and Marcovich were asked if they could return to Hanoi with some concrete proposals to move things a step closer to the conference table. They agreed and this time asked for visas in the normal fashion through Hanoi's diplomatic mission in Hanoi. They were refused. Why? Marcovich believed that, as on many other occasions, Johnson's "other hand" decided to intervene in diplomacy, authorizing a series of violent air raids on Hanoi itself, hitting among other targets a power station less than a mile from the city center, a hospital and the Long Bien bridge spanning the Red River, across which all traffic to Hanoi and the South passed from the port city of Haiphong and from China. These raids were taken in Hanoi as Washington's true response to the Aubrac-Marcovich mission. Was Kissinger aware that Johnson would again treat such a peace gesture from Hanoi as a sign of "weakness?" Marcovich still gives him the benefit of the doubt, believing that Kissinger was as frustrated as the two amateur diplomats.

Back in Hanoi in October, after talks with Premier Pham Van Dong and Nguyen Duy Trinh, I reported for Associated Press:

> There is no possibility of any talks or even contacts between Hanoi and the U.S. government unless the bombardment and other acts of war against North Vietnam are definitively halted . . .
>
> Hanoi is in no mood for concessions or bargaining. There is

---

the progressive American industrialist Cyrus Eaton to bring together East-West scientists to defuse some of the tensions of the Cold War, starting with a search for formulas to facilitate nuclear disarmament.

an absolute refusal to offer anything—except talks—for a cessation of bombardment. The word stressed is 'talks,' not 'negotiations' . . .

I quoted Nguyen Duy Trinh as saying that his offer of talks in the January 28 interview was still valid and that they could be "meaningful", but whether they would be "fruitful" or "productive" would depend on the United States ·

> One difficulty that foreign diplomats have in persuading Hanoi to make any new peace gesture in what one of the leaders referred to as a "credibility gap" between what President Johnson says and does. Because of experiences in certain earlier private and secret moves—which no leader with whom this correspondent talked would precisely specify—there has been deep skepticism about any public statements or private feelers coming from Washington through diplomatic and other channels . . . I know of no leader who believes that President Johnson is sincere in stating that he really wants to end the war on terms that would leave the Vietnamese free to settle their own affairs, or that he does not intend to keep a permanent United States presence in South Vietnam . . .

The above dispatch was based on the disgusted reactions of President Ho and other DRV leaders to the hypocrisy of President Johnson in his San Antonio speech on September 29, especially the following gems:

> "Why not negotiate now?" so many ask me. The answer is that we and our South Vietnamese allies are wholly prepared to negotiate tonight.
>
> I am ready to talk with Ho Chi Minh, and other chiefs of state concerned, tomorrow.
>
> I am ready to have Secretary Rusk meet with their Foreign Minister tomorrow . . .
>
> I am ready to send a trusted representative of America to any spot on this earth to talk in public or in private with a spokesman of Hanoi . . ."

The crux was that the DRV was upholding an important principle of international law—that one does not negotiate under duress unless it is to surrender. What equality in negotiations could there be when one side is bombing the other, demanding some price for the cessation of that bombing, or threatening to restart the bombing in case it has been temporarily halted? "How can one speak of negotiations with a gangster when he has a pistol prodding into your back?" was how President Ho once expressed it to me during a breakfast discussion. Meanwhile "Operation Rolling Thunder" went on as U.S. air power set out relentlessly to destroy every man-made structure north of the 17th parallel, except in Hanoi and Haiphong, to the point where pilots were complaining that they had run out of targets. But life went on, supplies continued to roll south; what the Americans destroyed by day—as far as communications were concerned—was repaired by night.

In the first week of December 1967, returning to Phnom Penh via Paris after having given evidence of U.S. war crimes at the Bertrand Russel War Crimes Tribunal in Roskilde, Denmark, I received a telephone call from John Dean, first secretary at the U.S. Embassy in Paris. Could I possibly have lunch with him at his flat the following day? Somewhat mystified, I agreed. A short, affable man, Mr. Dean introduced me to Mr. Heyward Isham, a tall professorial-type who explained over a pre-luncheon whisky that he was a member of the State Department "task force" on Vietnam and that his own particular job was to follow up any prospects for peace or negotiations. Mr. Dean explained that he himself maintained some intermittent contacts with the North Vietnamese diplomatic mission in Paris for the same purpose. They had invited me in order to probe for any additional information I could give them about the Nguyen Duy Trinh interview which could provide leads for getting negotiations started. For such a laudable purpose I had no inhibitions, taking advantage of the occasion to say how regrettable it was that the standard reaction in Washington to any Hanoi peace gestures was that they were signs that the North Vietnamese were weakening so they must be hit still harder to hasten the final collapse. First of all this was nonsense. Despite the destruction, the economy was in good shape; the bombs had only heightened morale and determination. But such an attitude by Washington rendered any further initiatives from Hanoi, or even any contacts, impossible, in my view. The Vietnamese seemed convinced that as long as the United States persisted in such illusions fresh initiatives were useless.

By the type of questions these two diplomats asked, I had the impression that whoever they were reporting to (I assumed it was Averell Harriman, President Johnson's ambassador-at-large on the Vietnam question) realized that the bombings were getting nowhere and that it was high time to think about negotiations. There were questions as to where and at what level talks would take place, what parties would be involved and what sort of an agenda there would be. This was the real stuff of pre-negotiations. I knew the answers to some of the questions because I had written about them. For others I could make a reasonably intelligent guess and to some I simply replied, "I just don't know".

Obviously they knew they could count on my discretion in taking a risk by talking with me. Journalistically, it would be a great "scoop" to reveal that "private discussions" were going on in Paris to set up Vietnam peace talks. It was an example of the sort of role a journalist can occasionally play when normal diplomatic processes have broken down. An independent journalist has none of the restrictions of the diplomat who has to be conscious every minute that he represents his government, for the slightest error or indiscretion can complicate his country's conduct of foreign affairs—not to mention his own career. A journalist can sometimes be the "drop of oil" that gets clogged machinery moving. But this is possible only if he can repress that professional yearning to see everything important that he knows in the next day's headlines, and if he does not have an editor on his back demanding just that.

I felt that I was privy to the most serious effort yet to discover a basis for negotiations. It had taken over ten months since the Nguyen Duy Trinh interview to get down to the concrete details of how a conference might be set up and even by the nature of their questions Messrs. Dean and Isham revealed their own views on this. It seemed clear to me that once the decision was taken to open talks, practical details were not going to stand in the way.

Taking the Nguyen Duy Trinh interview and the meeting with Dean and Isham together, I was more than ever convinced that the Vietnam revolutionaries were going to win, although at that time I was convinced that it was going to be a negotiated victory. Despite the fact that Westmoreland was still boasting that he had virtually defeated the NLF forces in the South and only had to deal a few more blows in the frontier areas and it would be all over, I was certain that more lucid views were circulating somewhere in Washington; otherwise I would not have been lunching with senior officials of the State Department.

Shortly after that lunch, on December 29, Nguyen Duy Trinh, at a reception to a visiting Mongolian Delegation, offered a sop to the Washington semantic experts by repeating his earlier formulation but changing "could" to "will hold talks" with the United States and adding "on all questions concerned." The State Department began to show interest—not because the mood of the verb had been changed but because the mood in Washington had changed, and the futility of counting on bombing to bring a change of DRV policies had started to dawn on all but the lunatic fringe among the Washington hawks.

Chapter 9.

Unusual Aide-Mémoire

If the North Vietnamese made a maximum diplomatic effort to mark the Têt of 1967, they made a maximum effort of another kind, together with NLF in the South, to mark the Têt of 1968. The aims of both were the same—to bring the United States to the conference table and to add a new dimension to the struggle by opening up a new diplomatic battlefront. Experience had shown it could not be done by the soft method of declarations and interviews or by high rank peace-makers hurrying between the capitals of the world drafting formulae and official notes. So the violent way had to be used to blast American policy-makers, including the President and his generals, out of their illusions and bring them down to earth. And it succeeded fabulously well. Don Oberdorfer, of The Washington Post, who had devoted a large, well documented book to the single subject of the Têt offensive, summed up part of what it meant in his Foreword:

> This is the story of one of the great events of our time and how it came to be ...

> It is the story of a turning point, when people and nations swung round to new opinions and new courses. To depict the military action without its political consequences, or to depict the political action without the moving elements in the field, is to miss half the story. In the history of the Têt

offensive, a sense of relationship, of connection and disconnection in space and time, is as vital as a sense of drama.

The Têt offensive by the Communist forces in Vietnam in early 1968 was the high point of military action in the second Indochina War and, in all likelihood, the only battle of the war anyone will long remember. The plan of action—a simultaneous surprise attack on nearly every city, town and major military base throughout South Vietnam—was audacious in its conception and stunning in its implementation. The repercussions were on a scale to match . . .[30]

The Têt offensive was indeed one of the greatest feats in the history of warfare until that time. Above all, it deflated the bragging of U.S. generals, especially that of the Commander of the U.S.-Saigon forces, General William C. Westmoreland. He and other U.S. generals were proven to be bungling amateurs, out-manoeuvred on the battlefields; their intelligence services hopelessly incompetent; their much-publicized gadgetry of super-detection, laughable. They had failed to spot the movement and concentration of scores of thousands of troops around every major town and base, including three battalions around Westmoreland's own headquarters at Saigon's Tan Son Nhut air base and a company of commandos outside, and soon inside, the U.S. Embassy in Saigon. They had failed to spot the movement of hundreds of thousands of tons of supplies into position in and around every major city. What movement had been spotted was wrongly evaluated. Five days before the attack, Westmoreland did have some inkling of things going on, but sounded the alert in the northernmost sector only as if an invasion from the North was coming! He and his generals boasted that detection techniques were so perfect that "no Vietcong could cook a pot of rice undetected." An hour before midnight on January 30, 1968, they were cooking pots of rice by the tens of thousand around over one hundred cities and towns, around every U.S. and South Vietnamese base and almost on the steps of the U.S. Embassy!

Without any planes, helicopters, tanks or armored cars— and precious few trucks or Jeeps—the NLF moved their forces into position around some 140 towns and cities, and scores of military bases throughout the length and breadth of the coun-

---

30. Don Oberdorfer, *TET, The Story of a Battle and its Historic Aftermath* New York: Doubleday, 1971.

try, striking simultaneously with a minimum of one battalion of troops per target. (Except in some special cases, like the U.S. Embassy, where smaller commando groups were used.) It was one of the most humiliating defeats for U.S. military technique and intelligence that such an attack could take place. Oberdorfer relates that the first flash reached the State Department just as four of his colleagues from the Washington Post were being briefed by security on how well the war was going, with the usual collection of "captured communist documents" to show that the Vietcong were at their "last gasp." After a few slips of paper had been passed to him, the briefing officer, "with a thin smile" announced: "It appears the Vietcong are attacking the Embassy in Saigon." The journalists had been called in for a special "pep talk" because their paper had started to become skeptical of victory prospects!

Over seven years after the event, a CIA officer testified to a sort of conspiracy between the military and the CIA to fool press and public as to the real state of affairs and thus to defuse the activities of those inside and outside Congress that wanted the U.S. out:

> "Although our aim was to fool the American press, the public and the Congress", testified former CIA analyst Samuel Adams before the House Intelligence Committee, "we in intelligence succeeded best in fooling ourselves. The intention was to show that the enemy was not growing stronger, that the U.S. side was winning the war."

He said that he had received a secret cable to this effect from the U.S. ground commander in Saigon, General Creighton Abrams (who succeeded General Westmoreland as overall commander in South Vietnam in June, 1968). The U.S. intelligence agencies had agreed to stick to the figure of 300,000 for the "enemy forces", although they knew their true strength was about twice that number in order "to prevent the press from drawing an erroneous and gloomy conclusion".[31]

This is only one more bit of evidence as to the difficulties and dangers of trying to take a war away from the Pentagon. This deliberate faking of intelligence is a precise counter-part of the Pentagon analysis and White House conclusions that

---

31. As reported in the *International Herald Tribune*, Paris September 19, 1975.

Hanoi peace gestures signified that the North was hanging on the ropes, ripe for the knock-out punch. Either Johnson and his State Department and Pentagon aides were fools, incapable of intelligent analysis, or they were knaves, guilty of something very close to treason. The official U.S. figures of their Têt offensive losses between January 29 and March 31 were 3,895 killed and about 10,000 wounded. Even so the intelligence fakers tried to present the whole affair as an American victory, inflating by several times the losses they inflicted on "Vietcong" and North Vietnamese troops. There was another reason to present the adversary's total troop numbers as far below the real number. They had to be presented as "invaders" from the North, whereas the overwhelming majority, especially at the time of the Têt offensive, came from the villages and countryside of the South, where they encircled the bases and towns. With their lack of any modern transport how could it have been otherwise? To conjure up the picture of an army of 600,000 invaders from the North and the fantastic supply problem this would entail would make the U.S. air effort look totally futile, and intelligence twice as stupid. The U.S. Command in Saigon and in Washington were thus continually caught up in credibility gaps that only lies could paper over.

Rep. Otis Pike, of the House Intelligence Committee put a belated finger on this when he summed up the Samuel Adams testimony:

> *"You are saying that political decisions were made, after which the intelligence was shaped to fit the decisions that had been made. This is what you mean by your charge of corruption. Is that correct? The intelligence was intentionally made corruptive to comply with political decisions that had already been made. Is that correct?"*

> *"Yes sir," replied Adams.*

All this duplicity made the business of moving the confrontation from the battlefield to the conference table very complex. Normally a lot of probing goes to try to find out what the other side wants and then find the means of giving maximum satisfaction on all that is reasonable. The difficulty was to know what the United States wanted since U.S. policy-makers from the President on down were afraid to reveal to their own people, to the world at large and sometimes even to their own negotiators what they really wanted.

What the North Vietnamese and NLF in the South wanted was clear—a total independence and a united country, preferably through negotiated settlement. No one on their side had any shares in armament industries or saw in war a possibility for quick promotions or a chance of stuffing their pockets with dollar aid or a cushy job as a provincial governor. The sacrifices of the Têt offensive would gladly have been avoided if the Têt diplomacy of the previous year had worked. But the whole story of the Vietnamese War was that the United States consistently slammed all doors to anything but the violent blood-letting solutions of the battlefield. I have written it so often that it sounds banal to repeat: Vietnamese revolutionaries have one sole yardstick to judge the results of any military action small or big—the political effect. The political effect of the Têt offensive more than met their expectations.

In terms of assessing casualties, the U.S. considered March 31, the end of the Têt offensive and related operations. This was also the day that President Johnson chose to make a major speech.

Gathered in my hotel room (because I had a good short-wave radio) at Hanoi's Ton Nhat (Reunification) Hotel on that memorable evening, were American author Mary McCarthy, CBS chief foreign correspondent Charles Collingwood, U.S. writer Franz Schurmann and, for their second visit, the American journalists Harry Ashmore and William Baggs. We had all been involved in some way, and with varied motives, to get the war stopped and it seemed highly appropriate that we should be in Hanoi together to hear what was to be the most dramatic statement from any president on the Vietnam war.

> There is no need to delay the talks that could bring an end to this long and bloody war. Tonight I renew the offer I made last August—to stop the bombardment of North Vietnam. We ask that talks begin promptly, and that they be serious talks on the substance of peace. We assume that during these talks Hanoi would not take advantage of our restraint . . .

> Tonight I have ordered our aircraft and naval vessels to make no attacks on North Vietnam, except in the area North of the demilitarized zone where the continuing enemy build-up directly threatens allied forward position and where movements of troops and supplies are clearly related to that threat. The area in which we are stopping our at-

tacks includes almost 98 percent of North Vietnam's population and most of its territory. Thus there will be no attacks around the principal populated areas, and in the food-producing areas of North Vietnam . . .

It turned out next day that the bombings were to continue in an area 200 miles north of the demilitarized zone, where a good 20 percent of North Vietnamese lived and which was an extremely valuable food-producing area. It meant also that the same tonnage of bombs that had been used against North Vietnam as a whole would now be concentrated in the "pan-handle", through which ran all North-South communications.

> . . . Now as in the past, the United States is ready to send its representatives to any forum at any time, to discuss the means of bringing this war to an end. I am designating one of our most distinguished Americans, Ambassador Averell Harriman, as my personal representative for such talks . . .

As he went off into vague generalities, there were shouts to turn off the radio while we compared notes to make sure we had properly understood and to brief Ashmore and Baggs who had come in late. Then there was a rush downstairs to toast what we all felt was the real beginning of the end. It was only a few minutes later that a Vietnamese friend came to ask what we thought about Johnson's decision to withdraw from the Presidency! We had turned off the radio too soon!

It turned out that Johnson's "any forum at any time" did not include Phnom Penh (proposed by Nguyen Duy Trinh in an interview with Charles Collingwood a few days later) nor Warsaw where the U.S.A. had been negotiating with the Chinese for several years, nor Paris. But the latter city was eventually accepted, reluctantly by Johnson, as a site for a conference.

Thus, on the last Sunday of May 1968 (the talks having started on the 13th) I found myself having lunch with Averell Harriman, who was named to head the American delegation, in his suite in Paris's prestigious Hotel Crillon, together with Charles Collingwood and one of Harriman's chief aides, Daniel Davidson. It was an informal affair, Harriman in shirt-sleeves and braces, starting off over drinks by thanking me for a service I had rendered in helping arrange the release of some U.S. POW's as a "goodwill gesture." He reminded me that he had been especially designated by President Johnson to try to do something about the release of POW's. But after the first ex-

changes it was clear that he wanted my views on the real negotiating aims of the North Vietnamese, and if there were realistic areas of agreement. Harriman, then 77, created an atmosphere that made discussion easy. A table had been set out on a
sun-filled terrace overlooking the beginnings of the Champs-
Elysées and the U.S. Embassy. It was clear that he had plenty of
time. So after explaining that everything I would say was purely
my own personal opinion, I took the opportunity of giving the
background to the long history of Vietnamese struggle against
foreign invaders, culminating in modern times by their resistance wars against the French and now against the United States.
That was one aspect. Another was that they had constantly
felt cheated of the fruits of their victories (the Geneva Conference for instance) and that it was normal that they held the
United States responsible for that and most of their troubles
since. Harriman said he was particulary concerned that the
North Vietnamese had not respected the 1962 Agreement on
Laos, which he had helped negotiate. I replied that the affairs of
Indochina had to be seen as a whole and that 1962 was precisely
the year that President Kennedy had started U.S. intervention
in South Vietnam. This could not but upset any agreements on
Laos. The original 1954 Geneva Agreement was a delicately
balanced affair. The concept of a unified Vietnam and neutralized buffer zone states of Laos and Cambodia had been a sound
one. The United States had worked to upset this, with disastrous
results. Similarly, as far as I knew, the 1962 Agreement on Laos
was a good one, but how could it but be affected when the
United States started moving into South Vietnam by setting up
a U.S. Command in Saigon in February 1962. And if one looked
at things through Vietnamese eyes how could they but see the
United States, as just the most recent, of a whole series of great
powers which had tried to seize their country and transform it
into their colony.

Harriman's reply was that it would be a mistake for the
North Vietnamese to believe the United States was in Vietnam
as a new colonizing power. Her interests were only to prevent
the North taking the South by force: limited and short term
interests. "By the size and permanence of the bases and installations you have put in, it looks as if you've come for a long
stay," I remarked. "Anyway the Vietnamese can be excused for
thinking that."

"They must understand," said Harriman, "that when our

military move into any part of the world they want the most and best of everything they can have". At that point Davidson intervened for the first time. "You only have to look at the sort of bases we abandoned here in France, with grass growing out of runways three feet thick, to understand that the size of bases has no relation to permanence of stay."

"If you could persuade the North Vietnamese of that," I replied, "then you may achieve something." Harriman laughed and said: "If the North Vietnamese can persuade us that they don't intend to invade the South and we can persuade them that we don't intend to hang on in the South, then we've got the basis of an agreement." I agreed that suspicion of each other's motives was a big obstacle to be overcome.

As Harriman was obviously in a receptive and leisurely mood, I went over what I had witnessed on the spot and assessed as an endless series of U.S. blunders in Asia: consistently backing reactionary forces which could not stand on their own feet, starting with China, and American support for the Kuomintang in 1945. Blunders that had cost the people of Asia very dear—and the United States also. Harriman at one point looked up sharply and said, "Ah, I was not in State (the State Department) in those days and I could agree with much that you say". I said that I mentioned it because I hoped that on this occasion the chance would not be thrown away because of some errors of misjudgment, North Vietnam was the one country that could stand on its own feet in Southeast Asia, and not the satellite of anybody. He did not comment but asked me what I thought of the NLF leadership and their policies in the South. When I gave a very positive appreciation, he said: "Yes, I read their political Program before coming to Paris. It is realistic and reasonable", and, turning to Collingwood, he said: "It's a very interesting document. You ought to get hold of it."

At one point Harriman raised the question of the presence of North Vietnamese troops in the South and the fact that their delegates in Paris refused to admit this made negotiations difficult. (The Paris talks at this stage were aimed solely at getting a complete bombing halt as a prerequisite to full negotiations but the Americans were still demanding "reciprocity" as a quid pro quo for halting the bombings.) I explained that the Vietnamese were a very flexible people and that if a good agreement were in sight, there would be no North Vietnamese troops in the South by the time it was signed.

Altogether we spent four hours together and I left Harriman feeling that he was sincere in wanting an end to the war, on reasonable terms, and would be more than pleased if he were the one to negotiate a settlement. What more honorable way could any diplomat end his career! It was neither his fault, nor that of his opposite numbers at the conference table that this did not come about. From the moment that the North Vietnamese delegates became convinced of the sincerity of Harriman and his deputy Cyrus Vance they began to make things easy for them. This is clear from the brief references to the conferences made by Harriman in the book which he later wrote.[32] This is not the place to go into the wearisome details of the negotiations that led to the limited agreement to end the bombings. Suffice to say that Harriman several times thought he had fulfilled his negotiating brief and got the assurances that President Johnson wanted, only to find the brief had suddenly been changed. Finally, agreement was reached in time for Johnson to announce on October 31st, 1968, that the bombings would be halted on November 1, and a four-party conference with NLF and Saigon representatives participating would start on November 6. (The announcement came a few days too late to prevent Senator Humphrey getting an extra fraction of a one percent switch in the vote to win the presidential elections on November 5). On October 29th, however, President Nguyen Van Thieu, who had gone along as an obedient puppet until then, suddenly revolted and said he neither wanted a bombing halt nor the November 6th conference. The first pretext was that he couldn't get his delegation to Paris in time, followed later by a series of other objections. Explaining this in his book, Harriman writes:

There seems to be no doubt that through one channel or another Thieu was counseled to wait until after the American election. He was evidently told Nixon would be much harder-line than Humphrey, and he was warned that if negotiations began, Humphrey might be elected.

I don't in any way suggest that President Nixon knew anything about this. But some believe that if we had started actual negotiations during the week before election day, it might well have made the small, but vital difference in the

---

32. W. Averell Harriman, *America and Russia in a Changing World* New York: Doubleday and Co., Inc., 1971.

outcome of the election. If Hubert Humphrey had been elected President, we would have been well out of Vietnam by now...[33]

There followed the period between November 5 and the inauguration of President Nixon on January 20, when the chances of a negotiated peace were deliberately frittered away by Nixon's new team and their manipulations of Thieu in Saigon. The pretext was the famous "shape of the table" argument, or the seating arrangements for the four-party conference. Although this argument was primarily a stalling device to prevent any substantive discussions until President Nixon had formally taken over and picked his own negotiating team, there was an important point of principle involved, that none except those that followed every phase of the conference could appreciate. The general opinion was that "everyone had gone mad"! The DRV and NLF negotiators wanted a round table, as originally proposed by Harriman, or a square table which reflected the four-party nature of the talks. The Saigon delegates, wanted an oblong table to symbolize their idea of an "our side-your side" concept, they obviously sitting with the U.S. delegates. It seemed an innocent enough proposal, except that it was intended to push the NLF out of South Vietnam. This was precisely what the Saigon side proposed later at the first meeting, namely that "your side" withdraws all its armed forces from the South. NLF forces should also be withdrawn! In the end, a variant of the round table formula was agreed on—just four days before Richard Milhous Nixon was sworn in as president. Harriman wrote of this period:

> During the period between the election and inauguration, we worked hard to get negotiations going. I am not very good at making a case for the enemy, but the North Vietnamese did disengage in the two northern provinces, of I Corps. That had been an area of some of the bloodiest fighting involving Americans—Khesanh and the like. The North Vietnamese had a large force there. They took 90 percent of their troops out, and half of them above the 20th parallel some two hundred miles to the North. There was almost complete disengagement, so much so that it permitted General Abrams to take the first Cavalry Division out of I Corps to the III Corps for increased action there.[34]

---

33. Ibid., pp. 136-7.
34. Ibid., p. 137.

Most of the substantive business of the earlier conference had been arranged at private talks during the breaks for tea instead of at the open sessions which each side used as a tribune to influence world opinion. Thieu's delegation sabotaged this, as Harriman regretfully noted. (He resigned as chief negotiator as soon as Nixon took over.)

> When I left Paris in January 29, we had arranged that the two sides, with two on each side, would sit down privately and talk together. There is no doubt in my mind that Thieu scuttled those negotiations, and he did it consciously. He announced on January 29 that he was not going to sit down in private, and one of his spokeman said: "Whatever we have got to tell the communists we have already told them in Paris, and it is not necessary to have private meetings with them." This was, of course, nonsense, because they knew that we got nowhere in those public discussions and that whatever progress was made had to be done privately. So there were no private talks among the four...

> Unfortunately, the tea breaks did not continue after January 20, 1969...[35]

> My partner, Cy Vance, stayed on in Paris for a month under the new Administration, and during that period Ambassador (Cabot) Lodge (who had succeeded Harriman, W. B.) had no private talks on substantive matters. I understand he didn't attempt to have such private talks for two months...[36]

The conclusion of Harriman was that it was Thieu in Saigon who was chiefly responsible for any lack of progress in efforts to end the war. (Having been a loyal public servant for over half a century or so, he was hardly likely to point his finger at the really guilty party—the U.S. government—so his criticisms of Nixon's policy were somewhat oblique.)

> Why should we give Thieu the right to dictate American policy? I can't conceive why anybody should give a veto to a foreign potentate, no matter who he is.

> We should want to stop this fighting in Vietnam. To me the Vietnamization of the war is an immoral thing. We have no right to perpetuate the fighting. Every effort should be made to end the human tragedy that is going on in South Vietnam...

---

35. Ibid., p. 139.
36. Ibid., p. 140.

Our political objectives in Vietnam cannot be achieved by military means. We can expand the war to include Cambodia, Laos, North Vietnam and China, and even the Soviet Union, but this war cannot be won. This is not the fault of the United States but the nature of the problem that exists there ...

"Vietnamization" of the war was the much publicized "peace plan" that Nixon promised the American and Vietnamese people. He had won the election by promising "peace," but had thrown away the best hope for a negotiated settlement by using Thieu to sabotage the Paris talks, so he could engage in a massive build-up of Vietnamese troops to "change the color of the corpses" as his ambassador in Saigon, Ellsworth Bunker was quoted as saying. Harriman denounced Nixon's "peace plan" in language about as strong as could be expected from one in his position.

The Administration's program of Vietnamization of the war is not in my opinion a program for peace, but it is a program for the continuation of the war ...

Furthermore, the Vietnamization of the war is dependent on an unpopular and repressive government ...

He complained also that Nixon had downgraded the negotiations by leaving in charge of the U.S. delegation (after Lodge had resigned) Philip Habib, who had been the third on Harriman's original negotiating team, and was very strongly rumored to be an important agent of the "Company" (CIA).

It was becoming increasingly clear to the DRV and NLF leadership that it was going to take another "aide memoire" or two to blast some sense of reality into the Nixon administration.

Chapter 10.

Expanding the War

As the winner of the 1968 elections on the "peace ticket," Nixon was the one who expanded the war in Vietnam to its furthest dimensions, accepting the advice of the most far-out of the Pentagon hawks, not to mention that of his National Security Adviser, Henry Kissinger. The talks dragged on in Paris, the blood continued to soak into the mud of Vietnam's rice-fields while Nixon's military men armed and groomed a South Vietnamese army not only to repress their own compatriots, but to carry the war to their neighbors in Cambodia and Laos, and, in the designs of Nixon to North Vietnam as well. Westmoreland and his successor Abrams had sighed for the chance to "clean up the sanctuaries" in Cambodia, the only thing that had prevented complete victory! The image was conjured up in the U.S. press of an enemy always eluding the final blow by slipping across the border. As the Cambodian Head of State, Prince Norodom Sihanouk, had always refused to permit "hot pursuit" operations, he had first to be replaced by a compliant U.S. puppet. Thus the coup which overthrew Sihanouk's neutralist regime on March 18, 1970. It was soon found that America's new "man in Phnom Penh", Marshal Lon Nol, could not stand on his own feet. Resistance forces were hammering at the gates of the capital within a few weeks, having taken over vast areas of the countryside, including provincial capitals and district centers in which Lon Nol's forces were never able to set foot in the five year's bitter struggle which followed. A full-scale rescue operation was thus launched by U.S.-Saigon troops on April 29-May 1, followed by three more actions up to May 6, bringing the total of invading troops up to over 50,000 and making it by far the biggest U.S.-Saigon operation for over three years. Preceded by the most massive air bombardments since the start of the Vietnam war, including for the first time B-52 bomber raids against towns, wiping out half a dozen frontier towns in as many minutes, the U.S.-Saigon forces tried to combine the task of putting down resistance to the Lon Nol regime with that of "cleaning up the sanctuaries" and dismantling the "Vietcong Pentagon".

Thus, in his "search for peace", Nixon had another bloody and expensive war on his hands, not to mention an unprecedented explosion of wrath in the U.S., culminating in the shooting death of four students at Kent State (Ohio) University.

Oddly, but typically, enough—as was the case with the initial U.S. intervention in South Vietnam—the Americans did not bother to go through the motions of informing the Phnom Penh regime. Lon Nol complained that he had not been "consulted in advance" and that the operations "were a violation of Cambodian territorial integrity" and that he was "considering a protest." (It never got beyond the "considering" stage.) To encourage their flagging zeal the South Vietnamese troops had been promised all the booty they could lay hands on and they went on a rampage of pillage, rape and murder.

What the U.S.-Saigon Command succeeded in achieving by their Cambodia operation was that if *there ever were* Vietcong sanctuaries in Cambodia, they had now been spread virtually over the whole country. Of course, there were supply dumps in the frontier area (just as there were on the Moroccan and Tunisian side on the frontiers with Algeria in the latter's national liberation struggle against the French), but by the time the U.S.-Saigon forces had reached them, 90 percent of the supplies were in the hands of the fast-expanding Cambodian resistance forces. For the purpose of propping up the Lon Nol regime for a few years, the operation succeeded. The cost was an inevitable death sentence for Lon Nol and his closest collaborators when the time came to settle accounts. The Saigon regime simply annexed the "Parrot's Beak" area where Southeast Cambodian territory approaches most closely to Saigon, as well as the islands off the

south coast and set up a naval base at Neak Luong on the Mekong, where no Cambodians could enter, some 40 miles east of
Phnom Penh. Cambodians who asquiesced in this and in inviting
U.S. air power to devastate the countryside would one day
clearly be judged as traitors. But President Nixon claimed to be
greatly satisfied:

> We have witnessed the visible proof of the success of Viet-
> namization as the South Vietnamese performed with skill
> and valor and competence far beyond the expectation of
> our commanders or American advisers. The morale and
> self-confidence of South Vietnam is higher than ever be-
> fore...

> With American ground operations in Cambodia ended, we
> shall move forward in our plan to end the war in Vietnam
> and to ensure the just peace on which all Americans are
> united...*

The following year it was Laos that was the center of Nixon's "peace-seeking" operations. "If only we could cut the Ho
Chi Minh Trail," the hard-liners had been sighing for years,
"then we've really got the war won." They could have found
no more sympathetic ears for such sighs than those of President
Nixon unless it was those of his National Security Adviser,
Henry Kissinger. On February 8, 1971, Saigon forces invaded
Laos, with the United States supplying air support, including
planes and helicopters for transporting parachutists and commandos.

A U.S. State Department declaration the same day explained
that the mission:

> will make the enemy less able to mount offensives, and
> strengthen South Vietnam's ability to defend itself as US
> forces are withdrawn from South Vietnam. It will protect
> American lives. This ground operation by the South Viet-
> namese against the sanctuaries will thus aid in the Vietnami-
> zation program...

Two days after the invasion started, the fire-eating South
Vietnamese vice-president, Air Vice-Marshal, Nguyen Cao Ky,
stated that the invasion force would remain in Laos "until the
dry season finishes at the end of May", and that "we may even
launch ground attacks on North Vietnam."

---

*President Nixon reporting to the American nation on June 30, 1970.

Norodom Sihanouk, who was visiting Hanoi at the time, was later to tell me that on February 10 he was dining with North Vietnam's greatest soldier, Vo Nguyen Giap. It was a leisurely dinner and over coffee, Giap played some records. Sihanouk said he could contain himself no longer and said: "I feel guilty, mon général. I have taken up too much of your time. I simply cannot understand you giving me so much of your time when such a tremendous battle is going on in South Loas."

"Oh that," replied Giap with his calm, gently ironical smile. "That's been prepared long ago. Our Pathet Lao comrades have everything necessary to deal on the spot with that. There's no need for me to bother. It has been expected for a long time. I listened to the radio today. Thieu says his troops will remain in Laos until May or June. In fact what's left of them will be out by the end of March at the latest."

"And they were" added Sihanouk solemnly, his eyes wide in admiration: "The last had left by March 25. Giap is a military genius, undoubtedly the greatest strategist of our time and one of the greatest of all time."[37]

The South Laos campaign was a debacle from the first day. Claims by Saigon to have captured Tchépone, the main town in the area, by March 6, were proved false as were claims by the Americans that the north-south main oil pipe-line had been cut —the briefing officer had been holding up a bit of cut pipe-line from somewhere else! The invasion of Laos was supported by a massive U.S. operation just south of the 17th Parallel. It was a grandiose scheme which successive American commanders had longed to launch but were fearful of the cost. Now that the "color of the corpses" had been changed, those same generals could encourage their puppets to "press on." Maximum aims were to cut Indochina in two at its "narrow waist" by occupying South Laos right across to the borders of Thailand and then pushing east to occupy North Vietnam, at a point just north of the 17th parallel. It must have looked beautiful in the Pentagon map room. A solid barrier, inches thick on the military maps, from the Pacific Ocean to Thailand, through which not a case of ammunition, nor sack of rice could pass. Commander-in-Chief Nixon would have succeeded where previous presidents had failed!

---

37. I have used the version as published in *My War With The CIA*, by Prince Norodom Sihanouk, as told to Wilfred Burchett, New York: Pantheon Books, 1972.

These pipe dreams were shattered when the Pathet Lao (and certainly their North Vietnamese allies) launched a devastating counter-offensive on March 12 and the invasion force plunged into head-long retreat. Photos on the front pages of the world press at the time showed South Vietnamese troops fighting to get aboard helicopters or hanging on to the landing skids —scores of them to be jolted and shaken to unmarked deaths in the jungle-covered mountains. Some slight inkling of the extent of the disaster came from a TV appearance of Nixon on March 22.

> . . . The South Vietnamese went in without any American advisers, with only American air support against very heavy odds numerically on the ground. They fought extremely well. Now they are withdrawing. They are having all the problems of an army withdrawing. Some of their units have not done so well but 18 of their 20 battalions, as General Abrams has pointed out, are doing extremely well, and he says they will come out with greater confidence and greater morale than before . . .

What sort of morale and confidence they retained after leaving most of their heavy weapons, practically all their artillery, tanks and armored cars and every last one of their trucks behind is not difficult to imagine. And these were elite troops, the best that Saigon had. At the height of the counter-attack, when Delta 1, the main Saigon base, was attacked and the survivors evacuated, 37 out of 40 U.S. helicopters were shot down, the largest number in any day during the Vietnam war. The official overall losses were put at 105 helicopters downed, with 66 crewmen killed, 91 wounded and 27 missing. (This was on the Laotian side of the frontier only.)

There had been no comparable military debacle in Indochina up till that time. From the moment the Pathet Lao and North Vietnamese struck, there was only one thought in the minds of the South Vietnamese troops—how to escape. And at Command level, how to recuperate as many of these crack units as possible. The Americans diverted B-52's from strategic bombing missions to bomb what they thought were Pathet Lao and North Vietnamese positions. But most of the casualties inflicted were on the South Vietnamese, inevitably caught out in the open while the intended targets were in deep underground shelters or caves long prepared for such an occasion.

At A Loui, only twelve miles from the Vietnamese frontier,

the command post of the ARVN (Army of the Republic of Vietnam) Armored Brigade was evacuated by helicopters on March 20. Three days later, the remnants of the Brigade straggled back across the frontier having lost over 100 of its 191 tanks and armored cars.

The evacuation of Delta 1, only 14 miles from the frontier, on March 22, was a fantastic shambles in which American pilots used their pistols against screaming South Vietnamese troops who killed one of their colonels in their panic-stricken rush to scramble aboard the few helicopters which managed to land. Once in the air, pilots deliberately dived and jolted their dangerously overloaded craft to jettison the surplus weight clinging to the skids so as to climb above anti-aircraft range. Three battalions of the crack Marine Regiment, lost 50, 60 and 70 percent respectively of their effectives and all of their artillery. On several occasions U.S. units refused to go to the rescue in the frontier area.

The "morale and confidence" of the survivors of all those units would be an interesting subject of investigation! Western press reports made it appear that only "North Vietnamese" troops were involved, it then being the fashion (imposed by the censor in many cases) that journalists must only refer to "North Vietnamese" troops if reporting military activities in Cambodia or Laos. An occasional reference to "Viet Cong" was permissible in the case of South Vietnam and Cambodia. From my own observations during several visits to widely separated battlefronts in Laos, the battle-hardened Pathet Lao forces, veterans of 25 years of unremitting combat by that time, would have played a major role in repulsing the South Vietnamese invasion. A Pathet Lao communiqué of March 24 claimed that over 1,000 Saigon troops had been captured out of 15,400 enemy troops (including 200 Americans) put out of action altogether. (The Americans admitted a total of 167 pilot and crewmen casualties.) 496 planes and helicopters, 586 tanks, armored cars and trucks, 144 artillery pieces and over 5,000 other weapons had been destroyed or captured, according to a detailed Pathet Lao accounting of the campaign. It was a crushing defeat for the Saigon Army and the Vietnamization "export model."

The Chairman of the U.S. Senate Foreign Relations Committee, Senator William Fulbright, comparing the results with the optimistic briefing given by Secretary of State William Rogers as to the expectations of this operation, accused the Nixon administration of either "massive deception" or "massive misjudgment."

In the months that followed, taking advantage of the terrible mauling of Saigon's élite units in South Laos, plus the routing of other units, which in parallel actions tried to push into Cambodia to recapture the strategic provincial capital of Kratié on the Mekong river, the NLF launched a series of commando raids at bases in the northern sectors and in the strategic Central Highlands. These were especially devastating in the "three frontier" areas where the borders of South Vietnam, Laos and Cambodia meet.

On the diplomatic and negotiations front, there were some important developments in 1971. Presidential elections were due to be held in South Vietnam on October 3 and two candidates announced they would oppose dictator Nguyen Van Thieu. One was vice president Nguyen Cao Ky who had become increasingly critical of Thieu following the South Laos debacle (and the absurdity of his own predictions). The other was General Duong Van "Big" Minh, who had played a leading role in the overthrow of the Ngo Dinh Diem dictatorship in November 1963, and had presided for 3 months over the triumvirate which had succeeded the Diem dictatorship, until he was overthrown on the grounds of being "too neutralist." The strategy of the DRV and PRG (the NLF Front had formed a Provisional Revolutionary Government in June 1969) was to facilitate these elections and provide a peaceful means for the removal of Thieu. The talks in Paris showed that the Nixon administration still used Thieu to block any possibility of a negotiated solution. Perhaps after the shattering defeats of "Vietnamization" in Cambodia and Laos, Nixon might be ready for a face-saving way of removing Thieu? That seems to have been the thinking behind the presentation of a 7-point plan by the PRG's foreign minister, Madame Nguyen Thi Binh on July 1, 1971. A key passage in the second of the seven points stated that the U.S.A.

> must really respect the South Vietnam's people right to self determination, put an end to its interference in the internal affairs of South Vietnam, cease backing the bellicose group headed by Nguyen Van Thieu, at present in office in Saigon, and stop all manoeuvres, *including tricks on elections*, aimed at maintaining the puppet Nguyen Van Thieu. (My italics, W. B.)

Most of the rest dealt with technical details of troops withdrawals, ceasefire, release of POW's, and the setting up of a three-way government in the South, but the 5th point was clearly intended to point to the new type of relations that could exist between a non-facist South Vietnam and the U.S.A.

> South Vietnam will pursue a policy of peace and neutrality, establish relations with all countries regardless of their political and social régimes, in accordance with the five principles of peaceful coexistence, maintain economic and cultural relations with all countries, *accept the co-operation in the exploitation of the resources of South Vietnam, accept, from any country economic and technical aid without any political conditions attached, and participate in regional plans for economic cooperation.* (My italics throughout, W. B.)

The reference to "tricks on elections" was to the fact that Thieu was pushing through a series of measures which made it virtually impossible for any free choice, even for such candidates as a "Big" Minh or Nguyen Cao Ky. (The "peace" candidate of the September 1967 presidential elections, Truong Dinh Dzu, who had beaten Thieu in Saigon and five nearby provinces was still in jail!"[38]

On July 15, "Big" Minh warned that he would step down if it became clear that the elections were to be a meaningless farce. He would not be "part of a masquerade", he said, just to create the illusion that Thieu's re-election was fair and democratic. He predicted that if U.S. Ambassador Ellsworth Bunker remained in Saigon Thieu certainly *would be* elected:

> Mr. Bunker is a specialist in elections of this kind. He succeeded in the Dominican Republic; he succeeded in Vietnam in 1967, and he will succeed again in October...

One of the built-in safeguards for eliminating rivals of Thieu's was that candidates had to be endorsed by 40 of the 190 deputies and senators of the Saigon parliament, or by 100 of the 545 provincial and city councillors. Each could endorse only

---

38. In the 1967 elections, Thieu officially received 1,649,561 votes, or 34.8 percent. Truong Ding Dzu was next with 817,120. Thieu failed to get first place in any major town, where there was some control over voting and counting. His majority votes rolled in from the provinces where Thieu's nominees were in charge at provincial and district level of every aspect of the balloting!

one candidate and endorsements had to be signed by provincial or city governors—all military officers appointed by Thieu, subject to military discipline or recall by him at any moment. Thieu had secured, in advance, enough endorsements—from 104 of the 190 deputies and senators, and from 452 of the 545 councillors—to make it statistically impossible for either "Big" Minh or Nguyen Cao Ky to obtain the required endorsements and signatures. Ky did obtain 101 signatures from the councillors, but 39 of these were invalidated by the provincial chiefs because they had already been used to validate Thieu's nomination. So Nguyen Cao Ky was disqualified.

On August 20, "Big" Minh withdrew his candidature from an election which he characterized as a "contemptible farce which will make the people loose all hope of a democratic régime and prevent any reconciliation among the Vietnamese people." The previous day Ambassador Bunker had urged Minh not to withdraw, but a spokesman for the latter stated on Minh's behalf that the general "felt the Americans merely wanted to use his name and reputation so that it would look to the world as if South Vietnam had chosen a President who wants to continue the war."

The one-man "elections" took place as scheduled and the official results showed that there was an 87.9 percent turn-out of whom 84.3 percent voted for Nguyen Van Thieu. The U.S. Secretary of State William Rogers conceded that the elections were "not pristine and pure, and neither are ours for that matter."

At that time I was in New York covering the debate on China's admission to the United Nations. A day of two after the "elections" my telephone rang, and the following dialogue took place.

"Is that Mr. Burchett?"

"Yes, it is."

"I am Dick Barnett, one of Dr. Kissinger's secretaries. Dr. Kissinger heard you were in town and wonders whether you would care to have breakfast with him next Tuesday."

"In principle—yes."

"Then at 9:30, at the western wing of the White House."

"I have a bit of a problem."

"Oh, (very coldly) what is that?"

*"My movements are restricted to within 25 miles of the U.N. headquarters."**

"Well in that case, I don't know what to say. I don't know anything about this."

"Under the circumstances I propose to ignore that restriction."

"I propose to ignore the fact that you have raised that matter. So you will come?"

"Yes. At 9:30 A.M. on Tuesday at the Western Wing?"

"Present yourself to the Marine guard with identification. You will be escorted to the Western Wing, and I will take you in to Dr. Kissinger.

"Agreed."

As the weather had turned foggy and I did not want to miss the appointment, I travelled down to Washington by train wondering (a) what Kissinger wanted to talk to me about, China or Vietnam, and (b) what would happen if anyone checked my passport and discovered I was violating the 25-mile restriction. I had left my passport behind, retaining only my UN accreditation card as identification. At the hotel I registered under a slight variation of my name. At 9:30 exactly, I presented my accreditation card to a Marine guard in a sentry box and within seconds, another Marine appeared to escort me the few score yards to the Western Wing, where a woman secretary asked me to wait a few moments. Who should appear, but a smiling Kissinger himself. As far as I could recall the conversation later, it went something like this, starting as he escorted me into his office adjoining the reception room.

K. *"I've wanted to meet you for a long time. I've read a lot of what you've written, and found it interesting."*

B. *"I've read some things that you've written also and found them interesting."*

By that time we were seated, Henry behind his desk, myself on his right. Someone came in with a tray and served breakfast: coffee, toast and shelled soft-boiled eggs in a glass for Henry;

---

*Because of my problems over the Korean and Vietnam wars with the Australian government, I was travelling on a Cuban passport!

coffee (how I was longing for my habitual tea) and scrambled eggs on toast for myself.

K. *"What have you read of mine and what did you find interesting?"*

B. *"The series of foreign policy articles—the idea of multipolarity instead of bi-polarity in foreign relations which I found interesting and I suppose the Chinese did also."*

K. *"Ah yes, those dealing with negotiating an end to the Vietnamese war. But I had forgotten you also had a China background. What do you think of Chou En-Lai?"*

B. *"First I must explain that I have known him for over 30 years. He is an outstanding leader, with unique experience in international affairs."*

K. *"I quite agree. Of course he's a revolutionary, but I can appreciate someone who has dedicated his life to his ideals. Actually I wanted to speak to you about Vietnam. When were you last in Hanoi?"*

B. *"Not since 1969, shortly after Ho Chi Minh died. But the night before I left for the UN, I had dinner with minister Xuan Thuy, who heads the North Vietnamese delegation to the Paris peace talks."*

K. *"How is he feeling about things?"*

B. *"Very relaxed, very confident, very pleased that for once both the Soviet Union and China are in agreement in supporting their 7-point peace plan. And, by the way, I have the feeling from the official reactions to that plan, that no one in the State Department has ever seriously studied it."*

K. *"What makes you say that?"*

B. *"Because if your real aims are as those stated, this plan gives you everything you want. Point five for instance."*

K. *"You mean the one dealing with neutrality?"*

B. *"It goes much further than that. It provides for foreign economic investment, regional economic cooperation, an opening to the West and by implication normalized relations with the U.S.A., etc."*

K. *"Frankly, that 7-point plan is a bore."*

B. *"Frankly I should think it must be much more of a bore to be stuck with the sort of regime the U.S. is stuck with in Saigon."*

K. *"I won't comment on that. But we cannot just dump that regime and the North Vietnamese have not advanced any realistic things that we should do to change it."*

B. *"I believe they think it is not a question of what you should do but that you should stop doing some of the things you are doing. For instance you would not allow a single alternative to Thieu in the presidential elections a few days ago. You insisted on a one-man election when there was a real possibility of peaceful change."*

K. *"The North Vietnamese were responsible for that also. One of the troubles is that they are too suspicious."*

B. *"But surely history gives them the right to be suspicious. They have had their pockets picked by the West too often not to be suspicious."*

K. *"I agree, but they are also an intelligent people. They must know that the United States in 1971 is not the United States in 1954 when Dulles was trying to expand into Southeast Asia. The United States of 1971 is moving out. They should understand that. Moving out completely. No troops, no bases. Total withdrawal. The North Vietnamese are also a heroic people. I admire them. I wish they were on our side. We have no wish to punish them. What sort of a man is Pham Van Dong?"*

B. *"A great man. Exceptional intelligence, quick grasp. A very sensitive man. A Vietnamese Chou En-Lai."*

K. *"Really? I consider Chou En-Lai a great man. Who is more important—Le Duc Tho or Xuan Thuy?"**

B. *"Le Duc Tho is a member of the Political Bureau of the Lao Dong party, Xuan Thuy is a member of the Central Committee and a former foreign minister."*

The telephone rang and Kissinger replied: "I'll be there in a few minutes. He listened, scribbled a few notes, then dictated some comment into what I realized was a communiqué announcing Nixon's forthcoming visit to Moscow, with Nixon on the other end of the line. As I rose to go, Kissinger said:

"You may tell your Vietnamese friends of our conversation. I don't know whether you know or not, but I have

---

*Le Duc Tho, a veteran leader of the Vietnamese revolution, was officially "senior adviser" to the North Vietnamese delegation and arrived in Paris always at critical moments in the negotiations. Xuan Thuy, a former foreign minister, headed the negotiations delegation.

*been working on this Vietnamese problem even in the time of the Johnson administration. Anyone who thinks I am less eager to see a settlement because I am with the Nixon administration is simply not correct. I hope that our conversation will contribute to overcoming some of the obstacles to agreement. The fact that I am receiving you on the eve of my second visit to Peking should convince your Vietnamese friends of the importance I attach to this."**

B. "What is the main obstacle?"

K. "The North Vietnamese are too impatient. They are not willing to await the political consequences of our withdrawal. They want everything too quickly."

And with that we parted. My impression was that of a vain man, but a good listener, and one capable of persuading anyone with whom he spoke of the sincerity and reasonableness of his viewpoints. I felt by the abruptness with which he had changed the conversation that I had stung him on the question of the Thieu régime and United States blocking of any electoral procedures to change it. What I did not know was that less than a month prior to our meeting, Kissinger, on September 13th, had broken off a series of twelve secret meetings in Paris, seven with Le Duc Tho and Xuan Thuy together and five with Xuan Thuy alone. A major purpose of these meetings had been to try to break the deadlock in the Paris talks, which could only be done by changing the régime in Saigon. Those of us who had assiduously followed the weekly sessions of the Paris Conference, had no inkling that such secret talks were going on. The fact that they had, was revealed by President Nixon in a dramatic TV address on January 25, 1972. What amounted to patient pleas by Le Duc Tho for a removal of Thieu by reasonably fair elections, were described by Nixon as "demands to overthrow the government of South Vietnam."

By permitting one-man elections, the Nixon administration had once again bolted the door against any but battlefield solutions.

---

*Kissinger's forthcoming second visit to Peking had not then been announced. By telling me, he probably wanted to show that he counted on my discretion, in that as in other matters, Nixon's visit to Moscow was announced the following day.

Chapter 11.

Kissinger and the Christmas Bombings

If 1970-1971 were years of major military initiatives by the U.S.-Saigon forces with the invasions of Cambodia and Laos, in 1972 the initiative was clearly with the forces of the PRG-DRV. And if the previous two years had badly shattered the export model version of Vietnamization, the home version was to be put to its severest test till then. 1972 was the year in which Nixon tried out two more of the hawkiest war-winning formulae—Senator Barry Goldwater's "Bomb and mine Haiphong and other harbors" and General Curtis Lemay's "Bomb 'em back into the Stone Age." (Known as "Killer" Lemay in World War II for his advocacy of indiscriminate bombing of civilian targets, he had headed the U.S. Strategic Air Command.) If it were the Têt offensive which brought the U.S. to the conference table in 1968, it was the PRG-DRV "Spring Offensive" of 1972 which produced the signature of an agreement to end the war.

The maintaining in power of Nguyen Van Thieu by the device of the one-man electoral farce made nonsense of everything being discussed in Paris—either at the open conference or in the Kissinger-Le Duc Tho secret talks. Nixon had served notice that although he was interested in getting most GI's out in time for the 1972 presidential elections, he was determined to hang on to South Vietnam as a neo-colony, teleguided from

Washington and equally determined to hang on to Thieu as the most effective instrument for this. Terms like "self-determination", used by U.S. negotiators in Paris, were negated by Thieu's constant, brutal repression of all opposition forces, including the death penalty for anyone advocating "communism" or "neutralism." Nixon counted on his trip to Peking in February, and to Moscow in May 1972, to maintain his "peace-seeking" image. The TV cameras would enforce Kissinger's doctrine of the "averted gaze"—namely that you could continue to get away with bloody murder as long as you could divert the public gaze away from the scene of the crime! (I covered Nixon's trip to China. When did a President ever get so much free TV time in an election year? Or against such a décor? Nixon revelled in it with a gluttonous appetite for the TV cameras. He wore make-up even in the daytime, addressing his electorate from the Great Wall, the Ming Tombs, the Forbidden City— toasting Chou En-Lai in the Great Hall of the People! Where was the Vietnam war in comparison? It was the Greatest Show On Earth! He signed the bill with scarcely a glance. Recognition that Taiwan was part of mainland China; peaceful coexistence as the basis of foreign policy; no great power hegemony in the Asian-Pacific region.)

The effect of what Nixon-Kissinger believed they had achieved by the China visit was immediately apparent in Paris. On March 23, after having suspended the weekly conference intermittently from February 10 onwards, while stepping up the bombings in Vietnam, U.S. delegation chief, William Porter— the fifth since the talks started—announced that the United States was indefinitely suspending the Paris Conference. It was a declaration in ultimatum-type language, phrased in a manner most calculated to slam the door to any resumption. Addressing the DRV-PRG delegations, Porter said:

> We believe it would be preferable to await for some sign from you that you are disposed to engage in meaningful exchanges on the various points raised in your and our proposals. Our side will be alert to signs of that nature, which you may send through any convenient channel ... If you do indicate a desire for serious discussion, you will understand, I am sure that *we may need to explore your intentions rather fully prior to agreeing to meet.* (My italics, W. B.)

The sign came just one week later, as did the reaction to the

China visit, when there was another *aide mémoire* from the PRG-DRV forces, a reminder that the Vietnam War refused to go away, and that it had to be settled with the Vietnamese and not the Chinese or Soviet leadership. It came from the big guns and rocket-launchers which blazed into action along almost the entire length of the 17th parallel. 153mm howitzers, 130mm field guns and the devastating 122mm Soviet-built rockets laid down a thundering barrage as a prelude to the greatest offensive of the war until then. This time it was not a matter of simultaneous guerilla attacks against towns and bases all over the country but a classical, tank-supported assault which quickly over-ran all Saigon positions immediately south of the demarcation line. And of General Abrams' "great confidence and morale" of the Saigon forces, there was not a trace.

Within three days, the northern half of Quang Tri province, adjoining the 17th parallel, was in DRV-PRG hands, except for the provincial capital Quang Tri and the port of Dong Ha. Massive use of U.S. air power—including B-52 bombers flying tactical support missions—slowed up, but could not stem the advance. Dong Ha was captured on April 28, and Quang-Tri on May 1, the first provincial capital Saigon had lost since the start of the war. In the meantime, several other widely separated fronts had been opened up, notably by PRG forces operating about 200 miles south in the Central Highlands around Kontum and the Binh Dinh coastal province, as well as at Loc Ninh and An Loc, a good 350 miles to the South (all distances given in straight lines). Saigon's Third division, defending Quang Tri, fled in disorder, panic-stricken troops throwing away their weapons and tearing off their uniforms. A brigade of the supposedly élite Marines also fled, but not in such disorder. (General Hoang Xuan Lam was relieved of his command of the 1st northern military region: the 3rd division commander, General Vu Van Giai was arrested; the head of the Marine Corps, General Le Nguyen Khang was also relieved of his command, all of which was hardly a good advertisement for Vietnamization of the war!)

At Hoai An, about 40 miles north of Qui Nhon, the provincial capital of Binh Dinh province, the Saigon troops also threw away uniforms and weapons without a fight. Fleeing troops of regular army and elite units fought with each other over vehicles and loot (the central market of the old imperial capital of Hue was completely gutted by fire as a result of armed brawls between drunken 3rd division and Marine troops). Some idea of the state of morale is contained in the following dispatch from the *Guardian* (London) correspondent on May 3, just after the fall of Quang Tri:

> The performance of much of the ARVN (Army of the Republic of Vietnam) regular infantry has been poor. American advisers from Tan Canh, for instance, where two regiments of the 22nd division broke under attack, have been as scathing as etiquette permits...

Amongst the first to flee from Quang Tri, incidentally, were 75 American military advisers. The fact that they were whisked away by helicopters at the first sign of the impending disaster, must have contributed to the general panic of the troops they were supposed to advise—especially their commanding officers! The *Guardian* dispatch continues:

> A combination of confused tactical concepts, together with the poor performance of some units had, in each case, quite negated the initial performance of slowing the Communist advance. Attempts to break the circle of North Vietnamese forces, to locate and engage their units away from the threatened town and off the flanks of the threatened road, have been on the whole half-hearted and unsuccessful. Instead there is the blind dependence on the air kill concept. Based on the reasonable view that the North Vietnamese have limited manpower, supplies and weaponry, this merely asks the defenders that they hold while aircraft strike again and again at the converging enemy...

Full-scale bombing of North Vietnam was resumed on April 6, followed up by B-52 bombings of Haiphong for the first time on April 16, resulting in 244 civilians killed and 513 injured, mostly in the first surprise raid in the small hours of the morning. Twenty-five warships of the U.S. 7th Fleet, including four aircraft-carriers, had moved into the Gulf of Tonkin early in April and joined in the general battering of coastal towns and villages on the pretext of halting the movement of supplies to the South. As U.S. experts estimated that it would take seven or eight months for such actions—even if they were effective—to have any effect on the battlefields of the South, it was clear that the bombings were not aimed at the battlefields but at the conference table. In the South itself, the U.S.-Saigon forces had completely lost any initiative and were reduced to defensive reactions wherever the PRG-DRV forces chose to strike.

On April 26, there were clear signs that the offensive had

achieved its purpose. On that day, President Nixon announced three things: (1) American troops would continue to withdraw, seeing that "Vietnamization had progressed sufficiently;" (2) He had "directed Ambassador Porter to return to the negotiation table in Paris tomorrow;" (The conditions so arrogantly laid down by Porter just a month previously, were conveniently forgotten.) (3) "Air and naval attacks on military installations in North Vietnam will be continued until the North Vietnamese stop their offensive in South Vietnam." Hanoi, while never openly confirming that its troops were operating in the South—in order not to support the American contention that this was the main problem—had stated on April 11, that:

> Wherever there are U.S. aggressors on Vietnamese territory, all Vietnamese have the right and duty to fight against them, to defend the independence and freedom of their Fatherland . . . [and repeated the exhortation to the people in the North:] to liberate the South, build up the socialist North and proceed to the reunification of the country.

The renewed conference soon broke down because the DRV-PRG delegates wanted a Geneva-type comprehensive agreement which combined military and political solutions. The United States wanted to separate these two questions. The Saigon delegates wanted no agreement at all. The United States, in other words, wanted its responsibilities to end with the safe withdrawal of its remaining forces and the return of its POW's, but did not want to accept any responsibility for dismantling the fascist dictatorship it had imposed. This should be a matter exclusively between the PRG and Saigon. Also Nixon was banking on his Moscow visit to get the Soviet Union to put pressure on the DRV-PRG leaders to settle on his terms. (In Peking, Premier Chou En-Lai had refused to discuss the Indochina situation when Nixon raised it, stating that the talks should deal only with Chinese-American relations but advising Nixon to deal directly with the leaders of the national liberation movements in Indochina if he really wanted to settle the wars there.) Ambassador Porter suspended the Paris talks again on May 4 and on May 9, just two weeks prior to the start of Nixon's visit to Moscow, U.S. planes started dropping mines into the harbors of Haiphong, Vinh, Quang Khe and Dong Hoi as well as into the estuaries of all North Vietnam's important rivers. The Paris talks resumed on July 13 and the secret talks between Le Duc Tho and Kissinger a few days later.

At the public sessions it seemed that a breakthrough had come on September 11, when Madame Nguyen Thi Binh proposed a formula which, while accepting the separation of military and political questions, provided for a three-party transitional government to be composed of the existing Saigon regime, the PRG, and neutralist elements not connected with either of the belligerents. The reality should be accepted that there were two armies and two administrations in the South as well as a "third force" which could act as a bridge between them. Thieu violently attacked the proposal, as he did anything which involved less than the total extermination of the PRG-NLF. He vowed he would "never sit down with the Communists" nor share power with any other Communists "disguised as neutralists."

After secret talks and shuttle diplomacy by Dr. Kissinger, which grew in intensity as the date for the 1972 presidential elections approached, it was announced in Hanoi on October 26 and confirmed by Dr. Kissinger at a Washington press conference later on the same day, that full agreement had been reached. Hanoi published a summary, of the text which Kissinger confirmed as being correct. The Agreement had been finalized during five Kissinger-Le Duc Tho meetings, starting October 8, and ending on the 17th. It had been agreed that "bombings and other acts of war" against the DRV would be halted on October 21, the Agreement initialed the following day and signed in Paris on October 30. Hanoi also released the text of a telegram from President Nixon to Premier Pham Van Dong, dated October 20, which stated:

> The U.S. side appreciates the goodwill and serious attitude of the Democratic Republic of Vietnam. The text of the Agreement can now be considered complete . . .

Because of a few "complex points", however, President Nixon proposed that the initaling and signing be postponed by 24 hours. Pham Van Dong replied to Nixon's telegram on the 22nd, giving his government's views on the "complex points," accepting the postponement on condition the Agreement was signed "exactly on the 31st." Nixon replied the same day accepting Pham Van Dong's views as "satisfactory."

At his press conference, Kissinger said that "peace is at hand" but adding ominously that full agreement could be had

> in one more negotiating session with the North Vietnamese negotiators . . . We did agree that we would make a major

effort to conclude negotiations by October 31, and it is true that we did from time to time give schedules by which this might be accomplished. It was always, however, made clear, at least to us, and we thought we had made it clear in the records of the meetings, that obviously we could not sign an agreement in which details remain to be worked out simply because, in good faith, we had said we would make an effort to conclude it by a certain date . . .

Through this doubletalk, it was clear that Kissinger was already backing away from what had been negotiated. He pretended that the difficulties were mainly of a "linguistic" nature in discrepancies between the English and Vietnamese versions. It was certain that although "peace was at hand," nothing was going to be signed on October 31st—but the clear impressions for American voters going to the polls to re-elect "peace candidate" Richard Nixon on November 7, was that they could be quite sure that the Vietnam war would be over in just a few more days.

Late on the night of October 26, I talked with Nguyen Thanh Lê, the official spokesman for the DRV delegation from the start of the Paris talks. He assured me, as he did other journalists at a press conference the following day, that is was nonsense to speak of "ambiguities" or "linguistic difficulties."

Dr. Kissinger and minister Xuan Thuy worked for almost twelve hours—until very late into the night of the 17th—going through the Agreement, paragraph by paragraph, sentence by sentence and word by word—until there was total agreement on the texts. Dr. Kissinger had brought his own interpreter with him. He worked with ours until there was absolute agreement that the Vietnamese version was a faithful translation of the original English version. It was agreed that the Secretary of State would come to Paris and sign the Agreement with our foreign minister, Nguyen Duy Trinh on the 30th. At President Nixon's request, we later agreed to the 31st.

Why was Kissinger hedging? It seems that he was ordered by Nixon to get something on paper that would be good enough for him to beat the real peace candidate, George McGovern, but insert some built-in safeguards that would enable him to repudiate the Agreement later. The fact that Thieu, in Saigon, was giving an imitation of a puppet out of control, denouncing all the key provisions of the Agreement, was baloney. Nixon had the means of shutting him up any time he wanted. Instead, the Voice of America was giving fullest coverage to all of Thieu's utterances—including insults heaped on the head of Henry Kissinger. Thieu was being used by Nixon in 1972, as he had been in 1968, in an astonishing replay of the puppet making his master dance. This was a typical piece of Kissinger duplicity with something far worse, but in similar vein, to come.

On November 17, Le Duc Tho returned to Paris—he had left for Hanoi over a month previously, convinced that his work was done. Talks were resumed with Dr. Kissinger for six days, starting on November 20. Between December 4 and 13, there were eight more meetings, following which Kissinger flew back to Washington. At a press conference later, minister Xuan Thuy explained part of what had transpired.

> The American side tried to make a very great number of changes in the Agreement, 126 in all, affecting all nine sections of the document. It was a question of substantive amendments directed against the principles of the fundamental rights of the Vietnamese people and the right of self-determination of the South Vietnamese people. It is a question of modifications denying the existence in the South of two administrations, two armies and three political forces. The American side wished to perpetuate the division of Vietnam. We have rejected these modifications, but the Americans have always come back to them.

Xuan Thuy reiterated that the DRV delegates considered the Agreement as drafted a satisfactory document which should be signed as soon as possible. His delegation had made great efforts to remove any "ambiguities", and by the time Dr. Kissinger left for Washington, there was only one point still to be settled. It was agreed that he and Le Duc Tho would return to their respective capitals, remain in contact and try to settle the remaining point by an exchange of cables. Only if it were absolutely essential would they return to Paris for a final meeting. It was agreed, on Kissinger's insistence, that neither side would make any declarations or reveal the content of their discussions until the last point had been ironed out. It was only much later that I learned what this was. Kissinger demanded that Article 1 of the original agreed draft, stipulating that the United States respect the "independence, sovereignty, unity and territorial integrity of Vietnam as recognized by the 1954 Geneva Agreements on Vietnam" be buried much further down in the Agreement and replaced by Article 2, which dealt with the question of the coming into effect of a cease-fire. It was not "convenient" for U.S. public opinion to attach such importance, and give prominence to such questions as set forth in Article 1. It would be very difficult to persuade Congress to grant billions of dollars worth of reparations unless this was changed. On the other hand, if Article 1 was "de-emphasized" Kissinger could guarantee that the billions would be forthcoming. Le Duc Tho was, however, adamant on this point. First things came first and Vietnam's independence, sovereignty, unity and territorial integrity were very much a first thing. It was what 30 years of wars of national liberation had been all about. Kissinger's threats and attempted bribes were of no avail. It was on this point that the two men parted.

Xuan Thuy's press conference was in response to one given by Kissinger in Washington on December 16, at which he claimed that negotiations had broken down because of "obstructive tactics" of the North Vietnamese. He asserted, without giving details, that the DRV delegation had insisted on revising the whole agreement, a charge strongly denied by Nguyen Thanh Lê at a press conference a few hours later. Lê demanded that the Americans return to Paris and sign the Agreement as then drafted "without delay and without any alterations". He pledged the DRV "to strictly respect the entire text of the Agreement, and be prepared to sign it together with the American side, the sooner the better."

The scene then switched to Hanoi. Late on the evening of December 18, Premier Pham Van Dong received another communication from President Nixon. Either he agree to changes in the Agreement as Kissinger had proposed, or Hanoi would be heavily bombed. Within minutes, Hanoi's radar defense system picked up the blips of B-52s' already over North Vietnamese territory and heading straight for the capital.

"An ultimatum escorted by B-52s! We never deigned to reply," Tran Duy Hung, the mayor of Hanoi, was to tell me later. "But when we picked up those blips my heart missed a beat. As mayor I am also responsible for the city's defenses. I knew we had done everything possible and there would be no lack of courage on the part of our defense forces. But B-52s'? It was a case of the unknown. We knew of their great power, but at the defense headquarters, we all wondered how we could cope. The first bombs were already crashing down on Gia Lam, when a blip in one of the leading waves disappeared. I rushed out of the Command bunker—and there it was like a great torch, coming down quite slowly it seemed. People had come out of their shelters to cheer. I ran back into the bunker and ordered festive music played over the loudspeaker system with the announcement that one of the pirates had been downed. Amidst the thundering explosion of bombs and the din of the anti-aircraft guns came the gay music of victory. Later that night a second one was downed over Hanoi and a third on its way here.

"Fortunately," continued Mayor Hung, "Hanoi was largely empty. We started evacuating children on December 4, when at the first renewed session with Le Duc Tho, Kissinger used scarcely-veiled threats of bombing Hanoi. Later, we issued a general evacuation order, but most people wanted to stay so we did not press it. But people started leaving spontaneously after Kissinger's Washington press conference on the 16th—they drew their own conclusions without any special orders from us. It was a Sunday and they started leaving by the tens of thousands, children on the backs of their parents' bikes. Then we put the whole urban network of buses at the disposal of those who wanted to leave. 200,000 had left by the 18th and 300,000 more in the days that followed. All provinces afforded hospitality in our traditions of hospitality and affection. Everything was calm and orderly—not a trace of panic. People went to the peasantry who just naturally provided them with beds and food. One of our 'secret weapons' was that we had anticipated that Nixon's next move would be B-52s' over Hanoi.

"By next morning I knew we were going to be able to take it. I looked out from my terrace and there were the street cleaners at work, a little earlier than usual; sprinkler trucks spraying the streets. In the little public garden down below, a woman was watering the flowers and pot-plants as usual. There was an atmosphere of absolute order and serenity. The night had been terrible. No one could have slept. It had gone on for ten hours, with every wave of three B-52s' hurling down nearly a hundred tons of bombs. What with our batteries and missiles firing back at them, it was an inferno of explosions and flashes. But all the public services were working even better than normal.

"I toured the hardest hit areas—there were plenty of tears, but no cries or shrieks. At one place a man was tearing at a huge pile of bricks under which were his wife and three children. I told some workers to give him a hand. Later I came back and the man was weeping over the four bodies. When he saw me, he said: 'Excuse me. I gave way to weakness. That's just what Nixon planned. Now it's hate and vengeance. No more tears.' I was back in the area four days later and was told how he had labored day and night, helping the wounded, digging out people trapped in shelters without thought of hardship and danger. On that first morning rescue workers brought me an old woman of 70. She had carried forty people of all sizes on her back to safety. When I asked how it was possible, she replied: 'I myself don't know where I got the strength. I didn't think about it at the time.' "

On a table opposite the mayor's desk was a plaque with the serial number of the first B-52 shot down, and the helmet of the first pilot captured, Major Alexander.

"They got the shock of their lives," Mayor Tran Duy Hung said, with a reminiscent smile." They had been assured it was what they called a 'milk-run' operation. They thought they knew the limitations of the SAM-2 missiles. What they did not take into account was a Vietnamese secret of improving their efficiency. The pockets of the chief pilot shot down was stuffed with technical data on the model he was flying. He would never have been carrying it had there seemed the slightest risk of being shot down. It was very precious documentation for us because these were the latest B-52 D's and B-52 G's with no less than 17 electronic jamming devices to fool our radar warning system and especially conventional missile guidance systems. By the time the sun was up our electronics experts were working on how to counter those of the jamming systems which could affect the efficiency of our missile batteries."

To my question as to how they managed to shoot so many down (34 confirmed as having fallen in North Vietnam and an unknown number in Laos and Thailand as crippled planes crashed on their way back to their Thai bases), Mayor Hung said: "First of all there was magnificent coordination between our night fighters, which dived down through the fighter escorts straight at the B-52's, breaking up their formations, and our missile batteries and conventional anti-aircraft artillery.

"For the full answer," he continued, "you would have to talk with our scientists, especially Ta Quang Buu, (an Oxford-trained mathematician, who is minister of Higher Education and who negotiated the military clauses of the 1954, Geneva Agreement W. B.), because most of the brain-work, missile guidance-systems and such was done by his science students and post-graduates. But this much I can tell you as a non-specialist. They made the accuracy of the missiles independent of ground radio control by firing them in salvoes in the path of oncoming aircraft, with proximity fuses which exploded the war-heads when they were in effective range. So most of the enemy's complicated jamming devices were neutralized. Don't ask me how, but they managed to considerably increase both the range of the SAM-2's and the explosive power of their warheads. Our Soviet comrades were very astonished at this and also at the fact that we made them mobile by mounting them on truck-drawn tenders. Normally they are kept in fixed positions. The Americans could spot where they had been last by satellites, monitoring the flashes when they were fired; reconnaissance planes were continually over to spot the positions. But by the time the data was processed and the bombers came over, the missiles were elsewhere and the pilots bombed empty fields. We are very proud of our scientists and the heroism and skill of those who man our anti-aircraft defenses."

"The year 1972 was decisive for us," Mayor Hung said, in summing up the effects of the "Kissinger bombings," "but those twelve days at the end were the most decisive of the whole year. Nixon and Kissinger thought they could do better with the 7th Fleet and Tactical Aviation than with the ground troops they were pulling out. Finally they had to resort to their Strategic Aviation and got their B-52s' cut to pieces. This had to be done to get talks going again and reach an Agreement. Nixon is the most obstinate of all U.S. presidents and so he suffered the greatest defeat. All branches of his armed forces were beaten and the honor of the United States cut to shreds. The personality of Nixon has also suffered."

I visited the remains of some of the shot down planes. With typical Vietnamese humor, the carcass of one had been placed in the Hanoi Zoo, "alongside less dangerous beasts of prey like tigers and panthers," said Mayor Tran Duy Hung, whom I accidentally encountered there as he was checking up the layout of some statistical and other explanatory materials. Children were clambering over its huge wings and examining the twisted entrails and defused bombs spilling out like unlaid eggs. Tail fins and part of the wings of another were sticking up out of a duckpond, a score of yards from a primary school in the city outskirts.

"The sound was unimaginable," said Nguyen Dinh Tranh,

watchman at an electric powerhouse, whom I found cleaning and stacking bricks from a pile of rubble that had been his home in Kham Thien street, in the most populated area of downtown Hanoi. "It was a roaring, thundering sound that blotted out everything else—even the sound of buildings collapsing on top of us. Waves of air kept knocking us to the floor of the shelter. My mother and my six-year-old child were buried with me in the shelter, but when the 'all clear' sounded we fought our way out through the bricks and rubble. I rushed to our next-door neighbor's house and dug through the rubble to their shelter— all five of them dead. We went from one pile of smoking rubble to another calling to our friends, helping them out from the mountains of ruins."

Kham Thien street—an area which includes scores of narrow lanes feeding into it—had been hit on the night of December 26, one of the rare occasions in which successive waves of B-52s' broke through the defenses and dropped their loads neatly along the entire 1½ mile length of the street, cutting a swath of destruction about 500 yards wide. 215 people were killed, a large proportion of the 1,318 officially listed as killed between the nights of December 18-19 and 29-30. Had 90 percent of the population not been evacuated, the casualties would have been scores of times greater. Those remaining in the city, with few exceptions, were those engaged in essential work, disciplined and nimble enough to move quickly into the shelter system. (Nixon used the low civilian casualty figures as proof that "only military targets" were being bombed!)

North Vietnam's air raid warning and shelter systems were like none other I have seen. Apart from some group shelters at places of work and residence, there were millions of individual concrete cylinders in the pavement or ground, with room for one person to stand or squat with their head well below ground level. Loud-speaker systems supplemented the air raid sirens by bringing a running commentary as to the distance of the planes, the moment to get into the shelters and the moment when the heavy concrete covers should be slid into position. Such shelters gave protection against everything but direct hits of heavy bombs. Including the group or individual shelters at place of work and residence, there were three shelters for every resident, one for shoppers or people on their way back and forth to work. The same system existed in the villages, except that they consisted of cylindrical holes dug into the ground at homes, fields and roads and paths in between.

Over 40,000 tons of bombs were dropped on Hanoi alone in 500 B-52 attacks between December 18 and 30. In the same period, 15,000 tons were dropped on Haiphong, killing 305 residents and wounding another 882, according to official statistics. When I saw the extent of the destruction it was difficult to believe the casualties had been so light, but the city had been almost completely evacuated.

World public opinion was aroused as never before at the horrors of what were known as the "Christmas bombings" in the outside world, as the "Nixon bombings" by the Vietnamese and what I think could also be called the "Kissinger bombings." The Swedish prime minister, Olaf Palme, described them as an "outrage" and compared them to other atrocities perpetuated in modern history by names such as "Guernica, Oradour, Babi Yar, Katyn, Lidice, Sharpeville, Treblinka..." The U.S. Chargé d' Affaires was withdrawn from Stockholm as a result and Sweden was asked by the U.S. State Department not to replace its ambassador to Washington. There were expressions ranging from disgust and indignation to cold reproof from countries normally regarded as the closest friends and allies of the U.S., such as Japan, West Germany, Italy, Austria and Australia. By adopting "Killer" Lemay's "Bomb 'em back into the Stone Age" advice, it was Nixon and Kissinger who were seen as the Stone Age cavemen as far as millions of people throughout the world were concerned. Olaf Palme spoke for mankind when he said: "Nazi Germany and Fascist Italy collapsed completely because their leaders lost all sense of conscience... In the history of nations, no Head of State has deceived the national conscience as Nixon has done..."

Among the qualities of the DRV leadership is that they are never taken by surprise. They never allowed themselves to be disarmed by the image of Nixon the "peace-maker," or to be taken in by his and Kissinger's promises. They believed from the outset that, as a last card, a Nixon or some other president would attempt to wipe out Hanoi and Haiphong. Ho Chi Minh prepared the North Vietnamese people for this from the very first bombing raids. Within weeks, every public building, factory and school in North Vietnam displayed banners with the words of Ho Chi Minh to the effect that the Americans might destroy Hanoi, Haiphong and many industrial installations, but that, as he expressed it in his Testament,

> Our mountains will always be, our rivers will always be, our people will always be.
>
> The American invaders defeated, we will rebuild our land ten times more beautiful.

I wrote at the time of the first bombings, after discussions with "Uncle" Ho and other North Vietnamese leaders:

> The idea that the threat of destroying Hanoi and Haiphong would bring Ho Chi Minh to the conference table on Washington's terms betrays a desperate ignorance of Vietnamese sentiments and traditions. If the Vietnamese people in the first resistance were prepared to burn their own towns and set fire to their homes with their own hands, they are not likely to fall to their knees because the enemy destroys their town and homes or threatens to do so.[39]

On December 24, Nixon sent another communication to Pham Van Dong, stating that the bombings would continue until the DRV accepted the U.S. version of the draft Agreement. Hanoi's only reply was to continue to shoot down the B-52s'—not to mention a number of the supposedly "invulnerable" F-III swing-wing fighter-bombers. The rate at which the B-52s' were being shot down was causing great concern at Strategic Air Command headquarters. (Reuter reported at the time that the B-52 loss rate was such that if it continued, SAC would be out of planes within three months.) The U.S. Defense Department conceded the loss of "only" 15 of the giant aircraft, plus 6 damaged, and acknowledged the loss of 93 airmen (killed, captured or missing) in the 12-day period. Nixon sent a very different communication on December 26, to the effect that the bombings would continue until Hanoi sent its negotiators back to the Paris conference table. To this, Pham Van Dong replied that the DRV delegates would never return to the conference table as long as the bombings continued. In a bit of fast footwork, Nixon replied that the bombings would be halted so the conference could restart its work on December 30. On this basis, Hanoi agreed to resume the talks and, waiting for a few days after December 30, to confirm that the bombings were really halted, sent Le Duc Tho back to Paris.

---

39. Wilfred Burchett, *Vietnam North* New York: International Publishers, 1966, pp. 119-120.

Le Duc Tho and Kissinger met for the first time since their fateful December 13 session on January 8, 1973. Journalists could see a not-so-confident Henry Kissinger go to the usual rendezvous. Instead of a smiling Le Duc Tho coming out with his hand stretched out in greeting as previously, Kissinger had to proceed, unwelcomed, and rap on the door. There was a size-able pause before it was opened and he was swallowed up from view. He was received icily by a wrathful Le Duc Tho who, for the following two hours, castigated him for the perfidious conduct of the Nixon administration in general, and Kissinger in particular. His only response was an occasional weary wave of the hand and to protest: "But I am not responsible for bomb-ing policies," which did not in the least convince the silvery-headed, veteran revolutionary, Le Duc Tho. (It was already known in well-informed journalistic circles in Washington that before leaving Paris on December 13, Kissinger had cabled Nixon: "We've Been Doublecrossed. Bomb! Bomb! Bomb!")

Kissinger could only sit and take it. As far as trying to im-pose terms on his counterpart, he had come to the end of his tether. He had no more leverage. His ace card of the threat of force, with sufficient application of force to make the threat credible had been played—and trumped. One of his favorite doctrines had been drastically devalued by the fact that it had been used. He had to go through the act of negotiating some retouches to the document as it was ready for signing on Octo-ber 31 and present it to the U.S. public, and the world, as some-thing wrung out of the North Vietnamese through the "Christ-mas Bombings." On January 23 the final draft was ready for signature on the 27th. Thieu, as will be seen later, was brought to heel by a large dollar gift and a pledge which meant in effect: "It's a scrap of paper. Sign it. Do what you want later, and we'll back you to the hilt." And he had it in writing from Nixon!

Thus, at a solemn ceremony on January 27, 1973, in the Paris International Conference Centre, foreign minister Nguyen Duy Trinh affixed his signature for the DRV, together with those of the U.S. Secretary of State, William Rogers, the for-eign minister of the PRG, Madame Nguyen Thi Binh and For-eign Minister Tran Van Lam of the Republic of Vietnam, to a document officially entitled: "Agreement on Ending the War and Restoring Peace to Vietnam." The text was virtually iden-tical with that which had been prepared in October, three months previously. Although I had covered the Paris Confer-ence from the beginning, I was not on hand to remind Nguyen

Duy Trinh that the signing ceremony was within a few hours of being the fifth anniversary of our historic interview which had played some role in starting the process which led to the signing ceremony.

By that time I was in Hanoi to taste the atmosphere when the signing of the Agreement had been consummated. Regardless of how it was implemented—and Thieu's off-stage noises in Saigon inspired no optimism—the Agreement represented an immeasurably important milestone along the infinitely difficult road of the Vietnamese Revolution.

Chapter 12.

The Têt of Peace

There were ugly gaps in the walls, and missing roofs and windows at Hanoi's Gia Lam civilian air terminal, but friends who I feared might have perished in the "Kissinger bombings" were there, flowers in hand, to greet me. Along the road leading from the airport, we were slowed down by a curious procession of vehicles: army trucks, horse and ox-drawn carts, hand-carts hauled and pushed by people of all ages, all piled to capacity with beds, cupboards, and chairs—the modest furnishing of an average Vietnamese home with old people and children seated on top or jammed in between. Weaving through this odd assortment of transport were men and women pedalling bicycles, usually with children perched in baskets in front and behind. It was all part of the Great Return. Bombing north of the 20th parallel had been halted for over a month, but aircraft batteries, manned on each side of the road, showed that nothing was being taken for granted. The press and radio had made cautious references to the possibility of a peace agreement finally being signed. This was sufficient for home-comers to start converging on the capital from all directions.

Gia Lam itself, an industrial suburb on the northern side of the Red River from Hanoi, was a mass of rubble, the big railway repair depot reduced to twisted steel and collapsed roofs through which one saw rusted wrecks of burned-out trains.

Rubble choked the footpaths and where facades of houses and shops still stood there were gutted ruins behind. Our car bump-bumped its way across one of the several pontoon bridges with the ruins of the big Long Bien bridge in the background, one span drooping into the river, a great gap where another had been—twinkling blue flashes testifying that welders were at work at what one felt was a puny effort compared to the magnitude of the task.

The animation and vitality of the people and the spick-and-span cleanliness of the streets as we entered the city proper was in sharp contrast to the depressing destruction along the road from the airport.

I arrived in Hanoi on the eve of the great Tết of Peace, one that will never be forgotten by those who participated. Tết is like the western Christmas and the New Year combined, a time of family reunions, of New Year hopes and plans, and as much rejoicing as the family budget permits. The narrow streets around the central market on the morning after my arrival were packed with early morning shoppers and ablaze with flowers, especially peach branches and tiny orange trees laden with miniature fruit glowing like little lanterns. Peach branches or orange trees—both if possible—are essential for a proper celebration of Tết. Never had there been such a profusion of flowers and everything from goldfish floating in glass spheres (both in a great variety of size) to paper flowers and dragons, festoons of fire-crackers—everything that shone and made for good cheer. Market stalls were piled high with fruit and vegetables, with the glutinous rice cakes and pastries that are specialties of the occasion. The crowd in the streets quickly swelled so that even cycling became impossible. Most of the young people—girls as well as boys—were in the olive-green uniform and camouflaged pith helmets of the Vietnam Peoples Army. But there were also thousands of families freshly reunited—children perched high on parents' shoulders, faces shining like the persimmons and oranges at the feast of color and good things on every side.

Suddenly there was the sound of banging drums and clashing cymbals and the crowd parted to receive a truck, swathed in red banners, from which young people handed out copies of an extra-special edition of the morning paper. Unprecedented huge, red-banner headlines, announced the Peace Agreement had been signed. As the trucks passed at snail's pace with many a halt, hundreds of hands reached out for the papers, and shoppers took a few minutes off to read the unbelieveably good news. The documents had actually been signed in Paris some 12 hours earlier, but with so many dashed hopes in the past, nothing was announced on the radio, or published until confirmation and full texts had been received from the DRV delegation.

As similarly decorated trucks and mini-buses slowly made their way along the main market streets handing out the good news, the loud-speaker system which for the previous eight years had so often sounded the grim warnings of approaching death and destruction burst into life and, punctuated with bursts of revolutionary music, announced the main terms of the Agreement and what they meant. On the main street corners, mountains of the special morning editions melted like snow in the hot sun and the vendor's hands were hard put to cope with the press of customers.

For the next three days it was the "let joy be unconfined" of officially-declared rejoicing. The stream of returning evacuees turned into a flood-tide. Never had Hanoi residents better cause to celebrate and never had good news come at more appropriate moment. Têt now provided the occasion for family reunions on a mass scale. Wives and husbands had been separated from each other according to their work, parents from their children, children from each other, schools were evacuated by classes, the tinier children sent to villages remote from communication routes (where possible with their grandparents). It was only by such measures that maximum survival could be assured. Now the long-separated elements of the families were converging for the greatest family reunions the capital had ever known. And the very first lines of the Paris Agreement were the most magnificent Têt gift that any Vietnamese could imagine.

> The United States and all other countries respect the independence, sovereignty, unity and territorial integrity of Vietnam as recognized by the 1954 Geneva Agreement on Vietnam.

Patriotic Vietnamese had been fighting for this for all their adult lives. Oddly enough the words "and all other peoples" were not in the October version of the Agreement, but were inserted—obviously with no objections by Le Duc Tho—during the January negotiations. This was typical of the emptiness of the pretensions of Nixon and Kissinger—that the most terrible bombings of the war had been necessary to bring about some fundamental changes in the text. All the essential points, the ones that one must assume Kissinger fought hardest against having included in the original text, remain. The key Article 4, for instance, that:

> The United States will not continue its military involvement or intervene in the internal affairs of South Vietnam

is word for word as in the original text. The adding of "and all other peoples" to Article 1, was designed to imply that the U.S. was not the only one who failed to respect the 1954 Geneva Agreement. Similarly Article 9 (c) states that:

> Foreign countries shall not impose any political tendency or personality on the South Vietnamese people.

whereas the original text states:

> The United States is not committed to any political tendency or to any personality in South Vietnam, and it does not seek to impose a pro-American régime in Saigon.

The change here, a slight gain for Kissinger, revealed by omission U.S. intentions to continue to impose a "pro-American régime in Saigon." 500 waves of B-52s' were employed as a red pencil to correct Kissinger's shoddy editing of the original version!

Any objective point-by-point comparison of the Agreement signed in Paris on January 27, 1973, and the summary as published by the DRV government of that to be signed on October 31, 1972, makes it abundantly clear that the changes did not justify the sacrifice of a single human life. The steadfastness with which the original text was defended reflects one more humiliating defeat for the Nixon-Kissinger strong-arm methods. Their aim had been to bomb the original version to smithereens. Instead they had to swallow it whole.

Apart from the military provisions for an end to all acts of war, the dismantling of all U.S. bases, a stand-still ceasefire in South Vietnam and provisions for supervising these arrangements, the Agreement laid down the precise steps to be taken for a political solution in the South, including: (Article 11) non-discrimination against individuals or organizations which collaborated with one side or the other and the introduction of broad democratic liberties—freedom of press, association and assembly, freedom to choose one's place of work or residence, etc. All this in an effort to promote "national reconciliation and concord." The key article for bringing this latter about was contained in Article 12:

> (a) Immediately after the ceasefire, the two South Vietnamese parties shall hold consultations in a spirit of national reconciliation and concord, mutual respect and mutual non-elimination, to set up a National Council of National Reconciliation and Concord of three equal segments.

> The Council shall operate on the principle of unanimity. After the NCNRC has assumed its functions, the two South Vietnamese parties will consult about the formation of councils at lower levels.

> The two South Vietnamese parties shall sign an agreement on the internal matters of South Vietnam as soon as possible and do their utmost to accomplish this within 90 days after the ceasefire comes into effect, in keeping with the South Vietnamese people's aspirations for peace, independence and democracy.

> (b) The NCNRC shall have the task of promoting the two South Vietnamese parties' implementation of this agreement, achievement of national reconciliation and concord and ensurance of democratic liberties.

> The NCNRC will organize the free and democratic general elections provided for in Article 9 (b) and decide the procedures and modalities of these general elections.

> The institutions for which the general elections are to be held will be agreed upon through consultations between the two South Vietnamese parties. The NCNRC will also decide the procedures and modalities of such local elections as the two South Vietnamese parties agree upon.

The PRG concept of a three-way transitional government as proposed by Madame Nguyen Thi Binh on September 11 was thus retained in a somewhat downgraded form of a three-way advisory council. An ominous indication of how the U.S. intended to respect "self-determination" came in Nixon's broadcast statement of January 23, announcing the conclusion of the Agreement. After stating that final agreement had been reached that day and that this would bring "peace with honor" to South Vietnam, he stated in part:

> The United States will continue to recognize the Government of the Republic of South Vietnam as the sole legitimate government of South Vietnam,

a statement which Thieu never ceased to exploit by refusing to implement any of the terms of Article 12, for instance.

However, there was plenty to rejoice over in Hanoi; plenty of reasons for three days and nights during which the streets and parks were thronged with animated crowds, emotional re-unions occurring all over the place as friends met who hadn't seen each other during the years of evacuation. The explosions of enormous quantities of fire-crackers of all calibres replaced those of the anti-aircraft batteries. Mayor Hung had released thousands of tons of extra food and in the homes of various friends I visited there was no lack of food or the potent "shum shum" rice alcohol to wash it down. Even in the rubble of Kham Thien street, amidst pathetic hand-written notices on sticks poked into the rubble that such and such a child had survived and was now with "Uncle Nguyen..." or "Auntie Minh..." at such and such an address, there were also peach blossoms and orange trees planted outside makeshift shelters, thus contriving to soften the desolation. "The recent past was terrible, the pres-ent is difficult, the future is bright—and at Têt we always think of the future" was how a dimunitive, elderly woman summed it up, as she stepped back to survey the little orange tree she had just propped up between some bricks outside the ruins of her home—also in the Kham Thien area. Even during the holidays people were at work there, scraping mortar off bricks, neatly stacking them up and in some cases laying them without mortar in between to make walls of temporary dwellings.

What did the Agreement mean to Vietnamese? Firstly, that within 60 days there would be no more foreign troops on Viet-namese soil for the first time since a Franco-Spanish expedition captured Saigon in 1859. The bombings had been stopped and this time it seemed for good. The independence and unity of the country was recognized—and this time, as distinct from 1954 in Geneva—the Americans had put their signature to the Agree-ment. In whatever way Thieu would implement the Agreement in the South, this time—also as distinct from the 1954 Geneva Agreement—the revolutionary forces stayed where they were arms in hands until political solutions were implemented and the armies of both sides were integrated with a large part de-mobilized. The revolutionary forces in the South had their own government which was being accorded increasing international recognition.

"The Geneva Agreement gave us half the country 'red,'"

explained a peasant from the city outskirts, whom I found gazing with contempt at the B-52 in the Hanoi Zoo. "The Paris Agreement gives us half the South 'red.' That took 20 years. It will take much less to make the other half the South 'red.'" That was one of the best summing-ups I heard.

For the more politically sophisticated, Luu Quy Ky, for example, president of the Vietnamese Journalists Association, the Agreement was a document of the highest importance for the forthcoming struggle in the South. A "veritable political tribune" he said, "which provides the legal base for carrying on the struggle at a higher level. Our position and that of our comrades in the South will be for the strictest implementation in the liberated areas, the avoidance of any provocations, a demand for the same strict observance of the Agreement for the Saigon régime."

There was plenty for a journalist to do and see in those first few days. On the evening of the 28th itself, there was a ceremony at which Vo Nguyen Giap farewelled the advance group of VPA officers who were to go to Saigon as delegates to a four-party Joint Military Commission. The head of the group pledged to Giap that they would faithfully carry out their duty to observe the strict application of the Agreement. It was a solemn and rather moving moment and I was not the only one to have some inner doubts as to how many of them would ever return to Hanoi, in view of the torrent of abuse against the Agreement that continued to pour out of Thieu's headquarters. (Vo Nguyen Giap looked remarkably fit, incidentally, considering the report by U.S. intelligence sources in Saigon that he had been blown to bits by a delayed-action bomb in Haiphong just one month earlier.) The delegation was held up for 24 hours when they arrived the next day at Saigon airport because the authorities tried to make them fill in forms as if they were immigrants or tourists, whereas, according to the Protocols of the Agreement, they were to have the status of diplomats. Finally they were herded off into a barbed-wire enclosure at the Tan Son Nhut air-base, which was to serve as their residence and headquarters. This was the beginning of harassment and insults which ended only on April 30, 1975.

There was another ceremony to welcome a triumphant Xuan Thuy and his negotiations' delegation on their return from Paris. There were visits to Haiphong (two-thirds destroyed) and the coal mining center of Hongay, on the entrancing Baie d'Along north of Haiphong, which will surely become a major international tourist resort. Hongay had been 100 percent destroyed, not a building left intact. The city's pride, a fine football stadium on the outskirts of the city had been blown sky-high the very day it was to be formally opened! High quality Hongay anthracite is one of the country's most important export items—much appreciated in Japan amongst other countries —but the grading works and the nearby Campha wharf facilities had been blown to bits.

There was the arrival of Henry Kissinger on February 10, for a four-day visit to discuss, as had been believed, implementation of Article 21 of the 23 Article Agreement. It stated:

> The United States anticipates that this Agreement will usher in an era of reconciliation with the Democratic Republic of Vietnam as with all peoples of Indochina. In pursuance of its traditional policy, the United States will contribute to healing the wounds of war and to post-war reconstruction of the Democratic Republic of Vietnam and through-out Indochina.

This incidentally was the exact wording of the original version of the Agreement. Kissinger and his party were accorded all the courtesies of distinguished guests. They were met at the airport by Le Duc Tho. But Kissinger had not come to discuss "post-war reconstruction" although he would have had to be blind not to see a few hundreds of million dollars worth of civilian "wounds of war" just in driving from Gia Lam airport to his guest house! He had come to discuss the size of the bribe the U.S. was prepared to pay in return for a DRV pledge to abandon its compatriots in the South. It was as simple and crude as that, but his hosts continued to treat him and his aides with the good manners of a highly civilized people. No deviation from the official itinerary to drive past Kham Thien street, nor any invitation to visit the Zoo! The only concrete result of the visit was a decision to set up a Joint Economic Commission "charged with the task of developing economic relations between the two countries..." It was an affable, smiling Kissinger who arrived and a sombre, glowering Kissinger who left, four days later. (The Joint Economic Commission subsequently held a few fruitless sessions in Paris, then went into the indefinite adjournment when it became evident that the United States was interested only in buying the South for X number of billions of dollars.) A typical illusion of the U.S. leadership to think that a billion-dollar carrot could succeed where a B-52 stick had failed! President Nixon at one point sent a personal letter to Pham Van Dong pledging 3.25 billion dollars worth of aid to contribute to "healing the wounds of war!"

On the eve of Kissinger's visit, premier Pham Van Dong told me: "We will do everything for the integral respect of the Paris Agreement. It is the concrete expression of everything we have won and it opens up new prospects for the victory of the national democratic revolution in the South." On the question of U.S.-North Vietnam relations, in view of the Kissinger visit, the prime minister said:

"We are ready to normalize relations. But some problems have first to be settled. The question of the contribution to healing the wounds of war and aid for reconstruction, must be settled to the satisfaction of everyone. But we will accept no conditions. In all matters, our interests, our right, our sovereignty must always be respected." Referring to reports that the U.S. Congress would probably not approve the passage of funds to implement Article 21, premier Pham Van Dong said: "We will demand that the United States fulfill its obligations. If the people of the United States want to salvage their conscience, they will support this. But we will insist on freely disposing of funds that are allotted. We are absolutely determined to remain masters in our own country." On the overall question of implementing the Agreement, Pham Van Dong commented: "The United States seems to be bent on repeating the same old errors of closing their eyes to reality. The same old mistake of not seeing things that are extremely vital for everyone."

This was the viewpoint defended during Kissinger's visit to Hanoi and at the meetings of the Economic Commission in Paris. If Kissinger had been expecting to find some "last gasp" economic situation in Hanoi, with hands outstretched in the sort of dollar-grasping attitude that he was used to in South Vietnam and in so many other of America's beggar-client states, he must have been sorely disappointed. North Vietnam was poor in a material sense, yes, and the United States had done its best to make it poorer by bombing out of existence the little bit the North Vietnamese had. But it was also infinitely rich in national pride and dignity which, if Kissinger and his team had been sensitive, they would have noted. By the mercantile attitude of the U.S. delegates on the Joint Economic Commission—trying to buy half a country on the cheap—it seemed that they had not!

One of Kissinger's aides was discreetly on hand on February 12, to watch the departure of the first batches of U.S. pilot-POW's from Gia Lam airport. First there was a meeting in the bombed-out passenger lounge of members of the International Commission of Control and Supervision (Canada, Indonesia, Poland and Hungary) plus representatives of the Pentagon and the VPA, at which was agreed the modalities of the handing-over procedure. A representative of the U.S. Air Force then took his place at a table under a tent awning, with a list of POW's to be released, flanked at other tables by the ICCS officers. When all were in place, a camouflaged bus drew up and out stepped the pilots. Neatly dressed, sleek—obviously fit—one by one they marched to the desk, saluted, gave their names and units, and were escorted off to silvery Stratoliners waiting to fly them off to Guam.

A distraught-looking Pentagon official tried to catch up with each one and whisper a few words in his ear—presumably on what to say at the receiving end. Among the first to be released was one of the "Christmas bomber" pilots, his leg in plaster from an unanticipated "landfall." They were all in very different shape from the emaciated wrecks from the prisons of the U.S.-Saigon Command, slithering their way to freedom, as portrayed on Western TV, by propelling themselves with their hands—their legs withered and useless from years in chains in the Tiger Cages of Poulo Condor and elsewhere. Yet somehow it appeared in the U.S. press that it was the U.S. pilots that were to be pitied, not the tortured remnants from the U.S.-run prisons or the tens of thousands of orphans, widows and limbless victims of their activities!

As the first gleaming stratoliner took off with its load of pilots, an old friend, a Vietnamese historian, murmured: "Truly, times have changed. When we defeated the Mongols, we usually sent them back to China on our own horses or boats, with sufficient rations to see them on their way. We then sent delegates to Peking—once with a golden statue of the commanding general who had been killed—always with generous tribute and our excuses for having defeated their armies in regrettable incidents during which they had crossed our borders. 'Please spare us this in the future,' we said. Now at least there is an invader who sends his own transport to remove the captives, and even sends us an emissary to discuss the amount of *their* tribute."

Chapter 13.

Sowing the Wind

As far as the military part of the Agreement affecting United States interests were concerned, everything worked rather well. (As it had done with the French about 20 years earlier.) The U.S. got all of its pilot-prisoners and other POW's back in good condition; it withdrew the rest of its Expeditionary Corps without incident. As far as DRV-PRG interests were concerned, things were not so favorable. Article 5, for instance, stipulated:

> Within 60 days of the signing of this Agreement, there will be a total withdrawal from South Vietnam of troops, military advisers and military personnel, including technical military personnel associated with the pacification program, armaments, munitions and war materials of the United States and those of other foreign countries mentioned in Article 3 (a). Advisers from the above-mentioned countries to all paramilitary organizations and the police force will also be withdrawn within the same period of time.

Article 3 (a) referred to:

> The United States forces and those of other foreign countries allied with the United States and the Republic of Vietnam.

Article 6 stated:

> The dismantlement of all military bases in South Vietnam of the United States and of the other foreign countries men-

tioned in article 3 (a) shall be completed within 60 days of the signing of the Agreement.

This seemed explicit enough, but in practice such major bases as the huge air base at Bien Hoa, 15 miles north of Saigon, the capital's Tan Son Nhut airport, the huge aero-naval base complex at Danang, a major air base at Can Tho, in the heart of the Mekong Delta, and many others, were not dismantled. When this non-compliance of the Agreement was raised at the Joint Military Commission, the U.S. delegate blandly explained that these bases had been transferred to the Saigon authorities before the Agreement was signed and were thus outside its provisions.

On March 29, by which time all U.S. POWs were on their way home within the 60-day period provided for their release, the DRV accused the U.S. of "leaving behind over 10,000 soldiers disguised as civilian advisers," to which the State Department again blandly replied that there were only 8,500 Americans left behind in South Vietnam. They included over 5,000 Defense Department personnel under contract to the Saigon government for "maintenance, logistics, communications, automatic data processing and similar operations for the armed forces of the Republic of Vietnam..." A further 1,000 were attached to AID (Agency for International Development, a thinly disguised agency of the CIA), fifty more were assigned to the military attaché's office of the U.S. Embassy, etc. The dictionary meaning of words had lost it validity. U.S. corporation lawyers' expertise had been employed in drafting the Agreement to ensure that words did not mean what they appeared to. There were built-in loopholes according to U.S.-Saigon plans to continue the war. During the period between October 31, when the Agreement was not signed, and January 27, when it was, the United States had poured into South Vietnam heavy weaponry at an unprecedented rate, especially tanks, heavy artillery, planes and helicopters. Officially, these had been scheduled for delivery during the 1972-73 budgetary year.

As regards the ceasefire which was to go into effect at midnight (GMT) on January 27, it went into effect only in areas where the Saigon forces were in an obviously weak position. The most flagrant and ominous violation came the following day, when a regiment of Saigon's crack Marine troops launched a full-fledged attack against a PRG-held naval base in the Cua

Viet estuary just south of the 17th parallel, which had been in PRG hands since April 1972. The attack was preceded by air and naval bombardment and the Cua Viet base was temporarily captured. PRG troops counter-attacked, inflicting very heavy casualities on the Marines and recaptured the base on January 31. At the Joint Military Commission (JMC), where the PRG representative raised the matter, the Saigon representative claimed the base had been seized "ten minutes before the cease-fire was due to go into effect!" Cua Viet later became the PRG's most important port of entry for seaborne trade. It was one of the rare cases in which the PRG forces resisted such attacks, but there were no political considerations which could have justified ceding such a vitally strategic base. Instructions for the first few months were to cede territory in favor of political gains, thus demonstrating which side was for peace and which for continued war. In the Saigon-controlled area, the Paris Agreement was treated as a "subversive" document. Heavily doctored versions of it were published to prove that the Saigon régime was the sole legitimate government.[40]

Parallel to land-grabbing operations into the PRG-controlled areas, a vast para-military campaign was launched within the Saigon-controlled areas, not only as an intensification of the permanent effort to wipe out the "Vietcong" and their suspected sympathizers, but also to round up those suspected of "neutralist tendencies." The aim was to eliminate any potential "third force" candidates for the Council of National Reconciliation at national or local levels. A key provision in getting the ceasefire implemented was Article 3 (b) which stated:

> The armed forces of the two South Vietnamese parties shall remain in place. The two-party joint military commission described in Article 17, shall determine the areas controlled by each party and the modalities of stationing.

---

40. It was not only in Saigon that distorted versions of the Agreement were published. The official White House summary stated that the Saigon government "remains in existence, recognized by the United States, its constitutional structure and leadership intact and unchanged" and with the right to "unlimited economic aid" and "unlimited military replacement aid." Visiting Australia, after my Hanoi trip, I found the version as presented in the press—the original document of the Agreement not having been published—was that the "Christmas Bombings" had forced the DRV-PRG to accept something like surrender terms which included recognizing Saigon as the sole legitimate government of South Vietnam!

This was interpreted by the PRG as calling for an exchange of maps in the normal way to define the territories controlled by each side, with mutual withdrawals from respective enclaves in the other side's territory. This was clearly the intention of those who drafted the Agreement. There are frequent references to the "areas under the control" of each party, for instance the provisions in Article 3 (c) for:

> normal proficiency military training conducted by the parties in the areas under their respective control,

and even more so in Article 3 (d) which states that the JMC:[41]

> shall immediately agree on corridors, routes and other regulations (governing communications and transport) of one party going through areas under the control of other parties.

But Thieu's representatives refused any discussions of "areas under control." He had proclaimed to the world and to his own public for so long that he controlled 95 percent of South Vietnam that it would be embarrassing in the extreme to reveal the true situation on maps. His position on this was reinforced by accounts of various western journalists who mistook the PRG's disciplined, military passivity in the months subsequent to the agreement taking effect—even the fact that they could drive safely along the main highways—as proof that PRG forces were non-existent. Mine is the sole legitimate government, was Thieu's attitude. Did not President Nixon say so? And he acted as if this was indeed so, ignoring the fact that in Paris, on March 2, his own foreign minister, together with those of the PRG, the United States and 9 other nations, in the presence of UN Secretary General, Kurt Waldheim, signed a Declaration endorsing the Paris Agreement, thus giving international recognition to the PRG. The position taken by Thieu's representative at the JMC in Saigon and at the political conference which had started at La Celle-Saint Cloud, outside Paris on March 19, was that the PRG-NLF were virtually non-existent rebels to be exterminated. The only problem was with North Vietnamese invaders who must be made to withdraw.

Instead of delimiting the areas of control, Thieu demanded

---

41. The four-party Joint Military Commission was supposed to wind up its work within 60 days following the withdrawal of U.S. and other non-Vietnamese forces and the return of POW's. The two-party (PRG and Saigon government) JMC was supposed to continue to supervise the military aspects of the Agreement.

simply that the PRG pinpoint on a military map its bases and stationing points of its troops. Apart from a clear violation of the concepts of the political settlement, as Thieu had a complete monopoly of air power, one could well imagine the results of such disclosures. Indeed some of the early violations were the result of the PRG naming a point in its territory at which it would release POW's and Thieu's troops immediately launching an attack to try to seize the point. In adopting this absurd position, Thieu was backed to the hilt by the U.S. The "areas under control" of one side or the other were never delimited and Thieu's hands were freed to try to seize as much PRG-controlled territory as the relation of military forces and the PRG policy of maximum non-resistance permitted.

The land-grabbing technique was simple. Thieu parachuted commandos into a PRG-controlled area to establish a small base. He then claimed that his "long-established" base was encircled —a PRG violation of the ceasefire—and sent an armored column to "break the encirclement." With a monopoly of air power and heavy weaponry, he could get away with it, also with the setting up of his militarized administration in the wake of the armored column. Normally such units and columns would have been wiped out by the PRG's regional forces and village self-defense guerillas, without main force units being called upon. But instructions were to "bend over backwards" to respect the Agreement and not respond to provocations.

In the meantime the PRG delegation at the La Celle-Saint Cloud conference patiently tried to get the political provisions implemented—including the release of some 200,000 political prisoners. Their numbers had been added to by some 50,000 within a few weeks of the Agreement as Thieu's paramilitary and police units rounded up suspected "third force" potentials, especially intellectuals in Saigon and the provincial capitals. Taking his cue from the Americans who put their military advisers into civilian uniforms, Thieu switched the classification of political prisoners to common law criminals. As "communism" and "neutralism" had been decreed crimes meriting the death penalty this was simple! Thieu flatly denied there were any political prisoners. He refused even to discuss the setting up of the National Council of Reconciliation, claiming there was no such thing as a "third force," and by the most ferocious repression did his best to make this true. Democratic rights were more brutally suppressed than ever.

As a further measure to prevent the emergence of a "third

force", Thieu issued a decree calling on all political parties to register before March 27, 1973, with requirements that each party must have branches in at least a quarter of the villages in half of the country's 44 provinces, as well as in each city. Each branch must consist of five percent of registered voters. As this was regarded by his political opponents as a device to facilitate police repression by disclosing the names of party members, only three of South Vietnam's twenty-eight political parties had registered by March 27. The other twenty-five parties became automatically illegal. Amongst the three which qualified was the "Democratic" party, formed by Thieu in December 1972, when he realised that an Agreement was going to be signed and he might have to face up to some sort of contested election. No problem about mass membership! He simply ordered all officers to join up, which meant, apart from anything else, that provincial and district commanders—who controlled any Thieu-style elections—were members of his party. The other two parties, the "Liberal" and "Peasants and Workers" parties, were both run by Thieu stooges. At the opening meeting of the La Celle-Saint Cloud conference, the Saigon delegate said there would never be any elections until all "North Vietnamese troops had left the South". This in itself represented a violation of the Agreement, in which the question as to whether or not there were North Vietnamese troops in the South was avoided by a formula (Article 13) which simply stated:

> The question of Vietnamese armed forces in South Vietnam shall be settled by the two South Vietnamese parties in a spirit of national reconciliation and concord, equality and mutual respect, without interference, in accordance with the post-war situation.

> Among the questions to be discussed by the two South Vietnamese parties are steps to reduce their military effectives and to demobilize the troops being reduced. The two South Vietnamese parties will accomplish this as soon as possible.

The PRG delegates tried to get something going on this but met with flat refusals. As the "post-war situation" was one of unremitting land-grabbing attacks into the PRG controlled territories, it was obvious that whatever North Vietnamese troops were in the South would not be withdrawn until this stopped. No progress could be made on any single point that concerned PRG-Saigon affairs, except for an on-again off-again exchange of military POW's. At one point the Saigon side switched its stand on elections, demanding that a date be fixed and that this should have priority over all other matters. The PRG delegate pointed out that the pre-requisite for elections was the setting up of the National Council of Reconciliation, the restoration of democratic rights and the release of political prisoners.

When it became clear that there was not going to be any progress on the political provisions of the Agreement, the PRG decided there were no more dividends in "non-resistance." As far as public opinion in the South was concerned, they had made the point as to who was for peace and who for war. In October a "thus far and no further" order-of-the-day was issued to the PRG's armed forces stating that all further land-grabbing operations were to be resisted and the bases from which such attacks were made should be "punished."

Typical of the type of action that followed was one in Quang Duc province, at a point roughly 120 miles north of Saigon, near the Cambodian border. Three important bases, Bu Prang, Bu Bong and Dak Sone, which had been in PRG hands since April 1972, were occupied by Saigon troops, in the manner described earlier, who then claimed to be "encircled." General Tran Van Tra, who headed the PRG delegation to the JMC, protested five times, demanding an investigation by the International Control Commission. Thieu's delegate claimed the bases had been in Saigon hands "for years" and he objected to any ICC investigation. PRG forces attacked and retook the first two on November 4. Saigon replied by bombing their positions the following day. The PRG response to this was a "punishment" rocket attack on the big Bien Hoa air base on the 6th, destroying three fighter-bombers according to a Saigon communiqué—which meant the damage was far greater—and for good measure attacking and capturing the third base on November 7. There were many similar actions in widely separated parts of the country following the "resist and punish" order. As the main Saigon response was to launch ever bigger air raids against Loc Ninh, the unofficial "capital" of the PRG-controlled area, a second order-of-the-day was issued a month later ordering the recapture of all territory lost since January 28 and hard blows at the bases from which the Saigon forces launched their land and air operations.

On November 23, the Saigon Air Force launched wave after wave of bombers against a PRG base area in Tay Ninh province, about 60 miles north of Saigon. The PRG's declared response to this came on December 3, with a commando raid on the big Nha Be oil storage depot, in the southern outskirts of Saigon, destroying some 18 million gallons of petrol—a high proportion of Saigon's stocks at that time. By the turn of the year 1973-1974, the PRG claimed that virtually all lost territory had been recovered and very heavy losses inflicted on Thieu's forces. Also at the turn of the year, President Nguyen Van Thieu made two speeches which amounted to a declaration of war against the PRG and a formal tearing up of the Paris Agreement. On December 29, he declared there was no such thing as a "third force" in South Vietnam. It was "a term invented by the Communists to sow divisions among the people and facilitate their own seizure of power." So there was no need for a National Council of Reconciliation. There would be no elections, he said, and no political solutions negotiated at La Celle-Saint Cloud. On January 4, Thieu said that "as far as the armed forces are concerned the war has begun again" and the Communists" should not be allowed to remain secure in their bases to prepare attacks against the Saigon forces. "We should carry out our military activities not only in our own zones, but in the areas where their army is now stationed . . . "

These two speeches represented Thieu's real attitude to the Paris Agreement from the start, as translated by battlefield activities. They ended any illusion that the Agreement would ever be implemented as long as the United States maintained Thieu in power. It was a remarkable replay of Ngo Dinh Diem's denunciation of the 1954 Geneva Agreement—to American official applause—about one year after it was signed. At least the United States could claim it had not signed the Geneva Agreement and had played only a negligible—not to mention negative—role in the negotiations which produced it. But it had signed the Paris Agreement and had been a principal negotiator. Few who had followed events in Vietnam could have any doubts after Thieu's two speeches that the door had once again been slammed to any but battlefield solutions. What had happened throughout 1973 provided one more confirmation that Nixon and Kissinger, like Johnson and Dean Rusk before them, were incapable of accepting the fact that gestures for peace, and the kind of restraint the PRG had been showing, were not born of military weakness. They ceded territory—they did not stand and fight. Ha! They must be at their last gasp! Now is the time to hit and hit hard! It was the wearisome, old reaction of men who imputed to their adversaries their own concepts. It seemed impossible for them to grasp that the PRG's reluctance to fight back was born of a responsible attitude of avoiding blood shed—their adversaries' as well as their own—and to seek solutions within the framework of what was a very good Agreement.

There was one issue on which the PRG-NLF were uncompromising and that was on total independence and self-determination with the necessary freedoms to exercise that self-determination. This was central to all their efforts in the JMC and at the La Celle-Saint Cloud conference. And it was precisely this that the United States was determined to prevent at all costs. It was one more confirmation that, as in every phase of the Vietnam War, including negotiations, the United States rejected compromise solutions favorable to itself in favor of illusory total victories. There was a sort of masochism about it which reflected the total incapacity of American political and military leadership to face up to realities, or make a due appreciation of relations of force, not to mention maintaining any standards of international morality. No one could consider Kissinger a stupid man yet he continually acted like one as far as Vietnam was concerned. The old peasant, contemplating the remnants of the B-52 in the Hanoi Zoo, was infinitely more perceptive. Kissinger comes out of all this like a latter-day King Canute trying to sweep back the tide with a broom! In fact, the United States need never have been out on the beach. But in that first year of "peace," the United States "lost Vietnam," rejecting the best chance of salvaging something of American self-respect in favor of the gambler's "all or nothing" throw of the dice.

Later, Kissinger was to state that he

> always considered Indochina a disaster—partly because we did not think through the implications of what we were doing.

> We let ourselves down by entering too lightly on an enterprise whose magnitude was not understood, by methods which were inappropriate to the scale of the problem . . .[42]

42. In an interview with the American columnist, William Buckley, broadcast on September 13, 1975.

The truth is that at every critical point where there were options, the United States chose the most hawkish one—and this was never more true than when Kissinger was directing national security affairs and foreign policy. There was nothing haphazard about it, no faltering steps of a blindfolded Uncle Sam tottering towards a quagmire. It was "heads up and straight ahead" all the way, done without anything resembling the minimum norms of international behavior. Power was the only consideration and even here, a field in which U.S. technical facilities for scientific evaluations are unsurpassed, they failed miserably. Their estimates of the true relation of forces were always wrong. A major error in all the American calculations, including and especially those of the brillant Kissinger, was that they invariably left the people factor OUT. Conversely, if there was one thing that distinguished the DRV-PRG, it was not only that the people factor was invariably in, but was placed on top of everything else. People were the key, pivotal element in planning every strategy and tactic.

From the beginning of 1974, as Thieu's speeches had foreshadowed, the war heated up until it began to look like any year from 1965-1972—but without the Americans. The average monthly casualties among Thieu's troops, according to his own Command's figures, reached the highest level since the war began, with the exception of the period covered by the Têt offensive and its aftermath. Part of the price Nixon, Kissinger and Thieu gladly paid for "Vietnamization." Thieu's solution to political problems was simple—wipe out the "Communists" and expel the "North Vietnamese invaders." The only awkward question was how to do it. It was typical of Thieu's mentality and the cynicism of his American backers and advisers, that he thought, and was encouraged to think, that he could succeed where the United States, with 550,000 of its own troops, most of its Air Force and Navy, and half a million or more Saigon troops failed.

During the first half of 1974, major battles were fought in all four military regions, with Thieu's forces coming off second best in virtually every encounter. One of the earliest of these, the biggest battle since that at Cua Viet on the day the "ceasefire" was supposed to come into effect, took place between March 16-18, when some 3,000 Saigon troops pushed into a PRG-controlled area about 10 miles northeast of Kontum in the strategic Central Highlands. They were quickly encircled and defeated in a very bloody battle in which, according to the PRG account, they left 230 bodies on the battlefield and retreated in disorder. (Saigon conceded losses of 180 killed and wounded; claimed to have inflicted 440 casualties on the adversary, but did not dispute that the operation had been a costly failure.) As "punishment" for the attack, PRG troops took over three Saigon posts in the general area. By this time (and it was something noted more and more during 1974) the Saigon forces began to feel the effect of the American withdrawal. There was no longer unlimited air support to call on in difficult situations. They had been formed in the American image and were conditioned to rely on air support at the slightest obstacle. If a unit ran into trouble, it was used to pulling back and letting the fighter-bombers and helicopter gun-ships take over.

At the end of March, there was an unexpected flutter of hope at the La Celle-Saint Cloud conference, the United States having made some approving noises regarding a PRG six-point proposal presented on March 22.

(1) The Saigon government and the PRG would immediately issue identical ceasefire orders, providing for the implementation of the ceasefire agreements of January 27 and June 13, 1973, respectively, and would allow the ICCS to carry out its work effectively.[43]

(2) All prisoners of war and all political prisoners would be released, and persons not supporting either side would be allowed to choose their place of residence freely. This operation would be completed by June 30.

(3) Respect for democratic liberties such as freedom of speech, the press, assembly and political organization must be guaranteed.

(4) The National Council of National Reconciliation and Concord would be established by September 30.

(5) Elections to a Constituent Assembly would take place at a date to be fixed by the Council, within a year of its establishment.

(6) Both sides would reduce the size of their armed forces, after which the elections would unite to form a single South Vietnamese army.

---

43. The ICCS was paralysed by the lack of defined "areas of control" and because it could operate only on the basis of requests from the Joint Military Commission which could never agree about anything.

Doubtless prodded by Washington's slightly positive reaction—perhaps some military realists there were beginning to have some gnawing doubts about the staying power of the Saigon army—Thieu's delegation came up with a counter-proposal at the following meeting (March 29) which could have provided the basis for at least a dialogue. It suggested the setting up of four committees to settle "within 30 days," questions relating to democratic freedoms, setting up the NCNRC, the modalities of free elections and the question of the armed forces. Implementation of the ceasefire would be settled by these committees together with the JMC and ICCS. That all this could be done within two months was highly unrealistic, but the proposal seemed like a step forward. Nothing ever came of it. The Saigon delegation walked out of the weekly negotiating sessions two weeks later on the pretext of a PRG attack on one of their bases near the Cambodian border and at the following session they said they would boycott the sessions indefinitely "until the Communists have proved their goodwill by concrete actions for peace..." There were a few irregularly-spaced, desultory meetings after that, but no progress was made. The general feeling among those following the talks was that March 29 proposal had not been cleared with Thieu and the suspension of the talks was a way of steering the conference away from the "dangerous waters" of a possible comprehensive agreement.

On the same day that the political talks were suspended (April 16) the harrassment of the PRG delegates to the JMC was stepped up. Their diplomatic privileges, meager as they were, with withdrawn; telephone communications cut; permission to hold weekly press conferences cancelled. The prison-like atmosphere in which they lived in a remote corner of the Tan Son Nhut airport became even more intolerable. After unsuccessful attempts to make their plight known to the ICCS, the PRG withdrew from the JMC which automatically suspended the functions of the International Commission. It could only operate on the basis of agreed requests from the Joint Military Commission. There was precious little left of the Paris Agreement by this time.

As 1974 drew to its close, the situation as far as peace was concerned continued to deteriorate on all fronts: military, political and diplomatic. Implementation of the Agreement was at a total impasse. Instead of bending over backwards as in the past to avoid confrontations, the PRG forces were leaning forward on their tiptoes, hitting back hard at every Saigon initiative and taking the initiative themselves to keep the adversary off balance. The main interest shifted for a time to Washington, where there was growing reluctance to continue sending "good money after bad," or to do anything else to encourage Thieu to reject everything but battlefield solutions. The mid-term elections in November, reflecting nation-wide indignation over the Watergate scandal, injected a lot of fresh blood into Congress—most of it against the administration policy of supporting Thieu at any price. Or Lon Nol in Phnom Penh. Or the Rightists in Vientiane, for that matter, who were obstructing implementation of the 1973 Peace Agreement on Laos.

By the end of 1974, the tangled skeins woven between Washington and its puppets in Saigon, Phnom Penh and Vientiane, had come together in a Gordian knot that only some very sharp swords could sever.

If 1974 opened with the Saigon forces taking the offensive, it closed with them very much on the defensive. They were losing ground throughout the Mekong Delta and were in retreat even in areas guarding the northern approaches to Saigon. The year ended disastrously with the loss, in December, of the whole of Phuoc Long province except for the capital. 1975 was to open even more disastrously when the capital, Phuoc Binh, about 75 miles due north of Saigon near the border of Cambodia, fell on January 7, after a short seige. This was the first time a whole province including its capital had been occupied by the national liberation forces. The result was great panic in Saigon. Thieu declared three days of mourning and vowed several times that he would recapture the whole province. But nothing, in fact, was done except a series of savage bombing attacks against Loc Ninh and other PRG bases in neighboring Binh Long province.

The crucial importance of Phuoc Long for what followed was later explained to me by the head of the Provisional Revolutionary Government, Huynh Tan Phat, the former Saigon architect, who is general secretary of the National Liberation Front and prime minister of the PRG since its formation in July 1969. A trim, smiling man, 62 years of age when he moved into the prime minister's office in Saigon after the city's liberation, he had spent all the war years in front-line positions around Saigon. It was there that I had first met him during Têt, 1964. He is very typical of those Saigon intellectuals, like former lawyer Nguyen Huu Tho, president of the NLF and Chairman of the PRG's Advisory Council, who became experienced, battle-hardened revolutionaries in the course of the anti-French and anti-American resistance wars. In my four visits to the Liberated Areas, I had found their analyses of the situation always borne out by subsequent events—in sharp contrast to anything that American military and political analysts could produce. After our meetings in bamboo and thatch huts, or frontline dugouts, it was like a dream to meet Huynh Tan Phat, in September, 1975, in the prime minister's palatial offices in Saigon, looking as if he had been there all his life! One of my first questions was if he could sum up the main reasons for the dramatically rapid collapse of the U.S.-Saigon Command and its huge military machine of over a million men, with another million more in paramilitary, police and village "self-defense" units. He dealt with what he considered seven "fatal errors" of the Americans who, till the last, still made the major decisions on running the war, in his view.

"The main thing was," said Prime Minister Phat, "that the United States completely and consistently made false evaluations of the situation. Their leaders did this in all fields, making a series of fundamental errors. They thought that by their massive military aid to Thieu right after the Paris Agreement they would crush us militarily, drive us out of our Liberated Zones, penetrate our bases, force us to retreat to the frontier areas, then wipe us out and consolidate Thieu's control over the South. They had some successes at first. Partly this was because we wanted to demonstrate our loyalty to the Paris Agreement—who was for peace, who for war. Partly—to be quite frank—because of a lack of vigilance on our part, the enemy was able to push us back in certain areas and infiltrate some others. This was accompanied by most barbarous police and paramilitary repression in the Saigon-controlled areas. The essential was that our bases remained intact. So the first U.S. error was an incorrect evaluation of what Thieu was capable of doing. Also the Pentagon planners did not understand that Thieu's troops had had enough of war. Their morale was low, even when they were having some cheap successes pushing into our territory with little or no resistance.

"When we liberated Phuoc Long, this came as a great shock to Thieu. For the first time there were dissensions within his High Command. There were those—of whom Thieu was one—who favored an all-out effort to recapture the province. There were others who advised prudence and going over to defensive positions, the better to defend other strategic areas. The

result was that they did nothing except carry out massive reprisal bombings. We studied all this very carefully, their indecision
and weakness. As a result we advanced our own plans for the
general offensive which we had reluctantly decided was the
only way to break the impasse which the policies of Washington and Thieu had brought about. Inability to correctly evalu-
ate one's own forces and those of the adversary and accurately
weigh the correlation between them, making one's own plans
accordingly, can be disastrous", said Huynh Tan Phat, concluding his analysis of the first of the "seven fatal errors".

In a long analysis by General Vo Nguyen Giap and his
chief of staff, General Van Tien Dung, "The General Offensive
and Victorious People's Uprisings of Spring, 1975," written to
commemorate Ho Chi Minh's 90th birthday on May 19, less
than three weeks after Saigon was liberated, the authors describe the situation on the eve of launching the offensive as follows:[44]

> During two years of decisive warfare in 1973-1974, our
> people and our armed forces brought off great victories on
> all battle fronts. From December 1974, our compatriots and
> their armed forces in all towns of the Mekong Delta and
> the southeast regions brought off still greater victories. In a
> short time they wiped out thousands of enemy posts and
> liberated the province of Phuoc Long, the first province to
> be entirely liberated in South Vietnam. These large scale
> victories pushed the puppet administration into a situation
> of passivity and total disintegration, a non-reversible situa-
> tion which forced them on to the strategic defensive over
> the whole battlefield.

The authors claim that the United States strategic aim was
to clean up the whole of the Liberated Zones between 1973-1976
and place South Vietnam entirely under Thieu's control. Starting from the end of 1976

> They nourished the hope of peacefully building up and
> consolidating a U.S. neo-colonialist régime in the South,
> transforming it into a separate state within the U.S. orbit,
> thus keeping our country divided for a long historic period.

---

44. The analysis started appearing as a series of articles in the Saigon
Giai Phong, or Liberation Daily on July 5, 1975. The extracts quoted
were translated into English by the author from an unofficial French
translation of the original Vietnamese.

Part III

The Fall of Saigon

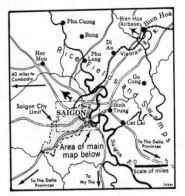

Key to Points of Interest

①	Caravelle Hotel	⑨	Police Headquarters
②	Central Market	⑩	Port of Saigon
③	City Hall	⑪	Presidential Palace
④	Majestic Hotel	⑫	Race Track
⑤	Me Linh Square	⑬	Railroad Station
⑥	National Assembly	⑭	Shipyards
⑦	National Cathedral	⑮	U. S. Embassy
⑧	National Radio Station	⤢	Main roads

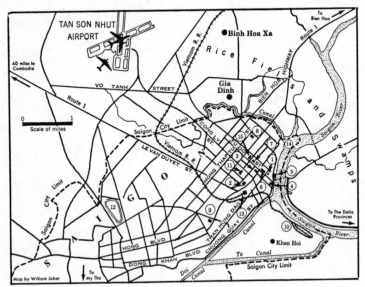

Chapter 14.

The Saigon Take-over

Towards the end of March, revolutionary cadres in Saigon got word to prepare for a seizure of power around May 1. Their main tasks were to neutralize enemy activity to the maximum; prepare to aid the VPA troops as they came in; seize strategic installations—electric power stations, oil depots, gas and water supplies—in order to prevent sabotage; and to do everything to ensure the city be taken intact and with minimum bloodshed. Among those who received the instructions was Huynh Van Tam, member of the NLF's Central Committee and head of its underground trade union organization. For years he had been one of the most "wanted" men in Saigon. A portly figure, with a bland, pock-marked face which fairly exudes optimism and good nature, Huynh Van Tam was popularly known as the "smiling Buddha" when I first met him in Algiers in 1964 (to arrange my second visit to the Liberated Areas). He recalls that he arrived in Algiers to open an NLF Information Bureau, on the same plane as William Porter, the new U.S. Ambassador to Algeria. Porter vainly expended much time and eloquence trying to persuade first, President Ben Bella, later President Boumedienne, to expel the "smiling Buddha," and close down the NLF office. In late 1966, Huynh Van Tam was assigned to return to Saigon to infiltrate and capture, as far possible, the puppet trade union movement. About the same time Porter was also transferred to become the political officer at the U.S. Embassy in Saigon. Having noted the smooth way in which Tam operated to win over most Third World diplomats in Algiers, it is reasonable to assume that it was Porter who spurred on Thieu's agents in their zealous efforts to track him down in Saigon.

"I had many hairbreadth escapes," he told me later. "On nine different occasions the police actually searched houses in which I was hiding." One of the first things he did after receiving instructions to prepare for the seizure of power, was to move into a "more secure and functional command post." This was nothing less than a cellar hide-out in the sumptuous and heavily-guarded headquarters of his greatest enemy, Tran Quoc Buu, one of Thieu's chief henchmen, a leading compradore-capitalist and land-owner, husband of nine wives and, more importantly, boss of the government-run, South Vietnamese Confederation of Labor. He was one of the most closely-guarded persons in the South, escorted wherever he went by a platoon of security guards. (On April 12, Tran Quoc Buu had been appointed head of a five-member governmental Advisory Council, one of Thieu's sops to those who were demanding he step down.)

"It suited me to set up business in Buu's headquarters," said Huynh Van Tam with one of his imperturbable smiles, "because no one was likely to look for me there and the cellar was an excellent place to keep in touch with what was going on in Buu's office on the top floor. Besides it fitted in with our guerillas' policy of 'grabbing the enemy by the belt! .."

In almost nine years of dangerous and difficult work, Huynh Van Tam succeeded in setting up revolutionary organizations, including Lao Dong party cells, in every significant enterprise in the Saigon area. His activists had heavily infiltrated the official trade union movement, including Tran Quoc Buu's headquarters, so successfully that Tam was able to set up his own command post there. Shortly after he moved in, he had in his hands—from the top floor—a far-reaching plan worked out by Tran Quoc Buu's agents, to sabotage main industries and installations in case the unthinkable worst happened and Saigon had to be abandoned.

"We foresaw," Tam explained, "that as the end approached, the puppets would almost certainly clamp down a curfew so that no one but their own sabotage squads could approach the factories. Our activists were told to do their best to stay on inside the factories, even during a curfew, and to seize power there; otherwise to try to seize power in their residential areas. By the 27th, detailed anti-sabotage measures had been received from factory organizations and were either approved or modified. A curfew *did* go into effect on the 28th, but most of our activists in the factories were able to bluff the managers by interpreting this to mean they must not even move out into the streets to go home. In the confusion they got away with it, and started to put the anti-sabotage measures into effect on the night of the 29th. Mines were dug up and defused; plastic explosive charges removed; agents charged with setting fire to fuel depots were 'neutralized'; other sabotage squads—none of them very enthusiastic—were either talked out of doing their work, or dealt with in some other way. The power plants, water works, oil and gas depots and other key installations were occupied by our people. By 10:30 a.m. on the 30th, when 'Big' Minh said he was ready to surrender, our organizations had taken over almost all the factories and a certain number of city districts. By 2:00 p.m., Peoples Revolutionary Committees had been set up in all city districts and precincts. Their primary task was to round up saboteurs and units of armed workers' militia stood guard at every factory and public utility installation. On that same evening, we were able to hand over to the city's Military Management Committee an inventory of all factories, installations, equipment and stocks of raw materials. Despite the curfew from April 28 and the May Day holiday, life returned to its normal rhythm on May 2. Victory was thus complete in all fields. Factories and public utilities had been seized intact; people's revolutionary power was established down to precinct levels."

There were those who claimed to be eyewitnesses in Saigon on April 30 who denied there had been any people's uprisings because there were no masses storming through the streets with muskets and butchers' knives—not even a replay of an assault on the counterpart of Leningrad's Winter Palace during the Bolshevik Revolution, although it was a VPA tank which smashed down the gates and led the way into the President's Palace! To admit a people's uprising would be to spoil the myth of the "invasion from the North." Also, it was impossible from Saigon's fashionable hotels to observe the quiet, well organized seizure of such substantial attributes of power as the industrial infrastructure that went on at every enterprise of any importance on the night of April 29-30.

Incidentally, the storming of the Winter Palace and the

crashing through the gates of Saigon's "Independence Palace," symbolized two diametrically different revolutionary strategies, each based on the concrete conditions of the respective societies. Storming the Winter Palace was the starting signal for a long, complex revolutionary war. Hoisting the NLF flag over Independence Palace marked the end of a still longer one. One revolution was based on the urban proletariat, the most revolutionary force in semi-industrialized, Tsarist Russia. The other was based on the rural peasantry, the main revolutionary force in predominantly agricultural and semi-feudal Vietnam. After the Winter Palace was seized and revolutionary power established in the cities, a Red Army had to be built up; the countryside liberated; the forces of counter-revolution and foreign intervention defeated in years of cruel, armed struggle. In Vietnam, a powerful, people's army was built up, based on a revolution in the countryside; its armed forces gradually encircling the cities to bring about that final fruition of the workers-peasants alliance. While the peasant armies shattered the bastions of military and administrative power, the urban workers took over the factories and centers of local power.

At the moment of victory, Huynh Van Tam moved out of his cellar to take over Tran Quoc Buu's offices on the top floor. Buu fled to the United States with his nine wives, the foreign reserves of the Nam Hai bank, which he owned, and everything else of easily transportable value on which he could lay his hands. (The suddenness of the collapse, however, forced him to abandon some 8 million dollars' worth of raw materials for his various enterprises!)

How was the NLF and Lao Dong party able to work inside the enemy's trade union movement and, at least partially, transform it from within to their own revolutionary weapon? The reason goes back to the time the NLF was formed and it was decided that although the main struggle would be in the countryside, when the final stage of people's war would be reached the cities must be seized. (In the anti-French resistance war, the stage of encirclement of the cities was also reached but the 1954 Geneva Agreement avoided the necessity of the final phase of seizing them by force.) To do this, the urban working class must play a leading role. After long discussions, it was agreed to work within the existing trade union movement.

"It was only because of fierce struggles waged by the working class that trade unions had even been set up," said Huynh

Van Tam, explaining what was the consensus of NLF and Lao Dong party opinion at the time. "Despite the enemy attempt to control them; despite the attempt to corrupt and divide the workers and infiltrate their ranks, the trade unions were objectively organs of the working class and not of the enemy. Because of this we were able to move into them and lead a struggle on two fronts. For better working conditions—the questions of wages and hours, of unjust dismissal and of democracy, the right of workers to elect their own leaders. But we also advocated struggle against the régime itself to prepare the way for an eventual seizure of power. We did not want to fall into the trap of reformism. The struggle on these two fronts had to go hand-in-hand, but with much discretion on the second point. Political consciousness at the lower levels was not sufficiently developed to accept sudden demands for the overthrow of the régime. We had one consistent, long-term strategy—advance the cause of the workers bit by bit; weaken the enemy bit by bit. Gradually the workers gained confidence in our activists who they saw were sincerely and courageously fighting for their day-to-day interests.

"There were many fierce struggles. Workers' leaders were arrested but good political struggles developed around demands for their release. Gradually we built up organizations in every factory, leaders and activists protected by the rank and file workers. It was this that led to April 29-30. Our struggle to win over the Saigon working class was part of the overall revolutionary struggle. It could be compared to a kettle of water on a slow stove. It may take half an hour to heat up, but suddenly within seconds there is a great commotion—and it boils. There is a radical transformation—water changes into steam."

Working within company unions, solidly controlled by the government, obviously had its complications. Huynh Van Tam cited the dilemma of dealing with the situation at the big Thu Duc electric power plant, where no less than one third of the 4,500 workers were police agents. Not just low-level informers, but taken off their normal work to attend agents' training courses and then returned to spy on their fellow-workers. "How were we to regard them?" asked Tam. "On the one hand, they were well-trained police agents camouflaged as ordinary workers; on the other, they took part in production so they were part of the working class. We decided to treat them as such but to work on them to reduce the enemy part of their activity; to win them back to their class viewpoint and also to arouse their sense of national pride. The results were quite good and some of them revealed the plans which we already knew about—to sabotage their plant."

He related another type of problem. At a naval repair yard which also had 4,500 workers on its payroll, only 2,000 actually worked there. The rest were registered because, as it was considered war work, they were exempt from military service. The boss pocketed their wages; the workers eked out a living as best they could, happy to have avoided military service. "What were we to do with 2,500 registered workers who knew nothing about ship-building or repairs? It was a racket, but on the other hand the workers had done this to avoid taking up arms against the people. We kept them on the payroll; gave them technical training and educated them at the same time on class and national questions. We must rely on such working-class elements and maintain vigilance, but not be sectarian about past activities under such abnormal conditions," said Huynh Van Tam.

There were only two cases in which sabotage of any importance was carried out. In neither case was this the result of workers' negligence. Three shells were fired into a 60,000-watt generator at the Thu Duc power plant but the damage was repaired within a week. A bridge pylon was damaged by electrically-detonated underwater explosives. It was repaired within a month. On the other hand, workers removed and defused many hundreds of mines—twenty from Vinatexco textile plant alone. Scores of tons of explosives were removed from other factories, power plants and oil depots. The utter failure of elaborately-conceived sabotage plans was an aspect of the "people's uprisings" which was obviously invisible to outside onlookers. Huynh Van Tam touched on another aspect—the failure of elaborately-conceived U.S. economic policies.

"From the time the Americans entered into negotiations in Paris" he said, "we learned in Saigon that they thought the 'worst' that could emerge would be a three-way coalition government with separate administrative zones controlled by Saigon and the PRG. Vietnam would thus be split in three instead of two, North Vietnam and two South Vietnams. In such a case economic confrontation would become the main battlefield. With their enormous financial, economic and technical superiority, the Americans were convinced that they could make nonsense out of whatever help the socialist world could give the PRG-controlled areas; or to the North which they considered had been sufficiently smashed to bits by their air power to retard economic development for a generation. By injecting vast quantities of dollars and industrial technique into the Saigon-controlled areas, they would create such prosperity as would smother any desire for reunification with the North. Nor would they have to fear any results of an electoral contest with the PRG in the South. While their political counterparts kept negotiations in Paris bogged down on the 'shape of the table' argument, U.S. economic experts worked on plans for a post-war 'economic miracle' for the South, based on industrialization at an advanced technological level.

"Politically, they wanted to create an economic base for a national and compradore-capitalist class and use it against the working class. They aimed at building up a capitalist class with a strong vested interest against any collaboration with the revolution in the South or any idea of reunification with the North. To this end, the United States invested some 12 billion dollars in building up industries and an infrastructure of roads and power plants to serve them. All of this from 1968 onwards, and all of it now in our hands, intact. So, while we still feel great hatred towards the Americans for all the suffering and irreparable destruction they inflicted on our country and we despise them for their intentions, which were the most perfidious possible, we have to feel somewhat thankful for the immense war booty, in terms of industrial equipment alone, that they had to abandon when we booted them out. It is now at the disposal of the Revolution and the needs of the whole of Vietnam."

Saigon now has some 500 big industrial plants geared to employ, when in full production, from 500 to 5,000 workers each, a total of about 300,000 industrial workers. Among some of the new factories is a polyester fibre plant, more sophisticated than any in the socialist world and most of those in the western world; an ultra-modern, Chicago-type pork processing plant where the pigs march in one end of the production line and come out on the assembly belts as anything from bristles to bacon; a pharmaceutical plant capable of supplying all-Vietnam needs in a very wide range of medicines; a fish refrigeration plant of huge capacity which deep freezes to below 50° (C) below zero; textile plants with an annual capacity of 250-300 million meters; various chemical, cellulose and paper-producing plants, and many others. All of them are very modern by world standards. Based on cheap labor, as in South Korea, the Americans had intended them not only to create a capitalist class absolutely dependent on the U.S.A., but to exploit them to flood the Asian markets with a wide range of goods at prices no other country could match. In Vietnamese hands, they would be used as a short cut to higher living standards for the whole people. I asked about qualified technical personnel and Huynh Van Tam replied with a big smile:

"The Americans trained the personnel to run these plants, many of them in similar factories in the U.S. Almost 99 percent of them have remained behind here. Probably a proportion would have left in the general stampede but the collapse was too swift and they were not the people to have either high priorities or big purses. They are a most valuable asset to us because of the high proportion of U.S. equipment. Some were trained as police agents as well, but we know who they are and they know that we know! We are used to handling such people; we know how to arouse their class spirit, their pride in the country and a vision of the future—their own and that of the country. The great majority of them sincerely want to contribute to making our country strong and prosperous. Even at the training establishments and factories in the United States, they got a feeling of the great prestige our country enjoys in the outside world. It is not difficult to arouse national pride these days, even among those who were our enemies!"

He conceded that supply of raw materials was something of a problem, as most of the plants were geared to U.S. parent-factories and depended on U.S. raw materials. "We can substitute some of this ourselves," Tam said, "we are already looking for suitable cotton-growing land, for example. Many other raw materials we can find in the socialist countries or through normal trade exchanged with friendly Third World or other countries. Our policy is also to normalize relations with the United States, but if the American leadership doesn't want this; if they insist on maintaining an economic boycott—so much the worse for them. We will find alternative sources and they will suffer one more defeat." His smile developed into a chuckle when I asked what had happened to the owners of all the new industries.

"That's where the Americans are really marvelous," he said. "They scared them all into running away. Ford with his predictions of 'blood baths'; Schlesinger with a 'million to be massacred;" Kissinger on the same line. We could have an inventory of factories, equipment and raw materials within a few hours, but not of the owners. It took us several days to realize that at least 70 percent of them had fled. They had the priorities and the big purses! We were forced to start administering, from the very first days, the greater part of Saigon's industry. We ought to send a vote of thanks to Ford, Schlesinger and Kissinger for their services to the Revolution!"

Thus, when most of the factories opened their doors again on May 2, they were under new management hastily improvised by the city's Military Management Committee. State control over the greater part of South Vietnam's industry was an imperative imposed by U.S. policy, the result of just one more colossal miscalculation by policy-makers who seemed incapable of ever seeing further than the end of their noses. The PRG had formulated most careful policies based on the expectation of capitalist ownership of industry and a coalition government in which national capitalists would have had their fair representation. That the most and best of private industry would fall into their laps on April 30 was the last thing that the PRG leadership—or that in Hanoi—had expected. For the factory-owners who remained, the new administration offered favorable terms for continuing their actvities and for state-private cooperation in running any enterprise which could contribute to the national well-being. Such industries were provided with capital, raw materials and encouragement to expand on a state-private enterprise partnership. A typical example of the latter such arrangement concerned a brand-new and very large plant for the manufacture of glucose and condensed milk which had not even entered production by April 30, but the proprietor of which had not fled. After three months of negotiations, mainly on the proportions of state-private control, agreement was reached on expanded operations on a 50-50 capital participation basis. Production then got under way on a scale almost sufficient to supply the whole of Vietnam's needs for glucose and condensed milk.

On September 2, the 30th anniversary of the setting up of the Democratic Republic of Vietnam and the first official celebration of the liberation of the South, Premier Pham Van Dong made an important speech in Hanoi in which, among other things, he addressed himself to owners of private enterprise in the South:

> We call on the national capitalists, who were formerly held back by foreign competitors, to put all their talents and ar-

dor at the service of the great cause of the nation now that our country has become independent and free . . . On the basis of an economic plan for the whole country, Ho Chi Minh City will have an important role in many respects and will broaden its foreign relations with countries in Southeast Asia and the rest of the world . . .

A more precise definition of the attitude towards the national capitalists was spelt out in a decree, signed by Prime Minister Huynh Tan Phat on September 10, 1975, dealing with measures to aid the national capitalists and hamper the activities of the compradore-capitalists and others guilty of speculation, black marketeering and hoarding of goods. Basic economic policy was defined as:

> To push ahead with the setting up of national enterprises in all sectors of the economy which can serve as a solid base for an increase in production; to strengthen the availability of goods, their distribution and the stabilization of the market, and to guarantee the people's livelihood.

> To encourage and help the national capitalists, small enterprises, handicrafts and small merchants to develop industry and trade useful to themselves and the national ecomony.

> To punish the compradore-capitalists who have continued until now to practice illicit hoarding; to disrupt the markets thus harming production and our people's daily life and preventing the onward march of our society.[45]

There followed a 14-point guideline for the application of these policies, six of which dealt with the type of aid and support available to the private sector. Briefly, the State would encourage and provide material aid to capitalists to step up production and expand their enterprises. The "right to ownership of their property and legitimate interests will be guaranteed by the State." Those owners who abandoned their properties and fled must have bitten their fingernails if they ever saw this document! But it was too late. They had made their choice and there was no question of their enterprises being restored to them. The State would also help private industry by providing raw mate-

---

45. The term "compradore" is usually associated with Chinese who served as intermediaries between the first western traders in Asia (in China they were at first not allowed ashore) and local merchants. Some made huge fortunes and went into business—mainly trading—by themselves, hence the term "compradore-capitalists."

rials and finding markets, and would also "associate its capital with that of capitalists desirous of contributing their capital, raw materials and technical 'know-how' to build up the economy." In the case of such mixed enterprises the State, while retaining the last word in overall management, would also "guarantee to the capitalists the right to participate in management, and to the distribution of appropriate profits." The State would also encourage and aid capitalists "who contribute their capital, technology and capabilities in building up the new economic zones."[46]

The compradore capitalists however, were clearly in for a bad time. Point 10 of the guidelines stated:

> Those who are guilty of hoarding and trying to control the economy; who disrupt the market and ally themselves with counter-revolutionaries, will be arrested and, according to the gravity of their crimes, will be punished and their fortunes may be wholly or partially confiscated.

In a discussion with Prime Minister Huynh Tan Phat, a few hours before he signed the decree, he explained that a sharp dis-

---

46. The term "new economic zones" usually refers to vast tracts of either virgin lands which, according to official figures of the former Saigon régime, amount to 7.5 million acres (3 million hectares) including 1.75 million acres (700,000 hectares) in the former guerilla base known as the Plain of Reeds which stretches from My Tho province northwest to the Cambodian border and 750,000 acres (300,000 hectares) of "abandoned lands" from which peasants had fled due to the "urbanization" bombings. The PRG offered special facilities—six months free rice and a small daily subsidy, help in building housing etcetera—to volunteers for the "new economic zones." Tens of thousands of demobbed soldiers and urban unemployed left Saigon and other big cities to build up a new pioneering life in these areas which in a few years will make a substantial contribution to the country's agricultural production. (The master plan provided for 800,000 people, 320,000 of them "activists", the rest family members, from Saigon to migrate to the "new economic zones", mostly in the Mekong Delta. In North Vietnam, an appeal was launched for 150,000 volunteers to open up virgin lands in the Central Highlands. This caused some American anti-war activists to mistakenly denounce "forced deportation of urban Vietnamese". It has been officially stressed by the Vietnamese leadership that this "de-urbanization" can only succeed if it is done on a voluntary basis. It is obvious that, compared to the sacrifices made during the war years and the feeling that most Vietnamese have for the land, this large movement of population will pose no great problem. A big movement in the North from the unhealthy swamp lands of the Red River delta to the highlands which started in the early 1960's was interrupted by the war.)

tinction was made between compradore and national capitalists. "The compadore-capitalists," he said, "controlled everything from purchasing to transportation and distribution of all commodities. They created great disorder in the market and plenty of difficulties for us. They act in their own financial interests but at the same time for the political interests of the U.S.A. and Taiwan. The Americans base their plans for sabotaging our economy on these people. We have to admit that we still don't have any organization capable of running economic affairs, especially marketing. It is not like most other fields in which we can improve on an existing administration. The Americans and their puppets, like the French and theirs, were quite content to let the Chinese compradores run economic affairs—virtually everything connected with supply and marketing was a closed compradore-capitalist world."

By withholding goods from the markets, the compradores created sudden shortages and price increases, inexplicable except by deliberate sabotage. A couple of weeks before the decree on economic affairs, the price of cigarettes from locally produced tobacco jumped three-fold overnight. That was the economic side of it. The political side was that rumors spread like wildfire in the Saigon market that the shortage of cigarettes was because Hanoi had commandeered all stocks and "shipped them to the North!" In the small hours of the morning on which the decree was announced, security forces swooped down on some of the most notorious Cholon compradores, including "Tobacco King", Siou Phong, listed as one of the nine main inner-ring compradores. Enormous stocks of tobacco and cigarettes were found in his warehouses. I was in Saigon's big central market on the day of the decree and the raids. It was fascinating to watch the prices being marked down by stall-holders as the radio announced the results of various raids on the warehouses. Down came the prices of textiles, by 30 to 60 percent when it was announced that in the warehouses of "Textile King", La Nghia, over 4 million meters of cotton, wool and silk cloth had been found, as well as 300 sewing machines which had virtually disappeared from the market. The go-downs of "Rice King", Ma Hi, were found to be bulging with sacks of rice. Multi-millionaire Ma Hi (his fortune was estimated at about 300 million U.S. dollars) had badly miscalculated with his hoarded rice, however! Peasants in the Liberated Zones had been encouraged to produce rice far in excess of their own needs ever since the

Paris Agreement. It was stocked away for just such an occasion as the liberation of Saigon by one means or another. Rice convoys followed hard on the heels of the armed forces during the final offensive and within 48 hours of the NLF flag being unfurled over the presidential palace, there was an abundance of rice on the Saigon market. For the first few weeks it was distributed free to the needy, on the basis of lists prepared by the local street committees. Later it was sold at below market prices through a network of state shops. So Ma Hi, who by that time was in Taiwan, did not make his expected profits on an artificially-created rice famine. Each of the compradore "kings", however, had his own monopoly, and between them they controlled every aspect of purchasing in the countryside and marketing in Saigon and other main cities.

"What was missing in the markets was found in the hoarders' warehouses," commented *Giai Phong*, (Saigon's Liberation Daily) after the first day's raids. "Huge stocks of grain, all types of food products, textiles, medicines—not to mention gold and diamonds." Replying the following day to a reader's query as to what a compradore-capitalist was, the paper explained:

> Compradores belong to the capitalist class. But they are to be distinguished from other capitalists and business people. What is typical of compradore-capitalists is that they always play a political, as well as an economic, role and always collaborate with imperialists and occupiers. They live off the misfortunes of the people, especially in time of war. They are profiteers of treason, the closest collaborators of the puppets. They emptied the markets of daily necessities to line their own pockets, but also to create political difficulties.

If the authorities waited over four months before cracking down on the compradores, putting up with all the consequences and discontent because of shortages and rising prices coupled with widespread rumors that "everything has been shipped North", it was partly because of the usual habit of studying all aspects of a problem very carefully before deciding on the solution. It was also because they wanted to have an overall economic policy which took into account all the bounties which had fallen into their hands and an embryo marketing organization to replace that of the compradores. In the days that followed the anti-compradore measures—which brought immediate relief to the whole population—Saigon's network of pharmacies received a wide range of medicines to be sold at fixed prices. A few days later, a cut-off date was announced, after which gasoline could be bought only through a state distribution network at prices far less than those on the "free" market. A certain amount of order began to be injected into the chaotic marketing system which the PRG had inherited and which had nothing in common with the revolutionary concept that service to the people should be the primary aim of economic activities.

"In the interests of the Vietnamese people," Huynh Van Tam explained, "and because of the objective requirements of the present era, we need to follow the socialist way. The realities of the situation in South Vietnam are such that they leave us no option but to take the socialist road, but we will do it in our own way which may be different to that of other countries." He referred to the fact that the majority of the people in the towns, including "large sections of the working class", had been educated to believe that their class interests "were identical to those of the bourgeoisie. The puppets carried on a national class struggle in their own interests and prejudiced people very strongly against anything remotely connected with communism or socialism," he said, "but the people now see that everything the State does is clearly in their interests and if that is what socialism is, they are beginning to say, 'Let's have more of it' . . ."

To a certain extent, one could say that just as the United States, in the long, drawn-out negotiations and the non-application of the Paris Agreement, closed all doors to anything but battlefield solutions, so also in the economic field by scaring most of the capitalists into flight and encouraging their compradore-capitalists allies to sabotage the economy, they slammed the doors to all but socialist solutions!

Chapter 15.

Order out of Chaos

"Saigon used to be known as the Pearl of the Orient. What we found was one great heap of garbage." This is how Dr. Nguyen Van Thu, in charge of public health and social affairs at the Saigon Military Management Committee, described the situation at the moment of the capital's liberation. "The public health services that did exist, were there to serve the wealthy," he continued. "Health services as they are usually conceived existed in only 4 of Saigon's 21 districts. In hospitals, for instance, there was no isolation of infectious disease patients from others in the same wards. Prophylactic medicine was non-existent. We found all sorts of epidemic diseases when we arrived, including cholera, typhoid, plague—not to mention venereal disease and drug addicts—especially those on heroin. According to old statistics which we are starting to update, over 3 percent of the Saigon troops were heroin addicts (much less than the rate among U.S. troops, W. B.) and 5 percent of the students, half of them girls. There were 130,000 drug addicts in Saigon alone and between 100,000 and 300,000 prostitutes. The latter figure is still difficult to determine because of the large number of part-time practitioners. There were also about 300,000 thieves and pick-pockets and 280,000 orphans of all colors, fathered by Americans—black and white—Australians, Thailandese, Filipinos, Koreans and Taiwan Chinese—all left unprovided for. This was part of the heritage of the U.S.-Saigon régime.

"To complicate the security problem still further," continued Dr. Thu, an old acquaintance from my wartime visits, "7,000 common law criminals took advantage of the flight of their guards on the night of the 29th, to break out of prison. On the following day, the streets were littered with discarded arms. Of course they went for the pistols and revolvers. Up till now, 300,000 soldiers and officers of the Saigon army have registered since April 30 and turned in their weapons but there still are a lot of side-arms unaccounted for. Still, the clean up so far enables us on this 88th day of Liberation (our discussion took place on July 28, a few days after my arrival in Ho Chi Minh city, W.B.) to walk around in comparative security...

"We had to deal with mountains of garbage," explained Dr. Nguyen Van Thu. "None had been collected for two weeks prior to Liberation. In some of the garbage heaps there were plague-infected rats. There was a scandalous shortage of garbage trucks—120 to serve a city whose population had swollen to three and a half-million. It was only due to the spontaneous aid of the people, especially students and other youngsters, that the streets are reasonably clean. We are trying not only to increase the number of garbage trucks, but to heighten people's consciousness about public health."

Two-thirds of the population had already been innoculated against cholera, plague and typhoid—and the work was continuing. Epidemic diseases were already under control, except hemorrhagic fever—transmitted by a non-malarial mosquito—which was still causing trouble (as I was to discover to my cost a few weeks later when I came down with this dangerous malady). Security forces and local people's organizations were carrying on a vigorous campaign against narcotics, but as Dr. Thu expressed it: "It is much easier to locate the drug addicts than the source of their heroin." Clearing up venereal disease was not so much a problem with the professional prostitutes as with the "secretly operating amateurs, wives of officers and soldiers who are on the streets and the biggest spreaders of disease." Those infected were supposed to present themselves voluntarily for free treatment, but the public also informed about cases they knew about. Because of rising food prices, Dr. Thu said: "There are many cases when patients don't want to leave the hospitals when cured—they may have to go hungry." He added that one positive aspect was a changed attitude among the Saigon doctors. "They used to treat only those who could pay well. But now, influenced by the correct attitude of our medical staff, they make no distinction between rich and poor. Before, you had to bribe everyone from the clinic or hospital doorkeeper to the doctors—and all in between—to get service. Now there are no more bribes. Perhaps a few discreet gifts of chocolate or a bottle of whisky, but there's real progress in this. After the VPA entered Saigon, doctors started going into the poorer suburbs where people are now getting medical service for the first time."

I asked how they managed for medical supplies, especially as a much higher proportion of the population was now getting medical treatment.

"There will be a real shortage of medicines in the months to come," he replied. "We have brought in our experience from the Liberated Zones, using traditional medicines and combining them with western medicines. But we are very short of the latter; short of doctors and medical personnel in general and especially short of anti-biotics, polyvitamins and medicines for treating malaria and liver complaints associated with chronic malaria. Because most medicines came from the U.S.A., the abrupt American withdrawal and drying up of medical supplies should have had an unfavorable effect on public health. In fact it didn't because we considered public health as a priority problem. Though massive innoculations—in keeping with our stress on prophylactic medicine—and by bringing medical care down to the poorer people who are the overwhelming majority of Saigon residents, we have brought some order into the chronic chaos of public health here. In this we were greatly helped by medical supplies from friendly countries."

I asked if he could make a comparison between the state of health in the Liberated Zones and that as he had found it in Saigon.

"In the rear areas, people's health was not too good due to lack of nutritive food and the fact that we only had a limited range of medicines. But even there, the standard of health was much higher than among the poor in Saigon-Gia Dinh because of over-crowded housing conditions, chronic malnutrition and the total lack of medical attention. I don't speak about the wealthy who had good food, good housing and access to medical attention. But even young men here from wealthy families, because they led an unhealthy life—too many drugs and night clubs—are narrow-chested, lethargic and somewhat effeminate compared to the sturdy, full-chested young men you find in the old Liberated Zones."

Regarding the many limbless ex-soldiers one saw in the streets—mostly in delapidated Saigon uniforms, Dr. Thu said:

"We have set up small factories to make artificial limbs and trained cadres to educate those that need them in their use—in batches of 300 at a time. Then we teach them trades according to their physical capacities—tailoring, typewriting, weaving, operating foot treadle machines—trades for those that can use their hands but not their legs, and vice versa. We had plenty of experience of this in rehabilitating bomb victims in the old Liberated areas."

In response to a question as to the proportion of doctors and medical students who had left for the United States at the time of the panic exodus, Dr. Thu replied: "Two-thirds of the students from the dental college left. The curriculum there was the same as in the United States and they were assured they could get good jobs there. At the medical faculty it was different because it was mainly staffed by the French. The French stayed on when the Americans fled, and so did their students. About 10 percent of all university teachers and professors fled—not as many as the Americans would have liked."

As he was also responsible for social affairs, I asked Dr. Thu how they had coped with the problem of the 7,000 armed jailbreakers.

"It was quite a problem at first," he replied. "They started committing common law crimes immediately. Hold-ups went on day and night. They were well-armed and usually worked in pairs on motorscooters, using snatch-and-grab tactics. They drove quite skillfully, weaving their way rapidly through the traffic after each attack, and generally got away with it. We had brought no police force into the city and we never had one in the Liberated Areas. Security was looked after by the local people. We never even had anyone to direct traffic—that's why you still see students doing it. Our troops were inexperienced and had orders to be impeccably correct with people. At first they fired at some of the criminals making their getaway, sometimes wounding civilians. Then we developed a technique. The moment a crime was spotted, a signal shot was fired and all traffic halted. People had to lay down on the footpaths. Those speeding away on their motorscooters were isolated. If they stopped also, or lay down on the footpaths, they were arrested by the public. There was no longer any sympathy with law-breakers as before. Of the 7,000, two thirds have been re-captured, including all the ringleaders. The rest are not very active but it's better to be vigilant in the streets at night."

Finally I asked Dr. Nguyen Van Thu whether he had brought into Saigon the pharmaceutical factories which he had helped set up in the jungle with U.S. petrol drums converted in-to sterilizers; pigs' entrails used as plastic tubing; bicycles on stands pedalled to generate light for emergency operations and scores of other such improvisations.

"No," he said with a smile, "but in general the personnel from those plants are now in Saigon. It is difficult for them to adapt from guerilla pharmaceutical production to the most ad-vanced forms. We have problems of mastering technology and management, but when these are overcome, we have very fa-vorable conditions to provide a very wide range of medicines for the whole of Vietnam. The question is how to make the best use of the very advanced equipment in new plants which the Americans had no time to destroy." Remarking that some val-uable equipment had been inadvertently damaged due to enthu-siastic, but inexperienced, guerilla personnel trying to put them into production, Dr. Thu mused:

"Carrying on the war was difficult, but trying to run a state even more so. We will continue mainly on the line of self-reli-ance as we have always had to do. But we are also going to need plenty of aid from outside."

A fact that all outsiders recognized, and none more com-pletely than those journalists who stayed on, was that life in Sai-gon was normalized very quickly. Order and security was es-tablished almost overnight and there was a smooth transition of power that astonished the world and confounded the high-level prophets of bloody disaster. In a 90-minute discussion with Prime Minister Huynh Tan Phat, part of which is referred to earlier, I asked why things had been normalized so rapidly and without any violent shocks.

"It may have appeared that way, but in fact we had plenty of problems," he said. "The fact that victory was achieved so rapidly had many advantages. We could seize important eco-nomic installations intact, great quantities of material all in an excellent state. But the very fact that victory was so complete also had its disadvantages. Even the fact that the enemy forces disintegrated and collapsed—but were not wiped out—objectively was a disadvantage. We had to establish revolutionary rule, but in a way appropriate to real conditions. We had won; the adversary was wiped out and we had plenty of divisions here to control the situation. But it is not only military force that counts—to think so was a fundamental error of the Americans and their puppets. It is political power that is decisive. Because of the nature of the régime and just because we had won so rapidly there was insufficient time to have adequate base organizations in the cities. We had élite vanguard forces among the working class but not broadly based organizations."

He went on to explain that while it was possible to build up, and maintain, conspiratorial groups such as Huynh Van Tam had organized, these worked within a legitimate trade union organization, whereas the degree of police surveillance was such that it was quite another matter for the NLF to try to maintain its own basic political organizations. While the conspiratorial groups were adequate when the moment came to seize power, they could not be the base for setting up an administration. There were, for example, districts in Saigon inhabited entirely by families of the puppet army. There was a belt encircling the city in which the residents were almost exclusively Catholics who had fled the North in 1954-1955, installed there on American advice as a sort of outer defense line to prevent the infiltration of revolutionary forces. In such places it had been impossible to develop any political bases because the population cooperated with the repressive system of house and family surveillance. After Liberation there was no problem about going into such areas with military force, but that was not the way to do it. It would have been a confession of political weakness.

There was also the problem of the 300,000 demobbed regular troops in the Saigon area, not counting paramilitary units. Part of them had not immediately laid down their arms. "They went underground," said Prime Minister Phat, "awaiting the chance to turn their arms against us. They were still under the influence of their reactionary superior officers. We could have gone in with a big stick, cordoned off the city, divided it up into sectors and conducted house searches, block by block. We had plenty of armed strength to do this. But we had to take into account the state of mind of the population. They had had enough of that sort of thing; they wanted an end to bloodshed. Their most heartfelt desire was for peace and an end to repression. How could we rally the population to our side by arbitrary measures of force? In any case, our fundamental policy was that of peace and national reconciliation. We intended to remain faithful to this. There was no contradiction between our policies and the people's yearning for an end to violence and the start of a truly democratic life. On the other hand we had to consolidate our authority."

The result was a step-by-step "soft" approach. The idea was to peel off layer after layer of the reactionary forces, isolating each from the other and separating the hard-core reactionary forces from the more malleable and potentially progressive elements at the lower levels. The first phase of this war was to call for the voluntary registration and turning-in of arms of the 300,000 officers and men known to be at large in the Saigon area.

"It was a non-violent way of doing it that the public could approve," Prime Minister Huynh Tan Phat said, "and it enabled us to separate the most stubborn and reactionary elements from the others. Also to disarm the majority of those who had retained their firearms. After registration, came the reorientation courses and here again, we were discriminatory. For the rank-and-file and NCO's, we gave courses of three or four days to explain what the war was all about as far as we were concerned; the difference between our aims and those of the puppets; what were to be the future tasks in building up a happy and prosperous future. After that they could return to their families. We won the overwhelming majority of those over to our cause with no friction at all. For the junior officers—second lieutenants to captains—the political courses lasted three to four weeks and were associated with some productive labor. After that the great majority were set free. This meant, as with the rank-and-file, that their full civil rights were restored and it was formally forbidden for anyone to refer to them as 'puppets.' We detained those who were really stubborn and unrepentant. These were proportionately very few—arrogant and unpopular with their fellow officers in the courses. They needed further re-education, and by hanging on to them we kept the most harmful and reactionary elements out of circulation."

After that, it was the mainly reactionary medium and senior officers—the majors, colonels and generals—who were left. They were given longer courses, the length depending on their attitudes, and were "out of circulation" during the period of consolidation of revolutionary power. It was obvious that the setting up of Military Management Committees at the top in

Saigon and a few other cities was to handle such problems and other aspects of public security with the necessary authority and power. In fact, this method meant that a broad amnesty had been granted. There were no such things as POW camps, nor any punishment or reprisals, in a formal sense, but a sincere effort to win over officers, many of whom had committed abominable crimes against their own people, to a state of mind in which they could become useful members of society. It was an amnesty associated with sufficient explanations and reorientation to create, as the prime minister expressed it, "favorable conditions for them to return to the ranks of the people." Doubtless the senior officers considered it "punishment" to have to attend such courses and to have to take part in productive labor. And of course they were under detention. But it was a punishment infinitely lighter than they had expected, or to that which they had been used to meting out to revolutionaries who fell into their clutches. And after a month or two, even the senior officers could end their detention and return to their own families if they showed that they sincerely regretted their past activities and were ready to use their talents in the work of national reconstruction. Prime Minister Phat considered that this method of tackling the problem had gained much prestige for the PRG. (Later, it was revealed that about 50,000 would be detained for upwards of three years—a large number but just five percent of the million whom former U.S. Defense Secretary Schlesinger and others predicted would be physically liquidated. The aim, as stated by the Vietnamese leadership, was not to punish but to integrate the 50,000 "hard-liners" into the realities of a Vietnamese society taking the socialist road.)

"It took the wind out of the sails of just those people whom the enemy wanted to work up against us," he said. "Because of the way we handled this, people understood much better that our policies were just and reasonable, and that there was no discrepancy between what we said and what we did. We gained people's confidence through this more than any other measure and it was largely due to this that we were able to normalize the overall situation so quickly. We had to restore order so as to normalize life. In doing it the way we did, we gave the lie to enemy propaganda about 'blood baths.' We recognized that the people in the cities were very much under the influence of the enemy. They didn't know much about us or our policies but our handling of the defeated enemy troops was a major breakthrough in gaining popular support. Once we had that, we could aim at the hard-liners among enemy officers and neutralize them. A decisive element in this was to mobilize the people also in struggling against the toughest, most reactionary elements who were prepared to continue to act against the revolution and the people's interests. Only by mobilizing and organizing the masses of the people could we consolidate power at all levels. This we did at 'phuong' and 'kham' (*phuong* is the lowest administrative unit in the cities, and *kham* is a neighborhood or street committee, W.B.) levels, which are the most important, constituting the real base of power."

With the military forces strong enough to deal with any emergency and a people's power structure building up from the street level, the prime minister said that the people themselves started to expose the hard-core, armed reactionaries who had hoped to carry on some sort of urban resistance, including the formation of "death squads" which the CIA had organized in some Latin American countries. "It was the people who knew where such elements were hiding out, but until they saw our strength and our just policies, they were too terrorized to take action," Prime Minister Phat said. "The time came when people in the neighborhood units started denouncing them or simply arrested them and turned them over to us. It would have been impossible for us to ferret them out and break up their organizations. With the people taking the initiative into their own hands it was done quickly and smoothly. This was a powerful factor in getting life back to normal. Without street-level support," Huynh Tan Phat insisted, "things would have been infinitely more difficult. For the first few months, when we had no police here, it was the young people, mainly students, who ensured order. The puppets had a very powerful police machine but they were incapable of ensuring public order. The young people did this in a few days, but only because of street level support. The people cooperated voluntarily and wholeheartedly. They knew these young people, but they didn't know us, so they were somewhat mistrustful of us at the beginning."

Speaking of the role of the intellectuals, Prime Minister Phat said that the majority quickly understood and appreciated PRG policies and this was true also of those known as the "Third Force," although, he added, the term was a misnomer. "The 'Third Force' could exist and have a role only as long as the enemy existed," he said. "It was comprised of patriots in opposition to the Thieu dictatorship, but it was not very strong, not a real 'force.' They have correctly judged our policies in action and, without any pressure from us, they have rallied to our side. This has been a big help in achieving national unity and reconciliation, which is our common goal." He considered that the counter-revolutionary forces were without any political base and thus very weak. They had counted on support from the Catholics who had come from the North, but the latter had become more and more divided, many having changed their political tendencies. The rank and file had been badly exploited by the Americans and the Thieu régime, many of them working in slave labor conditions inferior to those of local Vietnamese. "They see that we are against exploitation of any section of the population and that we are really for national unity," the prime minister said. "For the majority of the Catholics from the North, the agents of the Americans and the old régime have been completely discredited."

On the economic side, he said, there were plenty of difficulties which opponents had used "to sow dissensions and direct the discontent against us," and that although many very important enterprises had been taken over, they had been based on U.S. finance, raw materials, fuel and equipment. The new régime had inherited a total of 3.5 million unemployed for the whole of the South. Before Liberation there had been 1.5 million unemployed, but the figure had rapidly swelled, partly because of the U.S. withdrawal and cutbacks in dollar aid, but mainly by the addition of 1.5 million demobbed army men. The figure of 3.5 million did not include "American camp followers; prostitutes, hooligans and other riff-raff who lived off the U.S. presence and could not continue such roles under our administration," as the prime minister expressed it. The PRG had inherited an economy, plagued not only by unemployment, but by a galloping inflation, a currency that had been devalued almost every week prior to April 30, and bank vaults emptied of their gold and foreign exchange reserves. Due to the U.S. policy of forced "urbanization"[47] (sometimes referred to as

---

47. The "father" of "urbanization" was Dr. Samuel P. Huntington, a leading American political scientist, former head of the Faculty of Government, Harvard University (Kissinger's former faculty), and an adviser on military affairs to the Johnson and Nixon administrations. "Urbanization" entailed the application of maximum force—including B-52 bombers—to "empty the sea" in which successive U.S. military com-

"generating refugees") by bombing the countryside to empty it of peasants, pursued by the U.S.-Saigon command right up until the last days of the war, over half the population of the cities was non-productive. Some of the bombed-out peasants had returned to their villages immediately after Liberation; others had no villages to which to return, for they had been completely wiped out by "urbanization." A still smaller number had got jobs and a taste for city life and did not want to return to the land.

"South Vietnam used to be an important exporter of rice," Prime Minister Phat recalled. "But when the Americans introduced 'urbanization,' of which chemical warfare against agricultural production was an important element, the puppet régime was forced to import every year between 500,000 and 700,000 tons of rice. Saigon was fed like a beggar city on the American rice dole. We now have favorable conditions for developing agriculture. We will not import any rice this year; in 1976 we will have a small exportable surplus and from 1977 onwards, we will be back to our old position as an important rice exporter. Then we can begin to solve our foreign exchange problems. The South is rich in natural resources; the fact that we are in the tropical zone is very favorable for agriculture which will be our main economic activity. Gradually we will solve the problems of raw materials and fuel and restore our enterprises, which are now running on the average at only half their capacity, to full production."

I raised the question of the offshore oil deposits. According to some documents I had come across in Saigon, oil had been struck in exploitable qualities on October 24, 1974, southeast of Vung Tau, by Pecten, a South Vietnamese subsidiary of Shell Oil. A Saigon government report claimed that: "Oil spurted from the well with a flame 15 metres long. It was estimated that the well could yield 1,500 barrels of oil and 58 million cubic feet of natural gas per day." Pecten-Shell was only one of half a dozen companies, mainly American, which had been granted prospecting and exploitation concessions by the Thieu government. The first drilling had been started by Pecten two months

---

manders had failed to catch "the fish." Huntington's ideal status for peasants was to have them locked up like American Indians in reservations, living on carefully controlled hand-outs which would not permit an ounce of food being passed on to the guerillas.

before the strike at what was designated the "Coconut Nine" prospecting site.

"Yes," replied the prime minister. "There are big offshore oil resources—a very favorable factor for us. With high quality anthracite in the North; our hydro-electric potential and oil in the South, our fuel problems should be solved. We are already looking to certain countries for investment in helping to develop the oil deposits. This means we will accept technical help and investments, under certain conditions, even from those companies which started the prospecting work. We want to build up our country as fast and as well as possible. We are not interested in economic autarchy or a 'closed door' policy. We want to open up our country on conditions favorable to us and this means encouraging certain foreign investments. We need modern techniques—the best available—to develop our resources, as long as these can be had under mutually favorable conditions. The perspectives are excellent. Our reserves of hydro-electric power amount to ten times our forseeable needs." Prime Minister Phat noted that one such hydro-power station built by a Japanese firm at Dunhim, near Dalat at the eastern fringe of the Central Highlands (but which had never fully functioned due to guerilla activity) was being repaired by Japanese technicians and by the time it started functioning at full capacity early in 1976, it would supply more than half of South Vietnam's pre-Liberation electric power consumption.

Chapter 16.

Building the Future

It is hardly likely that there will be any monuments in South Vietnam to presidents Kennedy, Johnson, Nixon and Ford, but objectively they all played their unwitting and unwilling roles in the totality of the victory of the revolutionary forces in South Vietnam—and in latter years, in speeding up the process of reunification. The NLF, from the time it was formed, had worked out long-range policies aimed at facilitating a negotiated settlement, based on national unity, which reserved a voice in the nation's affairs for their adversaries. It provided for a non-socialist policy in the South; the sort of régime which could have facilitated the best relations with the then neutral kingdoms of pre-Lon Nol Cambodia and of Laos. These were sincere, long-term policies based on sacrifices as far as the tempo of the revolution was concerned, as a price willingly paid to end the bloodshed and restoring peace. The NLF was prepared to accept an administrative role far more modest than their real strength and the sacrifices their members had made.

The United States "grab-all, lose-all" policy was to scorn such concepts and even when some of them were incorporated into the Paris Agreement, to give Thieu a wink so loud that you could almost hear it—plus enormous quantities of arms to reject any but military solutions. The forces with which the NLF, later the PRG, were prepared to cooperate, (on the basis of detailed policies worked out during many months of discussion and much heart-searching; and solutions negotiated after five wearying years of public and secret talks in Paris), were totally crushed. That which could have been a vital role for "Third Force" elements, to encourage which the PRG was prepared to make concessions in its social and economic policies, had dissipated into thin air. The "Third Force" had been conceived as a bridge, and one of vital importance at that. But a bridge is a link between two elements, one of which had collapsed. From the beginning it had been the PRG which had encouraged and supported the "Third Force" elements and Thieu who had tried to hunt down and eradicate them. The fact that they did not, by definition, support one or the other of the belligerents, did not necessarily mean they were neutral. They understood which side supported national independence and which did not. They leaned heavily towards the PRG and were not likely to oppose the sort of policies that the PRG would naturally have adopted had it not been necessary to adapt its social-economic program to the expectation of taking part in a left-center-right coalition government of national union. There were economic problems —the abandoned factories—crying for a solution that meant the state taking over management. There were related problems such as the rational utilization of these huge modern plants which could best be solved on an all-Vietnam scale within a single all-Vietnam economic plan. The forces which would have opposed state participation in industry and economic integration with the North no longer existed.

Similarly, because of the same U.S. "grab-all, lose all" policies in Laos and Cambodia, there were no longer any risks of the PRG offending "Sihanouk-type neutralists" in Cambodia, or a "three-way neutralist" régime in Laos, by taking a socialist road, or hastening the process of reunification. The FUNK (Cambodian National United Front) had taken over power in Phnom Penh with a more radical social-economic program than that of the PRG, as a reaction to the immensely bitter war imposed on the Cambodian people by U.S. policies. The forces of the revolutionary Pathet Lao had taken over in Vientiane, facilitated by the same people's reaction to U.S. neo-colonialist policies there and by open sabotage by the United States and the right-wing forces it controlled, of every negotiated agreement.

These three parts of Indochina had come together with the northern half of Vietnam in a Summit Conference of the Peoples of Indochina on April 24-25 1970, the result of which was a pledge to coordinate the struggles of the three people while each retained its independence and sovereignty. The national liberation aims of each were endorsed by the others. The United States, in fact, had bombed North and South Vietnam into military reunification—its bombs and shells never respecting the dividing line along the 17th parallel; it had bombed into power revolutionary régimes in neighboring Laos and Cambodia and had certainly also bombed South Vietnam into taking the socialist road. It had bombed all three countries into a future in which socialist options were the only viable ones—each country doing it in its own way to solve the problems which arose during wars of resistance against United States intervention and aggression.

The compromises which the revolutionary forces in South Vietnam were prepared to make on a long-term basis to rally maximum support for that one supreme goal of national independence and freedom were made unnecessary by Washington's maximalist policies. The revolutionary forces emerged as the supreme masters of South Vietnam. The counter-revolutionary forces which could have been sharing power at the top and blocking every progressive measure, as they did for years in the three-way coalition government in Laos, went down to defeat, shattered, discredited, impotent and without the slightest possibility of revival. They had run their course, racing to their own destruction with the United States cheering them on. The PRG could decide on what policies it considered appropriate, freed from self-imposed restrictions but still pledged to take part in building up a united, democratic, neutralist, prosperous Vietnam. From its birth, the NLF had always proclaimed that it was not fighting for a monopoly of power, or decision-making, but to create the conditions for the Vietnamese people to make their own choice, decide their own options. This viewpoint found its most complete expression in the Paris Agreement. But despite what the United States leadership said for home and world consumption, the last thing it wanted for the South Vietnamese people was to exercise their rights of self-determination. That was what the war was all about!

A start towards building a socialist society was made by having to cope with a "Made in U.S.A." situation which left no alternative but for the State to move in. The case of the Sakymen woollen blanket factory was typical. Owned by a handful of Taiwan-Chinese, it employed 651 workers, 90 percent of whom were family members of Catholic evacuees from North Vietnam. Wages, in the immediate pre-Liberation period, were from 6,000 to 12,000 piastres per month, whereas members of the Board of Directors helped themselves to 280,000 per month. Any agitation for higher wages was immediately put down by the police. The owners had been able to pay for places aboard the first evacuation helicopters and had fled to the U.S.A.

"We were petrified with fear as to what the 'Viet Cong' would do when they arrived," said Le Thi Binh, a smiling young woman checking blankets for flaws in an inspection shed, when I asked about the first days of the takeover. "We had been told by our parents, the bosses and local priest ever since I can remember, what terrible people they were. We all felt that the end of the world had come when it was announced over the radio that everyone should report for work on May 2. Many of us thought this was a trick and we would be herded off to some concentration camp. What could we do? The factory was our life. Almost everyone turned up. In fact a very polite officer came along with someone from the trade unions. He was also very polite and told us of rights according to trade union regulations. Trade unions! We had been told this was an organization of the Devil! A tool of the Communists! But here was this polite young officer telling us to keep right on working, and the trade union man telling us we were entitled to a 100 percent pay hike for the lowest paid—which mainly meant us women—and a 40 percent rise for the highest paid. He explained this was possible because there were no more directors to grab all the profits. I wanted to rush straight back home to tell my parents. They had tried to persuade me not to return to the factory. And I could hardly wait to see our priest! No one had ever spoken to us so decently as the 'Viet Cong' and the trade union man."

Ba Dac, a stocky, bullet-headed member of the Military Management Board which now ran the factory, explained that he and some other cadres from the Gia Dinh Military Management Committee had come on May 2 to explain things to the workers. "We gathered everybody together and said the plant would continue to produce. The owners had fled, but there were stocks of raw materials to last at least until the end of the year and by then we would arrange supplies from elsewhere. We would guarantee wages, raw materials and markets and counted on the workers to guarantee production. The trade union representative announced the wage increases, which brought their wages into line with those at other textile plants, and also that the canteen lunch, which had previously been obligatory at a cost of 160 piastres, would be improved, without payment and optional. This alone was equivalent to a 33 percent wage increase for the lower paid workers. Wages would be guaranteed on a monthly basis—and not a day-to-day basis as before. The bosses used the daily system to lay off workers without notice, according to the fluctuations in demand for the blankets.

"There were smiles all around," said Ba Dac, "when we announced these things. After the workers had studied the trade union regulations and realized that they were the future masters of the factory, they denounced two reactionaries planted there to protect the former owners' interests. One was a Captain Tran Hoan Lan of the police, a relative of one of the owners, who had hidden in the factory instead of registering. A really bad type whose instructions were to organize sabotage in case the factory was kept in production. The other was of lesser importance and after a remolding course, he took a lead in persuading workers to join the trade unions. We never exerted pressure about this—even now less than two-thirds of the workers are trade union members. We want them to join up voluntarily when they are convinced of the real advantages of membership."

The average production per shift up to April 30, had been 700 blankets, now it was 900—1,800 per two-shift day—the increase, according to Ba Dac, due to better organization and improved morale. "Before, the workers faced real prospects of starvation," he said, "with a layoff always possible from one day to another. Now they know they have guaranteed jobs all the year round." The quality of the blankets was first class and I noticed that part of the production was being baled up for shipment to North Vietnam, where woollen blankets are in great demand for the winter months. The workers were obviously relaxed and those I spoke to at random expressed themselves as being very satisfied, especially at the fact—which each of them mentioned—that they had no more fears of lay-offs.

Among other interesting factories I visited was the Xedeco bicycle factory, in the same Binh Hoa district of Gia Dinh as the blanket factory. It had been set up under French ownership in January 1974, based on equipment and raw material from

France. It had started off with a modest production of 100 bicycle frames per month, with gears, chains and other parts supplied by other Saigon plants. After a few months, production had dwindled to almost nothing because of lack of market. An incredible situation in a city of over 3 million! At the beginning of 1975 production had stopped altogether and the owners returned to France, a few workers being kept on for maintenance. On May 8, Dung Van Xung, a stocky former soldier, with a rugged, determined face, was sent by the Gia Dinh Military Management Committee to look things over. With the help of the few workers left behind, he rounded up some 40 other former employees. "I got them all together," he said, "and told them we were going to need an awful lot of bicycles. The State would put up money and find raw materials and there would be no limits on output. They set to work with great enthusiasm, rapidly stepping up production. We turned out 600 frames in July and we will soon be producing 1,000 per month. We have been given the finance to add another workshop with more modern equipment and the work force will be expanded to over 200. We expect to turn out 500,000 bicycles within the next year, all from our own raw materials. Steel tubing will come from Bien Hoa (one of four new industrial zones set up within the framework of the "economic competition" plan, W. B.) and other plants will produce the gears, chains etc. We will do the assembly here." I spoke with Le Thi Lo, a woman lathe operator and asked how she was getting on. "Great," she replied. "I worked here under the French for 400 piastres a day and never knew from one day to another when I was going to be paid off. Now I get 500 piastres, but on a guaranteed monthly basis. Everything is changed, but especially the attitude towards us workers. We are consulted about everything—from how to step up production to the color of the frames. My husband was killed in the war and I have two children to support. The future seemed hopeless after the French owners left. Now everything has changed. I can see a decent life ahead for myself and the kids. Things get better every day."

Binh Hoa was a part of the "protective belt" around Saigon, inhabited mainly by soldiers' families, Catholics from the North and bombed out peasants. It had been a rural area, later incorporated into Gia Dinh as the population increased through "urbanization". At the administrative center Ly Hong Com, a gray-haired veteran with a smiling face, a member of the Binh Hoa peoples Revolutionary Committee, explained that the population was mainly very poor and that at the moment of liberation half of them were literally at starvation level. "Our most urgent task was to combat famine conditions and to provide jobs for the unemployed. Their numbers were swelled by 30,000 soldiers demobbed here. Army and administration personnel and their families accounted for about 80 percent of the population. About 20,000, of the district's 230,000 population, went straight back to their villages. "Of the 17,000-odd soldiers and officers who registered in Binh Hoa (the remainder of the 30,000 demobilized registered where their units had been headquartered), 15,600 had been through local remolding courses, 1,700 medium to senior officers had been sent to other regions" for longer courses. "We were taught by 'Uncle' Ho," said Ly Hong Com, "that the majority of Vietnamese are good. In their heart they will always be for the revolution, so in the remolding courses we try to kindle that spirit. But with many of the senior officers, imperialism changed them into wild beasts. Our task is to turn them back into human beings. The families of the junior officers and administrative personnel are very enthusiastic about the results of the courses. Before, their menfolk used to come home drunk and beat up their wives and children. Now they are polite and decent—they even give a hand with the house work. During the courses they got used to this by having to keep their living quarters clean by themselves.

"The people here had been conditioned to be totally hostile to us. They had wildly distorted views because of the enemy psychological warfare machinery. They believed there would be wholesale arrests and torture; that we would behave towards them as the puppets had behaved towards us. Some Catholics prepared poison to kill revolutionaries or to commit suicide if 'the worst came to the worst.' Instead we started distributing free rice to the needy. We found almost 60,000 people who were really starving to whom we distributed 670 tons of rice in the first few days. We still have 21,144 on our free distribution list—the rest have found jobs or have been helped to return to their villages. We provided work for unemployed, building houses, for instance, for those who are going to the new economic zones. We put rice on the market at 170 piastres per kilo whereas the free market rate was 220 piastres. The families of those attending the courses also get free rice, if they had no income due to their menfolk being away. People saw we were making a serious effort to solve economic problems and that there were no arrests or punishment. Those who returned from the remolding courses spoke well of us. In fact, for those who had served in the puppet administration it was less of a remolding course than one to reorient them so they could continue on in their old jobs but with an outlook that enabled them to fit the new society that is going to be built. We found that the overwhelming majority of these people were eager for this. The main thing is that they are patriots, proud to take part in building up a strong and prosperous society. They are objectively enthusiastic for such a society. Before, Binh Hoa was under a very tight grip of puppet repression. Our revolutionary bases were virtually exterminated and there were very few individual revolutionary cadres left. There were less than a hundred Lao Dong party members and sympathizers, but there has been great progress since. The majority of those soldiers and junior officers who went through the courses, have become members of the Liberation Youth Association and from being our enemies, they have become a great source of strength."

I asked about the attitude of the families of the senior officers who were being given much longer remolding courses.

"The main thing is that they can send food parcels, and exchange letters. The wives and children have a beneficial effect on them. Based on what they have seen of our activities, they encourage their husbands and fathers to study well so they can come back home quickly and take part in building up the new society. Every Vietnamese, including most of those officers, have a sense of relief that the Americans have gone and a secret feeling of pride that they are part of the Vietnamese nation which defeated French colonialism and American imperialism."

An example of the non-abrasive way in which the new administration neutralized potential opponents was at Go Vap district, in the northeastern corner of Gia Dinh province, an industrial suburb with many military installations but also a number of hamlets engaged in agriculture. Revolutionary bases were maintained here although virtually every cadre had been in prison for terms of up to ten years—and there had been a particularly vigorous uprising on April 30. Within two hours military repair shops and supply depots, police stations, a very big military hospital and a residential block for officers and their families were all taken over before the arrival of the main force units. The president of the People's Revolutionary Committee, Truong Thanh Son, an extremely forceful and obviously efficient cadre, explained a problem they had had with the Catholics:

"There were some reactionary Catholics who wanted to take advantage of confusion during the transitional period to raise the banner of counter-revolution in a very cunning way. We discovered that in 11 hamlets, working behind the scenes, these people had set up what they called 'revolutionary committees' with their own people in charge. They had acted very quickly and were quite well armed. The local people sent word to us and asked for armed forces to be sent. We sent some, but with instructions to act very discreetly. They gradually managed to infiltrate some sound, decent people into the pseudo 'revolutionary committees' and carried out propaganda among the peasants to unmask the imposters and replace them with real revolutionaries. Behind the scenes, the Catholic reactionaries carried on a steady propaganda urging people not to read newspapers, not to listen to the radio or watch TV and not to attend any performances of the art ensembles. Our cadres countered this by our own propaganda. The art ensembles based on our traditional music, dancing and folklore had such a popular appeal that no one could be kept away by priestly warnings. The ordinary folk knew they were being tricked. They worked to such good effect on the imposters, that at one meeting they got up one after another and asked to resign as they did not think they had 'sufficient merits' to direct administrative affairs in the new society. The political structure in these hamlets changed from one day to another.

"There was also a problem with a reactionary Catholic officer, Major Nguyen Van Huong. He had refused to register and circulated illegally within the province carrying on his counter-revolutionary activities. We could easily have arrested him but we decided it was not worthwhile making a martyr out of Major Huong. Better to get the local people to persuade him to register. We infiltrated a cadre into a hamlet where he was hanging out at the time. The local people were persuaded to organize a meeting at which Huong should be criticized. The meeting was arranged and Huong, not knowing what he was in for, accepted an invitation to attend. He was criticized to such good effect, that he got up and made a self-criticism and promised to register. Those present kept quiet, just let him speak, but they were very pleased at the outcome. He registered the following day.

"The reactionaries tried to regain some ground by organizing a demonstration for July 20, officially decreed by Ngo Dinh Diem, and perpetuated by his successors, as a 'day of shame' because the Geneva Agreements were signed on that day. It was going to be turned into a demonstration against us because we asked the Vatican's Apostolic Delegate to be recalled as was done with other diplomats accredited to the old régime. Our cadres called all the Catholics together and invited a general discussion of their grievances. Some of them took very reactionary positions at the meeting, but one thing they admitted was that the new government's policy was reasonable and that for the first time in their lives they could actually discuss problems with representatives of government. No one from any of the previous governments had ever come to discuss their problems! The demonstration was cancelled. The main point made by our cadres was that Vietnam was now independent and free. Catholics were also Vietnamese citizens and had the same right to protection and equality and to practice their rites as any other Vietnamese citizen, regardless of their religion. Government policies were patiently explained and although this probably had little effect on the hard-core reactionaries, it made a big impression on the Catholic rank and file and we have since had no problems with those hamlets."

This genius for neutralizing opponents by reasonableness in word and action was of decisive importance for the smoothness of the transition from fascist to revolutionary power. The economic problems of Go Vap were similar to those of Binh Hoa, and were settled in the same way. Free rice for the destitute; aid to get people back on to the land; the state moving in to get abandoned industries working; emphasis in expanding production in every field that contributed to building up the economy. As at Binh Hoa, the State had set up its own network of shops at which basic commodities—rice, cooking oil, salt, sugar and others—were available at fixed prices. The people could see that wherever the State intervened, it was clearly in their interests.

I visited a factory, the main production of which was a highly appreciated food seasoning powder based on monosodium glutamate which, according to a glossy advertising pamphlet put out by the previous owners, was produced by the world's newest and most advanced fermentation technique. The owners had been Kuomintang Chinese who had skipped off to Taiwan a few days before April 30, leaving some 570 workers unpaid and jobless. 60 percent of the workers, including all the specialized ones, were Chinese. Eleven engineers, ten from Taiwan and one from Japan, had fled with the owners. The plant remained idle until May 20, when workers were requested to turn up for work as usual. Explanations were made as to their rights and the benefits of trade union membership, the country's need for their products and the fact that the workers were now masters in the factories and a few similar eye-opening remarks. There was no problem in getting production started—the owners had taken the secret formula for the seasoning powder with them, but some shrewd old workers had managed to make a copy before they left. The engineers had also kept technical know-how from being diffused among the workers, but by pooling their experience with that of their own specialists, this difficulty was quickly overcome. By the time I visited the plant, (August 20) the work force had been expanded to 722, production had gradually increased from 120 tons a month—the maximum under the previous management—to 180 tons in July and it was expected to continually increase. The main reason, according to the trade union representative, was not the expanded force, but because of improved morale. Good quality canteen luncheons were available free and workers had access to foodstuffs at controlled prices. Only 40 percent of the personnel had joined the trade union till then—"they have to come to it voluntarily," the representative said, "but in any case all the workers now feel for the first time in their lives that there is an organization which bothers about their livelihood."

Within a few days and weeks of having come to power, the PRG somewhat unexpectedly, found itself managing a whole gamut of industry producing everything from steel to seasoning powder!

Chapter 17.

Total Victory

According to the lengthy analysis of the "General Offensive and People's Uprisings" referred to in earlier chapters, it seems certain that the offensive was orginally undertaken with the limited objective of bringing enough pressure on the U.S. and Saigon to implement the Paris Agreement and was not designed to bring about the total collapse of the Saigon régime. Included in the calculations was the possibility that the United States might intervene and even recommence the bombings against the North.

"After the great victory in the Central Highlands," wrote Generals Vo Nguyen Giap and Van Tien Dung, "our Party realized in time the new opportunity this presented; the new conditions, and immediately decided to put into effect a previously prepared plan for the complete development of the great strategic offensive on all fronts of South Vietnam to rapidly bring off a complete victory. In the meantime we had evaluated the capacity of the United States to intervene in various degrees and forms of activity, and we actively prepared for this eventuality.

"Our Party decided that even if the Americans ventured again to unleash war against us, we would still manage to bring off final victory, because we had all the necessary conditions to bring this about . . ."

Thus, if it was the Phuoc Long victory which was decisive

in advancing the date of the offensive into the Central Highlands, and the victory in the Central Highlands that provoked the decision to go all-out for final victory; it was the debacle at Danang that decided Giap to press ahead to take Saigon at a speed which made all previous notions of "blitzkrieg" look very out-of-date.

It was in applying this concept (total victory) that the operations of Hue and Danang were undertaken—organized and executed in one of the speediest actions history has ever seen. Immediately after the wiping out of enemy troops at Danang, we correctly assessed that the enemy must be on the verge of total collapse. The revolutionary war in South Vietnam had entered a phase of tremendous élan. Our revolution was developing at such a speed that one day was the equivalent of 20 years. Having thoroughly seized this strategic opportunity, we decided to conduct the general offensive to total victory ...

The lightning speed of the advance from that moment was such that it not only left the Saigon army and administration dumb-founded, but many of the revolutionary cadres, if not dumb-founded, at least gasping for breath. So much so that I found the atmosphere in Saigon for the first few weeks of my visit something of an anti-climax. "The greatest non-story of all time," remarked a western colleague, piqued at the lack of dramatic highlights to report. I wondered if the former Thieu forces were not licking their wounds and getting a second breath for a counter-offensive. Objectively, it was their best moment, with plenty of discontent over rising prices and shortage of foodstuffs and what seemed to be the insoluble problem of unemployment. After what had been a fairly generalized euphoria during the first weeks after Liberation, apathy seemed to have set in. The pep and vigor seemed even to have gone out of some frontline, veteran cadres I encountered. I raised the question when I ran into Ba Tu, who had twice been my interpreter during visits to the Liberated Areas. Frail, bespectacled, imperturbable and with a great sense of humor, Ba Tu had always been a tower of strength in tough situations. He laughed at my questions as to whether what seemed like an unnatural calm did not presage a storm. Were not the forces of reaction preparing a counterblow? Could the United States take a defeat of such magnitude lying down? Was I correct in sensing a certain apathy even among the cadres?

"In a way, you're right," he said. "Some of the steam does

seem to have gone out of us. But it's because it's we who are getting our second wind—not the enemy. They are down and out for ever. But we cadres were all geared up for the big political battles once the shooting ended. We all know the Paris Agreement backwards; we were braced for electoral campaigns; for tremendous political struggles over questions like reunification, or taking the socialist road. As for land reform, it had been carried out by the peasants themselves, so there would not have been much of a fight over that, but over almost any other question you could mention, it was expected there would be big battles for public opinion. All of a sudden it's finished. What sort of an electoral confrontation can there be? The puppets never did have any political power base. Their strength was exclusively based on American guns and dollars. We always said this, but it was difficult until now to realize how totally correct this was. Even the Catholic landlords from the North have been unable to react, to polarize any real opposition around themselves. Their great champions, from Diem to Thieu, and their super-champions from the United States, are gone, hated, despised and discredited. The reactionaries are absolutely incapable of staging any sort of a comeback.

"But you are wrong," continued Ba Tu, "to think there is nothing going on. Where policies have to be worked out, our top cadres are working day and night, formulating new tasks and methods of struggle appropriate to the situation created by the overwhelming nature of our victory. Meanwhile a lot of us at a lower level can take things a bit easier for a while. Don't worry," he said, clapping me on the shoulder, "there are going to be plenty of tasks soon, far more exciting than the political confrontation we were all thinking about. We will build up our country with the same dash and speed as went into the last offensive. We are only just beginning to realize—because we couldn't enjoy the luxury of thinking about such things before —how immensely rich the South really is. Normally at the end of any such protracted war, there are semi-famine conditions. Even in Western Europe after five years of World War II. We have had 30 years of war, but we had a relative abundance of rice, vegetables and fruit even here in over-populated Saigon within a day or two of the end of the war. We have great quantities of fruit and vegetables of the most diverse types. There will be a great riches from the sea once we get our fishing industry organized. It's a question of a rational exploitation and distribution of these riches, not for individual profit, but to rapidly increase living standards. We will encourage everything, private enterprise and foreign aid and investments—from capitalist countries too if they want to join in—which can provide short cuts for building up our economy. There's going to be plenty to do for all of us. But we cadres will have to readjust—be recycled for the new tasks. Even those who have performed meritorious services cannot rest on their laurels—or their medals—for the tasks ahead, mainly the transformation of our country into a rich and powerful nation."

A variation on this same theme came from Tran Bach Dang, a veteran cadre, member of the Central Committee of the Lao Dong party's southern section, responsible for propaganda. I had met him on all four previous visits and had always appreciated his frank and sober evaluations. At a discussion in February 1965, he had spoken of policies for the postwar period and I had thought his remarks of sufficient importance to send an advance chapter of my book, *Vietnam Will Win*, which incorporated them, to Averell Harriman when he had shown interest in NLF long-range policies at our Paris meeting. At that time I had asked Tran Bach Dang to define the contents of the four main NLF aims of neutrality, democracy, peace and independence. On democracy, he had said:

Democracy for us means a real national, people's democracy, based on the unity of workers, peasants, intellectuals and patriotic bourgeoisie of all tendencies. We are carrying out a national democratic revolution with the unity of all sections of the population as the basic element. We have to think of it at two levels, the present rather low level based on an alliance between workers, peasants and the lower strata of the bourgeoisie, which we consider a sort of people's democracy, and on the higher level of still broader unity which we are aiming at and which we could call a national democratic union to include the upper strata of the bourgeoisie.

Our present people's democratic alliance must approve measures acceptable to this upper strata as well. It may seem strange to outsiders to find communists fighting for the interests of the upper class, but we understand the vital necessity of unity at the highest level, not only now during the period of struggle but for the years of postwar reconstruction as well. But "unity" also has its specific content. It implies mutual concessions; we have elements who accept the word 'democracy' but think of it only in terms of bourgeois democracy, that is exclusively to protect the interests of the capitalists and landlords; there are others who think of it exclusively in the sense of expropriating the capitalists and landlords. "Unity" for us means harmonizing the various concepts.

We propose the formation of a national, democratic coalition government based on the highest attainable level of national unity. Within such a government there could be elements almost at the opposite end of the political spectrum from us; pro-Gaullist nationalists for instance, even pro-American nationalists as long as they break with the puppets and are for genuine national independence. We want a stable government which can be supported by every genuine patriot who rejects selling out the country's interests for a pocketful of dollars . . .[48]

How well-advised the Americans would have been to take this at its face value, when this concept was incorporated eight years later into the Paris Agreement! At our meeting in Saigon, I asked Tran Bach Dang—his hair a little grayer and face a little rounder than at our last meeting just nine years earlier—whether this was still valid.

"By and large, yes," he said, "but we had not foreseen that the Americans were going to push our enemy into committing suicide by staking everything on military confrontation, leaving us with a monopoly of power as the result. Some aspects of our policies, like some aspects of the Paris Agreement, have been bypassed by events. We are doing a lot of re-thinking now on problems to which we had not devoted much attention before, but which the speed and total nature of our victory now make solutions imperative. The great thing is that we no longer have to concentrate our energies on the sort of political confrontation we had envisaged but can get on with the real job of building up the country."

I asked whether Ho Chi Minh's famous phrase, "Nothing Is More Precious Than Independence and Freedom"—posted up all over Saigon—was wholeheartedly accepted, in view of the large number of people suffering material hardships because of the American departure and dollar cut-off? Was there any appreciable nostalgia for the return of the Americans, French

---

48. *Vietnam Will Win*, pp. 157-158.

or some other "protecting" power which could provide cushy jobs for a proportion of the upper and middle classes, not to mention a clientele for the hundreds of tailoring establishments, beauty parlors, curio shops and others in the fashionable quarters of Saigon?

"There are people, especially in Saigon," he replied, "who mock at the idea of independence and freedom. They pretend to be scared of the effects of us trying to stand on our own feet. Fundamentally they are scared of us—the Revolution. But even these elements appreciate the fact that they, or their sons, are no longer in danger of being picked up for military service. We may be a bit clumsy in taking over the reigns of power. Added to the fact that we have been fighting for over a quarter of a century, this is the first time in 117 years that Vietnamese in the South have had real power to run the country. So even our clumsiness has some virtue because the mass of the people see we are sincere even when we make mistakes. And we are accessible. People can come and talk to us at every level, from street committee up, to discuss their problems.

"In your contacts with a cross-section of society, you'll certainly hear plenty of criticism—from reactionary Catholics, from the families of generals, from intellectuals who think our explanations at the orientation courses are a bit simplistic, from ordinary people because of economic hardships we haven't been able to solve. Plenty of people are not very satisfied with some of the things we have done, or have not done. But even when they show dissatisfaction, we can see that it is at least tempered with satisfaction. No more press-gangs; no more dying on the battlefield; injustices and inequalities are less. And as we go along the positive factors will increase, the negative ones decrease. The greatest positive factor is that although the puppet army is still around physically, it has been dismantled. The enemy and all his organs of repression is destroyed as an organized force."

I asked, in view of the very large numbers of demobilized troops and officers, as well as leading officials of the old régime, still around, whether there was not a danger of them regrouping their forces and making trouble. There were plenty of grievances to work on and the CIA must be still around looking for weak points to exploit.

After listing the social and economic problems inherited from the fascist régime, Tran Bach Dang agreed that there were plenty of grounds for discontent, including the fact that famil-ies were upset because many civil servants as well as army offi-cers were away from their homes attending courses. "There is something abnormal in the situation," he said, "although life for most people has become more normal than in the past. The re-actionary Catholics, mainly the wealthy, privileged ones from the North, consider this a very favorable moment. But all they've managed is a few handwritten—not even roneoed let alone printed—leaflets and a few slogans scrawled on remote walls. Their agents are not very heroic. Objective conditions for starting something may seem great but the practical possibil-ities are non-existent, even though revolutionary power is still not set up everywhere. The reactionaries are frightened of their own shadows, their defeat has been so total. They fear that rev-olutionary spirits lurk behind every lamp-post.

"Some western journalists," continued Tran Bach Dang, "have raised the question of executions. After repeated warn-ings, a few gangsters caught red-handed at looting were tried by local people's tribunals and shot—the whole thing in front of TV cameras as a warning to others. But no counter-revolution-aries have been executed. We drew a line under everything that had happened up to April 30. Past crimes would be handled in a spirit of national reconciliation. This is not a question of hu-manitarianism, although we stand for revolutionary humanitar-ianism. It is because counter-revolutionaries represent no real danger. Incidentally, contrary to some western press reports, there have been no assassinations of any of the approximately 100,000 army men and cadres we have in Saigon. In our plan-ning, we don't even have to take into account the risk of coun-ter-revolutionary coup attempts." This from a leading cadre of the ultra-cautious, super-vigilant Vietnamese revolutionaries, was extremely categoric and convincing! He continued:

"The question of overall orientation of development is very important to grasp. We have no intention of doing anything that runs contrary to the people's interests. If today we cannot solve all the social problems, we will solve them in the near fu-ture. We didn't carry on our long struggle to rest on the laurels of past successes. We won't sit on our hands or go to sleep. We will build up a prosperous new country, astonishing the world by our victories in the battle of peaceful reconstruction as we did by those on the battlefield. Never before has our country been so rich. Everything is in our hands and the perspectives are infinite. All the elements are within our grasp to push on with the total industrialization of the country. And we'll do it, while taking fully into account the difficulties ahead."

To my question as to whether "national reconciliation" was a practical possibility in view of the terrible wounds and scars always left by a civil war—especially one that had gone on for three decades, Tran Bach Dang was convinced that it was. The speed and total nature of the victory and the flight abroad of the most reactionary elements had greatly facilitated this; also the fact that in its day-to-day activities the administration demonstrated that "national reconciliation" was not an empty slogan but a cornerstone of PRG policy. He considered this already a fact of life, even in Saigon, where far greater difficulties of security and public order had been expected. He pointed out that before April 30, the capital had been considered one of the world's most corrupt cities; one with the most complex social problems and one of the highest crime rates in the world.

"Frankly," he said, "we had thought the problem of public order and security would provide us with one of our greatest headaches. We thought that the so-called 'cowboys' and 'hooligans' would be with us for years to come and that social problems would be virtually impossible to control. We were worried about our lack of experience in this field. The former régime had a huge police apparatus but couldn't control public order. But now, after only three months, our crime rate is one of the lowest in the world, lower than Paris for instance. This is a product of national reconciliation. When the masses are masters, then society comes under control, and the action of the masses has been decisive in this. For every snatch-grab thief or looter, there are now a hundred people to chase after them. We could not estimate in advance the strength of the very fact of the revolution; nor the impact on the public of the good behavior, modesty and simple life of our armed forces and revolutionary cadres. Above all, it was the people who rose up and smashed the enemy's repressive machinery which was there precisely to thwart national reconcilation. When everyone was supposed to spy on his neighbor and denounce him to the police torturers, how could one speak of national concord and reconciliation? We helped the people to tear down the abnormal, unnatural restrictions on their day-to-day relationships and the traditional cohesion of our society immediately re-asserted itself. The family spirit, the good neighbor spirit, blossomed again as in the past. The old régime kept people apart by barbed wire and threats of jail if they even spoke to each other. We encourage them to get together, to discuss together and help solve each other's problems. At every level we foster national reconciliation."

"Is there not a terrible thirst for vengeance; for a settling of 'blood debts' as the Vietnamese express it, on the part of the hundreds of thousands released from the jails; those who have suffered at the hands of the torturers and hundreds of thousands of others who have lost family members and their homes," I asked. "What is the real attitude towards the former puppets?"

"People's attitudes are much influenced by those of our leadership," replied Tran Bach Dang. "For 30 years we have enjoyed great prestige despite the propaganda efforts of the enemy. If we advocate and practice national reconciliation, as was shown by our handling of the enemy's armed forces, then the people will follow our example. Especially those who have suffered most in the prisons—because they are also mainly revolutionaries. They understand the politics of leniency. There is also a great yearning to normalize human relations again. Even non-politically minded people can grasp that it is the only way to rapidly heal the wounds of war and build up a prosperous future. As for the former puppets, our position is this: Most of them were forced into working with the puppet army or administration for one reason or another beyond their control—by coercion or because of pressing economic reasons. One who blew up an American hotel, for instance, was a 'puppet' soldier —he was also a patriot. His was not an isolated case. We have to show understanding about this and not automatically regard everyone who served on the other side as a 'puppet' and therefore an enemy. That is why we have stated officially that those who have completed what I prefer to call their education courses are not to be referred to in the future as 'puppets'. At the Paris Conference, incidentally, it was our delegation which fought hard for the inclusion of a 'no reprisals' clause in the Agreement. All our cadres approve that Agreement in its entirety; they apply it in their day-to-day work and this sets a good example for the general public. The result is that your industrious colleagues have not been able to report a single case of the 'settling of accounts' that so many were prophesying before April 30. Many former enemy officers are now engaged in political activities and we encourage that. If they don't have political activities, how will they know how to orient themselves; what part to play in the tasks ahead? The revolution has won. They must live with this fact of life and make the best of it. That is why I prefer the term 'education courses', because these are designed to educate people about something of which they knew nothing before and to orient them regarding the policies which are going to govern the new society."

Tran Bach Dang's remarks on the attitude towards former puppets recalled a conversation with Madame Minh, the press officer of the PRG's negotiations' delegation in Paris, a few hours after the liberation of Saigon. (A Portugese friend had telephoned me the news just as I was leaving a Lisbon hotel to catch a Paris-bound plane and from Orly airport I had driven straight to the PRG headquarters at Verrières-le-Buisson, just outside Paris, where Madame Minh was already receiving a few friends and journalists.) A French colleague raised the question of "settling accounts." "There will be none of that," she replied. "We understand that in France and elsewhere in Europe, there was a settling of accounts with collaborators after World War II. It is a natural, human reaction. Our enemies committed unspeakable crimes; tortured and killed then robbed the families of the victims of their property for personal gain. But those who have the most 'accounts to settle' are revolutionaries. We have educated our people to abstain from revenge. We have made so many sacrifices in the past 30 years that the sacrifice of abstaining from revenge is small in comparison. Especially when the prize is national reconciliation. We draw a line under the past. But those who commit new crimes against revolutionary power will be severely punished." I wondered at the time whether it would really be possible to translate such an admirable attitude into practice. But it was done to the respectful admiration of the whole civilized world. It was not just a woman's heart that had been speaking but the considered voice of the Vietnamese Revolution.

My final question to Tran Bach Dang was about reunification—was it a priority item on the order of the day or not?

"Of course, it is," he replied. "It is the natural thing to do. In many respects it has already been done. The whole country is liberated—we have total independence. We are following a socialist path—there is no other. All elements are at hand to build socialism. But conditions in the North are different—they have been building socialism for over 20 years. You have been there and have seen the advantages—but our people in the South have not. So we have some problems. Our people struggled hard in the South against U.S. imperialism for independence, but socialism is a new idea for most of them. It's a matter of time. Even the national bourgeoisie and small compradore bourgeoisie in principle admit the necessity of taking the socialist road. But how to do it is still something of a puzzle. Let the people find their own way to socialism—start building it, and go on from there. This will take time and complete reunification may also take some time. As Communists, we know that the building of socialism is a question of realities. To do it completely, reunification is essential. How to bring this about is a question that we are studying very carefully, at various levels.

"Many of our comrades are anxious to know the exact date—they are impatient. They thought that reunification was one of the main aims for which they were fighting. While we were at war and there was a fascist régime in Saigon, non-reunification was understandable. But now that we have won, the whole country is liberated, the only irrational thing seems to be that we have not declared reunification. Some of our friends abroad are even indignant that we did not just declare this immediately. Of course nobody could stop us doing this tomorrow, and it is clear that reunification is advantageous for the whole Vietnamese people, as also for the whole anti-imperialist front. A nation of 50 million people tempered in arduous revolutionary struggle is an obvious asset. But we have to weigh carefully the advantages and disadvantages of the timing. One of the advantages of non-reunification that has been advanced is that Vietnam could have two voices at the United Nations, for a certain period. Later, that could become a disadvantage. Things could come to the point where the United States, which fears a united Vietnam at the moment, might say: 'One Vietnam is quite enough at the UN!' The time could come when the U.S. advocates reunification louder than anyone else. In any case, all aspects of reunification, the manner of it and the timing of it, are being minutely studied and will continue to be studied. The main thing is that it is entirely in our hands in discussion with our comrades in the North to decide how and when. One way or another our country will certainly be reunified."

Our discussion took place on August 8. Two days earlier the UN Security Council had decided by 14 to 1 (the U.S.) to place on its agenda the question of admitting both Vietnams to

UN membership. On August 11, when the applications were separately considered by the Security Council, each was accepted by 13 to 1, the United States opposing and Costa Rica abstaining. U.S. delegate, Daniel Moynihan, for the first time used the U.S. veto in blocking the admission of a new member, stating that his country "will have nothing to do with selective universality which in practice only admits new members acceptable to the totalitarian states." He had demanded that the admission of the two Vietnams should be linked to that of South Korea, a totalitarian state in the most complete sense of the term! Kissinger, who certainly authored the veto, thus torpedoed one of the most potent arguments of those within the Vietnamese leadership who argued that double representation at the UN was an advantage that merited postponement of reunification. Things moved swiftly after that.

At the Lima foreign ministers' conference of Non-Aligned Nations (August 25-30), North Vietnam, to the surprise of many, applied for membership—and was accepted. This brought all components of Indochina—the PRG, Cambodia and Laos—into the family of the Non-Aligneds. Although North Vietnam remained within the socialist camp, this was an important step in harmonizing the foreign policies of North and South, thus eliminating a possible obstacle to reunification.

Between November 21-25, delegations from North and South met in Ho Chi Minh City and decided on the momentous first concrete steps towards full reunification. Elections would be held in the first half of 1976, by direct and secret ballot, to a single general assembly on the basis of one deputy for each 100,000 of population. As the "supreme organ of the State of Vietnam, from then on, independent and socialist, the General Assembly," in the terms of the communiqué announcing the decisions, "would establish the leading state organs and adopt a new Constitution for a united Vietnam", the capital of which would be Hanoi.

Chapter 18.

Reunification

On April 25, 1976, an event scheduled for just 20 years earlier took place—nation-wide elections to an all-Vietnam National Assembly. This was the constitutional first step towards reunifying the country. According to the 1954 Geneva Agreement this should have taken place by July 20, 1956. But U.S. policies at the time dictated otherwise. And at that time, as distinct from April 25, 1976, the United States was strong enough to enforce its policies!

The only other all-Vietnam elections had been held 30 years previously—on January 6, 1946—to a National Assembly which gave legal form to the Democratic Republic of Vietnam set up as the result of the seizure of power by the Vietminh six months earlier, electing Ho Chi Minh as its founder-president. Although recognizing the Democratic Republic, France promptly set out to crush it, setting in motion a process which ended only on April 30, 1975. How much blood and tears flowed under the bridges and soaked into Vietnam's ricefields since, during the 30 years of separation and struggle!

It seemed legitimate to hope for some dispassionate appraisal of the historical significance of the April 25 reunification elections in the world press. But in the newspapers of France, the former colonial power and the United States—the would-be neo-colonialist successor—and their western allies, there were only the harsh and bitter words of those still licking the wounds of their defeat. "Freedom from the opposition is the only freedom this election can boast.." [49] was a typical comment from the western establishment press in bewailing the fact that there was not some western, "democratic", two or three party system electoral process.

By slamming the door to all but battlefield solutions for over 20 years, it was the United States which unwittingly influenced the tempo and manner of reunification. From 1955, when the Eisenhower administration pushed Ngo Dinh Diem into rejecting the all-Vietnam elections due the following year (Eisenhower was later to explain that 80 percent of the electorate would have voted for Ho Chi Minh), to October 1971, when the Nixon administration opted for a one-man presidential "election" and then supported Nguyen Van Thieu in repudiating the Paris Agreement, successive United States administrations rejected any democratic electoral choice for the Vietnamese people. Washington was thus ill-placed to criticize the manner in which the revolutionary leadership arranged their electoral affairs. The main western criticism of the April 25 election was that candidates had been selected "by the Communists": voters had no real choice; there was no western-style electoral campaign. Measured by western electoral procedures, the reunification election may well have seemed bizarre. For instance, instead of the American system of pre-selection of candidates by Democratic or Republican party "primary" elections at State levels, candidates in South Vietnam were pre-selected by the resistance committees of the NLF or its allies in the various electoral districts. They were obviously selected on the basis of their behavior during the resistance. There was no pretence that there was to be any risk of losing the fruits of 30 years of armed struggle on some sort of electoral gambling table in which the dice could be heavily weighted in favor of demagogy and opportunism.

In presenting the decisions of the North-South national electoral council, as to how the elections were to be run, its president, veteran revolutionary Truong Chinh said: "As far as the composition of the future National Assembly is concerned, favorable conditions must be created which will enable people to elect those really worthy of representing them in this

---

49. *International Herald Tribune* (Paris) editorial, 27/4/1976.

supreme institution of patriots deciding on the reunification of the country on the basis of national independence and of socialism. Counter-revolutionaries must not be permitted to infiltrate in any form whatsoever. The composition of the National Assembly must reflect the spirit of broad unity of the whole people within a national front on the basis of the worker-peasant alliance, directed by the working class..." Counter-revolutionaries, or those opposing reunification and socialism, had been disenfranchised, in other words. That was what the struggle had been all about. They would not have been disenfranchised in the South however, had the United States permitted the implementation of the 1973 Paris Agreement. They would have helped draft the conditions under which elections for a South Vietnamese National Assembly would take place, and it would have been that body which would have decided for or against reunification and socialism.

Instead of elaborate campaigning with brass bands, glamour girls and free beer in the American style, campaigning by candidates was forbidden. Another bizarre concept? As explained by the Saigon lawyer, Tran Ngoc Lieng, member of the South Vietnam delegation to the North-South Political Consultative Conference which drew up the modalities for the elections, the reason for the non-campaigning of candidates was the following.

"Everyone knows that in previous elections in South Vietnam, every candidate had the right to wage electoral campaigns, but to benefit from this right one had to lodge a financial security. And to undertake the electoral campaign, one also had to have money. This prevented honest people from posing their candidature because honest people in South Vietnam are usually poor and without financial resources. Thus only the rich and powerful could stand as candidates—and this power came from their fortune or from foreign sources. Secondly, to permit candidates to wage electoral campaigns is to create for braggarts and incompetents the conditions to deceive the voters and to indulge in all sorts of empty promises. Thirdly, by permitting candidates to undertake electoral campaigns is to disorient the voters. There are people who no one knows, who have not taken part in any struggle or honest social activity which could entitle them to be considered as representatives of the people but who dispose of propaganda means to bluff the naive and ill-informed and win votes. On the other hand, if candidates are not permitted to wage electoral campaigns, they have to be known for their merits or their revolutionary activities. The banning of electoral campaigns means that in putting forward their candidature they are not concerned with their own interests, but with those of the people. It is a duty, a heavy responsibility that they will have to fulfill if elected. It it not for them an occasion to run after wealth and fame.. "[50]

The chief tasks of the 492 delegates elected on April 25, 1976, were to perform the historic act of formalizing the reunification of the country; decide on its official designation, its flag and national anthem; elect a government; adopt a new Constitution and approve a five-year economic plan of national reconstruction.

United States policy towards Vietnam continued to be erratic, contradictory, perfidious—and above all—stupid. On March 26, 1976, the Ford administration sent a much-publicized message to Hanoi, through the latter's embassy in Paris, stating that Washington was interested in "normalizing relations." After some preliminary exchange of feelers, the Hanoi daily, *Nhan Dan*, denounced the offer as "a ruse, a merchandise offered by the Ford-Kissinger administration to the home market in this election year. . ." [51] That Hanoi's assessment was per-

---

50. If I devote some space to this subject, it is not only because of the obvious contrasts between Vietnam's reunification elections and the preparations for the 1976 U.S. presidential elections, but because my travels in newly independent countries have led me to the conclusion that there is an increasing rejection of the idea that the western system of parliamentary democracy is the only valid one. I have found leaders of the newly developing world increasingly irritated when their electoral systems are condemned according to their departure from the norms in vogue in the West. The first point raised by Tran Ngoc Lieng becomes perfectly valid when one learned that a leading contender for the Democratic party nomination in the 1976 U.S. presidential elections, Senator Henry Jackson, had to withdraw his candidature at an early stage of the "primaries" because his campaign committee had run out of money! Also the notion of parliament as a sort of debating society where representatives of sectional interests bicker over who gets the biggest slice of the national cake is rejected by those who have fought long and bitter struggles to gain independence. They want a unified, hard-working body devoted to getting on with the job of building up a prosperous and equitable society. A fact of life that the West has to get used to is that the end results of western-type parliamentary democracy are not all that appealing to hundreds of millions of people in Asia and Africa and the rest of the under-developed world. Partly because it was the image behind which the most tyrannical local despots and traitors sheltered.
51. *Nhan Dan* (People's Daily) of April 12, 1976.

fectly valid became apparent in less than a month when, on April 23, in response to some campaign prodding from Ronald Reagan, his rival for the presidential nomination, President Ford denied any intention of "normalizing" relations with Hanoi. In fact, the March 26 initiative was a sop to the hardheaded U.S. trading community which sees in a united Vietnam of some 50 million disciplined, industrious and talented people with rich natural resources to be developed, a most desirable trading partner. It followed a visit to Hanoi a month earlier by a U.S. Congressional Committee, headed by Senator McGovern, which discovered some very important facts.

That the United States was bound by the Paris Agreement (Article 21) to pay reparations to North Vietnam was public knowledge. What McGovern and his fellow congressmen discovered was that President Nixon had very solemnly promised 3.25 billion dollars of economic assistance of post-war economic assistance, spread over a period of five years and without any political conditions attached. A letter to this effect, dated February 1, 1973, and signed by Nixon was brought by Kissinger when he visited Hanoi on February 10-13, less than three weeks after the signature of the Paris Agreement. During that visit it was agreed to set up a Joint Economic Commission in Paris to work out details. An Agreement was drafted and a date—July 23, 1973—was set for the signing. At the last minute, however, the U.S. delegation made the signing conditional on a whole set of political conditions. These could be summed up as requiring Hanoi to renounce any further support for its compatriots in the South. More absurd still, Hanoi must use its influence to bring about a ceasefire in Cambodia, where things were not going the way Washington had planned.

Obviously 3.25 billion dollars was a lot of money and could represent a considerable short-cut along the road of reconstruction. But it fell far short of the 6 billion dollars' worth of bomb damage, scrupulously listed by the North Vietnamese authorities—excluding the B-52 "Christmas bombings" of Hanoi and Haiphong, for which Kissinger agreed a separate accounting could be made. There was nothing charitable about the Nixon promise to implement Article 21. Nixon and Kissinger knew that just as Japan re-entered the Southeast Asian markets through reparations payments for damage inflicted in World War II, so reparations in the form of industrial equipment delivered to North Vietnam would inevitably link the country to the U.S. economy. Soviet aid for the same period amounted to about 1 billion dollars—or less than one third of what the U.S.A. was proposing. The Agreement drafted in Paris provided that North Vietnam would spend 85 percent of the credits in the purchase of U.S. equipment, including a steel plant of 1 million tons annual capacity; various plants for the manufacture of building-construction and agricultural machinery; factories for heavy, medium and light industry.

Taken together with the American installations built up in the South, and the offer to U.S. oil firms to continue their prospecting and exploitation of South Vietnam's offshore oil fields, this represented a golden opportunity for the United States to get into the most stable trading area in Southeast Asia. And from a political viewpoint to help a unified Vietnam retain its independence in relation to the two major socialist powers and the western world. But the chance was thrown away because, in another of those incredible policy miscalculations, Washington had thought that a 3.25 billion dollar "carrot" could succeed where the B-52 "stick" had failed—and bribe Hanoi into abandoning the South.

"If the United States does not execute Article 21," Premier Pham Van Dong told a group of Americans in September, 1975, "they will suffer one more humiliating defeat in Vietnam." That defeat would obviously be the loss of a rich, stable and expanding market and the prestige loss of one more failure to fulfill international obligations.[52] It was predictable that the Vietnamese people would not permit the non-fulfillment of U.S. pledges to stand in the way of reconstruction any more that it could hinder reunification. And the two went hand-in-hand.

From the time of the liberation of Saigon until the end of 1975, the North had dispatched over one million tons of material and goods to the South, as well as tens of thousands of cadres and workers to help get the economy and administration off to a good start. From the beginning of direct American entry into the war, the North had increased its intake of students at the higher educational establishments by many times, deliberately training them in sufficient numbers for the tasks of post-war reconstruction for the South as well as the North. In

---

52. At the time of writing there were some signs that the U.S. oil interests and the trading community would exert sufficient pressure for the U.S. to reverse its policy of economic boycott.

his statement quoted above, Truong Chinh said that the elections "should be an occasion for all sections of the population throughout the whole country to throw themselves, body and soul, into the tasks of national reconstruction, the stabilization of living standards, the restoration and development of the economy, the development of education so as to gradually transform our country into a socialist land with a modern industry, a modern agriculture, a powerful national defense system, advanced in culture and the sciences. . ." There is little doubt that these goals will be rapidly attained, with or without the 3.25 billion dollars!

In a report presented to the DRV National Assembly at the beginning of 1976, Deputy Premier Le Thanh Nghi stated that virtually all industrial installations in the North that were destroyed during the war had been rebuilt, except for some, the reconstruction and expansion of which would be tackled according to the requirements and the new industrial capacity acquired in the South. Electric power production in the North was 2.4 times higher in 1975 than 1965, when the U.S. started its systematic bombing of the DRV. Compared with 1974, electric power output was up by 25 percent and coal production by 38 percent with a 34.5 percent increase in the output of the big central industries and a 10.4 percent increase in regional industry. As a result of major work during the war years to offset American bombings of the Red River dykes, and to improve road communications combined with extending the irrigation systems, 93 percent of the rice-fields for the winter-spring season and 84 percent for the summer-autumn season, have now been brought under irrigation. All this means that the North has got off to an excellent start in healing the wounds of war and laying the foundations for a big economic upsurge when the economies of both zones are formed into an integrated single unit.

"Our 45 million people," noted Le Thanh Nghi, in presenting a preliminary report on the new 5-year economic plan, "of whom about 21 millions are working people, including a rather notable contingent of scientists and technicians and specialized workers of both North and South Zones, constitute a precious capital for carrying out well the great economic tasks . . . In the South, the industrial sector and infrastructure have remained almost intact. A certain number of high capacity installations are equipped with quite modern techniques . . . The material and technical bases already acquired in the whole country, as well as the experiences accumulated, constitute the primary capital in effectively serving the socialist industrialization of the country. . ." The strategic tasks for the North and South respectively, as defined by Le Thanh Nghi were for the North "to intensify the construction of socialism and to perfect socialist relations of production," and for the South "to achieve simultaneously socialist transformation and the construction of of socialism. . ." A primary task for 1976 was to work out with the South (within two months of the April 25 elections) "the delimitation, the allocation and the reorganization of the various industrial branches throughout the whole country. . ." and the establishment of an appropriate 5-year plan. For the North alone, industrial production was planned to increase by twenty percent, including 21.4 percent for cement; 13 percent for coal and 11.3 percent for phosphate fertilizers. (As part of the registration for the reunification elections, it was discovered that the combined North-South population was almost 50 million).

That Vietnam will continue to defend its economic independence in the same stubborn manner in which it fought to conquer and defend its national independence is a foregone conclusion. Among the strategic tasks outlined in the Le Thanh Nghi report is that of "seeking by all means to extend economic relations with the socialist and other countries on the basis of independence, sovereignty and in the interests of building up an independent and sovereign economy. . ."

The effects of the victory of the Vietnamese revolution are incalculable. Wherever in the world people struggle for national liberation and independence, it is Vietnam which is taken as an exemplary model of "how to do it"—and this is not to detract from the magnificent liberation struggles waged by the Cambodian and Laotion peoples. Their leaders would be the first to admit that they were greatly inspired by the Vietnam experience, not to mention having been aided materially. If the pro-U.S. dictatorship in Thailand was overthrown and SEATO distintegrated; if Thailand and the Philippines asked the Americans to fold up their bases; if the U.S. Congress refused to finance pro-American puppets in Angola, this was because of Vietnam. If Kissinger had to go to Africa to pretend that the United States was the "black man's best friend" this was because of Vietnam. If elephants are on the run in southern Africa, it is because of black grasshoppers inspired by the Vietnamese variety. And if the captains overthrew fascism in Portugal on April 25, 1974, it was because the Vietnam experience convinced them that military victory in Portugal's African territories was impossible. Long discussions with student leaders in Thailand, with some of Portugal's "captains" and with leaders of national liberation movements in Angola and elsewhere in southern Africa have only deepened my convictions as to the globe-shattering importance of the Vietnamese example. At my first meeting with Lucio Lara, veteran Angolan revolutionary and general secretary of the MPLA, he brought me, for a signature, a tattered copy of *North of the 17th Parallel*, the first book I wrote about the Vietnamese revolution, explaining how precious had been the lessons of the Vietnamese struggle in the darkest hours of the Angolan revolution. Fretilin leaders of the national liberation movement in East Timor have also told me how their own considerable experience of fighting the Japanese invaders during World War II, has been enriched by their contacts with leaders of the Vietnamese national liberation struggle.

One anecdote perhaps sums it all up. It concerns the sudden, and for most observers surprising, collapse of the U.S.-backed Rightists in Laos, in May 1975. In Vientiane a few weeks after the events, I asked General Singkapo,[53] chief of staff of the Pathet Lao armed forces, what had happened so suddenly to change a situation which had existed for many years and in which the Pathet Lao controlled the countryside and the Rightists controlled Vientiane, Luano Prabang and other cities. "It was what happened in Saigon on April 30 and in Phnom Penh on April 17 that was decisive," he said, and went on to explain:

"Since the formation of the Provisional Government of National Union,[54] the Rightists continued their obstructionist activ-

---

53. General Singkapo Chunmali Sikhot, member of the Central Committee of the Neo Lao Hak Xat—Laotian Patriotic Front.

54. An Agreement to end hostilities in Laos, parallel to the Paris Agreement to end the war in Vietnam, was signed on February 21, 1973. As distinct from the Paris Agreement, a three-segment Provisional Government of National Union was actually formed in Vientiane but did not function any better than many such governments set up in the previous 20 years, following the 1954 and 1962 Geneva Agreements. The real administration in the Vientiane-controlled areas was the CIA front organization AID (Agency for International Development) which had its "capital" in the outskirts of Vientiane, until it was taken over by students in May-June, 1975.

ities. At every cabinet meeting there were unresolvable disagreements. The Rightists insisted on unanimity, but this was very rare to arrive at despite strenuous efforts by our side to be conciliatory. Even when they agreed to a proposal, they would block its implementation through their appointees at lower levels in the administration. This situation continued until the collapse of the puppet régimes in Cambodia and South Vietnam. Until then, our Laotian Rightists always counted on the backing of Lon Nol, Nguyen Van Thieu and, of course, the CIA. Their arrogance was based on that support. After the sudden collapse of the Saigon and Phnom Penh puppets our Laotian Rightists began to feel very isolated. On the other hand, inspired by the people's victories in the fraternal countries, our own people started rising up in the very centers of enemy strength. In the various ministries, junior employees started denouncing the corrupt, Rightist elements.

"May Day was a big shock for the Rightists in the government. They had wanted to ban all demonstrations in the capital, as usual, but we had our forces close to Vientiane by that time, and we firmly favored the demonstrations . . . It was the first time that workers and young people could legally hold May Day demonstrations and freely express their views in the capital. Besides slogans hailing international workers' day, there were others demanding strict respect for the peace agreement and for the removal of un-named officials opposing the application of the agreements. The strength and militancy of the May Day demonstrations just 24 hours after the liberation of Saigon struck terror in the hearts of the Rightist ministers. But the May Day demonstrations," continued General Singkapo, "were nothing compared to the nation-wide demonstrations of May 9, by which time the full importance of the victories in Vietnam and Cambodia and the impotence of the United States to halt the revolutionary tide, had sunk in. The May 9 demonstrations named half a dozen leading Rightists[55] who had to be ousted. These individuals panicked and fled across the Mekong River into Thailand.

---

55. The Rightists included Phoui Sananikone, several times prime minister who had been involved in numerous right-wing plots against the neutralist-inclined Vientiane governments, Defense Minister Sisouk Na Champassak, Finance Minister Ngon Sananikone, Health Minister Khamphay Abhay, and two secretaries of state for foreign affairs and public works.

"Following the departure of the Rightist ringleaders, workers in the ministries held daily meetings denouncing the chief henchmen of the departed Rightists and demanded their removal. Most of these individuals also fled the country once they were left without protectors . . . When even Thailand demanded that the United States close down its bases by March 1976, our Laotian Rightists realized that the tide had irrevocably changed against them and there was nothing to do but flee. They never did have any real roots in the country as far as popular support was concerned."

Thus the Laotian revolution ended in a "quiet" and bloodless victory. Plenty of blood, however, had also soaked into Laotion ricefields and stained the country's rivers since the day when an engineer, Prince Souphanouvong, fuming at the humiliation of his people under the French yoke, asked Ho Chi Minh what he should do about it. "Seize power from the colonialists," was the prompt reply. For the next 30 years this was what Souphanouvong and his originally small band of followers set about doing. Although it was not until December 1, 1975 that a People's Democratic Republic of Laos was proclaimed with Prince Souphanouvong as its president—the revolution in fact was won on May 9, with the abdication and flight of its most powerful opponents. Thus, within the space of 23 days the revolutionary forces in Cambodia, Vietnam and Laos—each in their own way—had victoriously completed a 30 years cycle of revolutionary struggle for independence and national liberation. Almost exactly five years earlier, the revolutionary leaders from the two halves of Vietnam, Cambodia and Laos had pledged—at the Summit Conference of the Peoples of Indo-China[56]—not to lay down their arms until their common enemy, U.S. imperialism, was totally defeated in their respective countries, and where possible, to coordinate their struggles. Rare are the examples in history in which such aims were so totally fulfilled and victories so closely coordinated! Or that victories had been won against such odds!

---

56. Held in South China on April 24-25, 1970, at the initiative of Norodom Sihanouk of Cambodia, the Summit Conference of the Peoples of Indochina represented an important landmark in the cooperation of the revolutionary forces of the former French colonies against the new enemy—U.S. imperialism.

Glossary of Names and Organizations

Bertrand Russell War Crimes Tribunal

The Bertrand Russell War Crimes Tribunal was set up on the personal initiative of the late Lord Bertrand Russell, internationally famous philosopher, writer and humanist. Two sessions were held in 1967, in Stockholm and Roskilde (Denmark) respectively at which an international jury, presided over by the eminent French philosopher and writer, Jean-Paul Sartre heard evidence from prominent scientists and legal experts plus reports from numberous teams of investigators which had collected evidence of U.S. war crimes in both North and South Vietnam. The conclusion was that grave war crimes, according to all criteria of international law, including Hague and Geneva Conventions and the Nuremburg judgements, had been committed. A number of U.S. Vietnam veterans gave evidence. A good summing up of the evidence and proceedings is given in: *Against The Crime of Silence* edited by John Duffield and published by O'Hare Books, New York, 1968.

Dien Bien Phu

The Battle of Dien Bien Phu, 13 March to 7 May 1954, in which the Vietnamese People's Army wiped or captured 17 battalions and 10 companies of the cream of French troops in Indochina, was the decisive defeat which brought France to sign the 1954 Geneva Agreements leading to the French withdrawal from Indochina.

General Duong Van "Big" Minh

Played a leading role in the overthrow of the Diem dictatorship in November 1963, and for three months headed a triumvirate government which in turn was overthrown in February 1964 by General Nguyen Khanh. "Big" Minh was accused of being "neutralist" and "pro-French". Nguyen Khanh was presented in the U.S. press as the "strong man" of South Vietnam and the United States' "man in Saigon."

Ho Chi Minh (1890-1969)

Founder-leader of the modern Vietnamese revolution. From 1919, when he submitted an 8-point memorandum in Versailles to the powers negotiating the post World War I Peace Treaty until he died in Hanoi on September 3, 1969 he worked and fought single-mindedly for the independence and unity of Vietnam.

Hoa Hao

The *Hoa Hao, Cao Dai* and *Binh Xuyen* were semi-religious, semi-political sects with, in the case of the *Binh Xuyen*, strong Mafia-type overtones, set up by the French to undermine and counteract Vietminh influence furing the independence struggle.

Huynh Tan Phat (1923—)

Saigon architect who headed the Democratic party, formed in 1945 from Saigon intellectuals and small business people to support independence and the resistance struggle against the French. Was successively chairman of the Saigon branch of the NLF; secretary-general of the NLF; Prime Minister when the Provisional Revolutionary Government was set up in June 1969.

Le Duc Tho (1910-)

member of the Political Bureau of the Lao Dong Party, a veteran frontline commander during the war against the French, Le Duc Tho was senior adviser to the DRV delegation to the Paris talks. His role was especially important in the bilateral talks with Kissinger. His arrivals from Hanoi were usually associated with some new moves at the conference table. In the final stages of the war Le Duc Tho helped direct military operations from a base in the Central Highlands and in the final stages from a forward headquarters about 40 miles from Saigon.

Marshal Lon Nol (1913-)

Originally one of Sihanouk's closest aides in the years after independence was ratified by the 1954 Geneva Agreements, Lon Nol alternated between the posts of Minister of Defense and Commander-in-Chief of Cambodia's armed forces until 1967 when he became Prime Minister. It was Lon Nol and the acting Prime Minister Prince Sirik Matak, who carried out the coup on 18 March 1970, which deposed Norodom Sihanouk as Head of State. After various internal intrigues and shuffling of leading posts, Lon Nol assumed the post of President on 13 March 1972, with virtually full state powers in his hands. He held that post until he fled to Indonesia on 1 April 1975 and from there to Hawaii.

Montagnard

A general term used to refer to some 60 ethnic groupings totalling about 5 milion tribal and sub-tribal groups who inhabit the mountainous areas of Vietnam. In the context used in this book the term refers to those living in the Central Highlands of South Vietnam.

NLF, National Liberation Front of South Vietnam

Established on 20 December 1960 in the jungle of Tay Ninh province, about 60 miles north of Saigon. It was set up to coordinate and direct armed struggle which had already broken out spontaneously in various parts of South Vietnam.

Ngo Dinh Diem (1900-1963)

Installed as Prime Minister in Saigon on 16 June 1954, at the height of the Geneva Conference, due to the efforts of Colonel Edward G. Lansdale of the CIA, Ngo Dinh Diem's role was to be the United States' "man in Saigon" with the primary task of ensuring the non-application of any Agreement signed at Geneva. A visceral anti-communist, Diem attracted the attention of the French colonial administration—in the late 1920's—by his zeal in denouncing Communists and reporting on their activities and, once he was given the power, of arresting them. As part of the process of the United States takeover from the French in South Vietnam, the pro-French Emperor Bao Dai, titular head of State, was deposed on 26 October 1955, and Diem took over as President retaining also the post of prime minister. As such he presided over the non-fullfillment of the most essential clause of the Geneva Agreement, the holding of nation-wide reunification elections, by July 20, 1956. This was the single, most important act—highly praised by U.S. Secretary of State John Foster Dulles at the time—which led to the long and bitter war. His tyranny and inefficiency led to his overthrow and assassination—with CIA blessing—on November 1, 1963, together with his Rasputin-like brother Ngo Dinh Nhu. A third brother, Ngo Dinh Can, the sadistically cruel dictator of Central Vietnam sought refuge in the U.S. Consulate at Hue after crowds tried to lynch him. Eventually the Americans handed him over to the new Saigon authorities. He was tried for some of his bloodthirsty crimes, and executed.

Nguyen Cao Ky (1930—)

French and US-trained air officer who rose to rank of Air Vice Marshall and commander of South Vietnam's Air Force. Prime Minister in 1965, he became deputy to Nguyen Van Thieu as Vice-President in 1967, but later fell out with Thieu when the latter forced him to withdraw his candidature in Thieu's one-man presidential elections of October 1971.

Nguyen Huu Tho (1910—)

Formerly a well-known French-educated barrister in Saigon, Nguyen

Huu Tho had been arrested in March 1950, for leading a huge demonstration in Saigon against the arrival of U.S. warships in Saigon harbor as the first tangible sign of U.S. support for France in the "first resistance war." Arrested by the Saigon régime again in August 1954, for having demonstrated in favor of the application of the Geneva Agreement, he escaped in 1961 and at the First Congress of the NLF, in early 1962, he was unanimously elected President. He is now vice-president of the Socialist Republic of Vietnam.

Nguyen Thanh Lê

Spokesman for the DRV delegation at the Paris talks, Nguyen Thanh Lê is deputy editor of Nhan Dan (The People) the daily paper of the Lao Dong party. His intelligence and incisive wit won him the admiration of most newsmen covering the talks.

Madame Nguyen Thi Binh (1927—)

A former student leader in Saigon, Nguyen Thi Binh was jailed by the French in 1951 and released only after the signing of the Geneva Agreement. She is a member of the Central Committee of the NLF and Vice-President of the Women's Liberation Association. At the beginning of NLF participation in the Paris talks, Nguyen Thi Binh was deputy head of their delegation. After the Provisional Revolutionary Government was set up in June 1969, and she was appointed Foreign Minister, she headed what became the PRG delegation. She is currently Minister for Education of the Socialist Republic of Vietnam.

Nguyen Van Thieu (1923—)

President of the Republic of South Vietnam. Became virtual Head of State as head of a military junta which seized power in Saigon in June 1965, became president through rigged elections in October 1967 and held that post until he resigned on 21 April 1975, fleeing to Taiwan five days later.

Pathet Lao

The Pathet Lao was formed in 1945 with Prince Souphanouvong as its head, to seize power from the Japanese in August 1945. From then until the 1954 Geneva Agreement, the Pathet Lao headed the bitter resistance struggle against the French. From 1954 until May 9, 1975, they fought an almost uninterrupted resistance war against various U.S.-backed puppet régimes. After the total victory of the Laotian revolutionary forces in May 1975, the name Pathet Lao was changed to that of the Laotian People's Revolutionary Party. The People's Democratic Republic of Laos was proclaimed in early December 1975 with Souphanouvong as its President.

People's Revolutionary Party

The southern branch of the Lao Dong party which, together with the Democratic party and Radical Socialist party, formed the political nucleus around which the National Liberation Front was formed.

People's War

General Vo Nguyen Giap, perhaps the greatest exponent and practitioner of People's War, explained in his book: *People's War: People's Army* what it had meant in relation to the struggle against the French: "Every inhabitant was a combatant; every village a fortress; every Party cell and village administrative committee a staff headquarters. The entire people took part in armed struggle, but fighting according to the principles of guerilla warfare, in small groups but always following one single line, following the same directives, those of the Party central committee of the Government." It is thus that the "grasshoppers" were able to vanquish the "elephants"!

Pham Van Dong (1906—)

Pham Van Dong is one of the great personalities of the Vietnamese Revolution. Student leader, organizer of the first underground trade unions, teacher of history and geography like Vo Nguyen Giap, he was arrested in 1929 and after a year in Saigon jails was sentenced to ten years detention at Poulo Condor. The equivalent of a death sentence. His dossier was marked: "Not to be returned to his country of origin. His release would constitute a danger to State security." Through books smuggled in from outside, Pham Van Dong turned the Poulo Condor prison cells into study classes in higher political education. After six years, he was released because a Popular Front government had come to power in France. Together with Vo Nguyen Giap he later left for political-military training in Canton, where Ho Chi Minh had established his headquarters. Also together with Giap he set up the first units of what was to become the Vietnam People's Army, and prepared the political ground for launching armed struggle. During a UN debate on the eve of the 1954 Geneva Conference, French Foreign Minister Georges Bidault described Pham Van Dong as a "non-existent phantom." But it was with this "phantom" as Foreign Minister of the Democratic Republic of Vietnam, that Bidault had to negotiate in the early stages of the Geneva Conference. Bidault was later disgraced and went into oblivion. Pham Van Dong was Prime Minister of the Democratic Republic of Vietnam from 1954 and is now Prime Minister of the Socialist Republic of Vietnam.

Poulo Condor

The Vietnamese name is Con Son, an island 60 miles due south of Saigon. Used by the French and successive régimes in Saigon as a penitentiary, it is known by Vietnamese as "Hell Island." Many of today's Vietnamese leaders, including President Ton Duc Thang and Premier Pham Van Dong, spent many years there under the French.

Rural Pacification Corps

The organization most hated and feared by the peasantry. It was primarily responsible for ferretting out suspected "Vietcong," their family members, sympathizers or friends—arresting, torturing, killing those on whom they could lay their hands. As those they were seeking constituted virtually the entire rural population one can imagine the breadth and depth of suffering for which this organization was responsible.

Prince Sihanouk (1922—)

Prince Norodom Sihanouk was named King of Cambodia by the French in 1941, abdicating in favor of his father in 1955, he became Head of State on the death of his father, King Norodom Suramarit in 1960. The neutralist régime which he headed was overthrown by a CIA-backed rightist coup in March 1970. In Peking, Sihanouk set up and headed the Cambodian National United Front (CNUF) and a Royal Cambodian Government of National Unity (RCGNU) to lead the resistance struggle and administer the liberated areas. Following the collapse of the American-supported Lon Nol régime on 17 April 1975, Sihanouk returned to Cambodia. Despite the decision of a special congress of the CNUF that he should remain Head of State, he resigned in April 1976. With his wife Monique and other members of the family, he lives in the royal palace in Phnom Penh, and the most recent news of him was that he was writing his memoirs.

Têt

Têt is the Vietnamese Lunar New Year, the great festive occasion of the year. Like the western Xmas and New Year combined, it is the traditional occasion for family reunions and as much festivity as anyone can afford.

Tien Van Dung

Chief of Staff of the VPA, who personally directed the battle of 55 days. The closest disciple of Vo Nguyen Giap, he had brilliantly applied the Giap concept of catching the enemy between dispersal and concentration of his forces.

Tran Van Huong (1903—)

Former Mayor Saigon, twice Prime Minister, later known as the "five-day president" holding that office between the resignation of Nguyen Van Thieu and the appointment of General Duong Van "Big" Minh, whose term of office was even shorter.

Truong Chinh

A senior member of the Political Bureau, and former general-secretary of the Lao Dong Party, Truong Chinh, together with Pham Van Dong and Vo Nguyen Giap, was one of the longest and closest collaborators of Ho Chi Minh.

Vietnam People's Army

Formed on 22 December 1944, with 32 members of what was then known as an "armed propaganda platoon."

Vietnamese Lao Dong (Worker's Party)

This was the successor to the Indochina Communist party, formed on 30 January 1930 and later dissolved in favour of the *Vietminh* or Patriotic Front. The Lao Dong in fact was the Vietnamese Communist Party, and officially adopted this name at the end of 1976.

Vietnamization

This was the name given to President Nixon's policy of an expansion of South Vietnam's armed forces proportionate to the gradual withdrawal of U.S. forces, or "changing the color of the corpses" as the U.S. Ambassador to Saigon, Ellsworth Bunker, expressed it. "Vietnamization" of the war was the real content of Nixon's 1968 electoral promise of a "peace plan" to end the war in Vietnam.

General Vo Mguyen Giap (1912—)

North Vietnam's Minister of Defense and Commander-in-Chief of the Armed Forces and founder of the VPA. He personally led the first action of the "armed propaganda platoon" and gradually developed into one of the world's leading military strategists. He first became known to the outside world as the victor of Dien Bien Phu, having personally commanded that battle.

General William Childs Westmoreland (1914—)

Deputy-Commander, U.S. Military Assistance Command, South Vietnam 1964; the same year promoted to Commander, which meant in effect Commander-in-Chief of all military forces in South Vietnam from 1964-68. Withdrawn after the 1968 Tết offensive, he was promoted to Chief of Staff of the U.S. Army. Unable to conquer territory and hold it in South Vietnam, Westmoreland was the inventor of the daily "body count" as the criteria of military progress.

Women's Liberation Association

The Women's Liberation Association was one of many such mass organizations affiliated to the NLF, including youth and trade union organizations, within which virtually everyone from children to old people in the liberated areas could make their contribution to the resistance struggle.

Xuan Thuy (1912-)

Member of the Central Committee of the Lao Don party and former Foreign Minister, Xuan Thuy headed the DRV delegation to the Paris talks.